E-Mail Marketing

FOR

DUMMIES®

E-Mail Marketing For Dummies®

Published by
Wiley Publishing, Inc.
111 River Street
Hoboken, NJ 07030-5774

www.wiley.com

WILEY

About the Author

John Arnold is a renowned marketing trainer and speaker as well as an entrepreneur and small business advisor. He has consulted with almost every type of small business imaginable and has personally taken more than a dozen small businesses from conception to fruition in the retail, service, nonprofit, and consulting industries, including a nationally syndicated radio show.

In 2006, John helped to pioneer a small business training program on behalf of the e-mail marketing company Constant Contact. Through the program, John personally taught e-mail marketing to thousands of small business owners, and his seminars and workshops have since become a trusted source for e-mail marketing strategies, tactics, and best practices. During John's tenure, Constant Contact was named #166 on Inc. 500's list of the fastest growing private companies, and in 2007, completed a successful Initial Public Offering.

John continues to train and advise small business owners as a Constant Contact Regional Development Director. He is a sought-after speaker and consultant for franchises, Chambers of Commerce, Small Business Development Centers, Business Improvement Districts, Visitors and Conventions Bureaus, and nonprofit organizations. John can be reached through the publisher or on his Web site at www.emailtrainer.com.

Dedication

This book is dedicated to the individual entrepreneurs who love the spirit of free enterprise and who live to share their personal passions with their customers and their communities.

I also dedicate this book to the One who causes all things to work together for good and reminds me that e-mail is not the most important thing in life.

Author's Acknowledgments

I would first like to thank my wife and kids for enduring my one-track mind while writing this book and for their belief in sharing life's experiences together. You guys are the best family anyone could hope for.

Next, I would like to thank Matt Wagner for running an ideal literary agency. This book wouldn't have been possible without his experience and guidance.

Special thanks to the super team of professionals at Wiley Publishing. I'd like to thank Senior Acquisitions Editor Steve Hayes for his patience in dealing with contracts and for helping me to understand the Dummies process. I would also like to thank my Project Editor Rebecca Senninger and my Copy Editor Teresa Artman for molding and shaping my material into purposeful thoughts and examples and for giving me so many ideas for improving the content in the book. Thanks also to my technical editor Ron Cates for his super-human ideas and inspiring personality.

Thanks also to Lavina Vohlken for helping me to obtain permission for many of the examples contained in this book and for keeping my office and schedule organized while writing. Thanks also to Harold Sullivan from SQV Technologies for providing the Web analytics examples in the book.

I would also like to thank the team at Constant Contact. The success of this book would not have been possible without Gail Goodman, Eric Groves, Robert Nault, Annette Iafrate, and many others at the company. Constant Contact's commitment to small business and in particular its investment in educational programs was paramount in my being in the position where I could author this book.

Finally, I would like to thank T.J. Carney for his outstanding legal counsel (the world doesn't need more lawyers, just more good lawyers), and Jon Schallert for his commitment to helping small business owners succeed and for first inspiring the momentum to write this book.

Publisher's Acknowledgments

We're proud of this book; please send us your comments through our online registration form located at www.dummies.com/register/.

Some of the people who helped bring this book to market include the following:

Acquisitions and Editorial

Project Editor: Rebecca Senninger

Senior Acquisitions Editor: Steven Hayes

Senior Copy Editor: Teresa Artman

Technical Editor: Ron Cates

Editorial Manager: Leah Cameron

Editorial Assistant: Amanda Foxworth

Senior Editorial Assistant: Cherie Case

Cartoons: Rich Tennant
(www.the5thwave.com)

Composition Services

Project Coordinator: Patrick Redmond

Layout and Graphics: Reuben W. Davis, Alissa D. Ellet, Shane Johnson, Barbara Moore, Melissa K. Jester, Christine Williams

Proofreaders: Cynthia Fields, Chris Sabooni

Indexer: Broccoli Information Services

Anniversary Logo Design: Richard Pacifico

Special Help: Brian H. Walls

Publishing and Editorial for Technology Dummies

Richard Swadley, Vice President and Executive Group Publisher

Andy Cummings, Vice President and Publisher

Mary Bednarek, Executive Acquisitions Director

Mary C. Corder, Editorial Director

Publishing for Consumer Dummies

Diane Graves Steele, Vice President and Publisher

Joyce Pepple, Acquisitions Director

Composition Services

Gerry Fahey, Vice President of Production Services

Debbie Stailey, Director of Composition Services

Contents at a Glance

Table of Contents

Introduction

• •

Communicating with consumers is easy, but getting them to pay attention isn't. Every successful marketing strategy entails cutting through the clutter, and few places are more cluttered than the average consumer's e-mail inbox.

E-mail marketing represents an opportunity to experience both the thrill of increased customer loyalty and steady repeat business as well as the agony of bounced e-mail, unsubscribe requests, and spam complaints. Whether you find thrill or agony in your e-mail marketing strategy depends on your ability to effectively deliver valuable and purposeful e-mails to prospects and customers who have a need for your information.

This book combines time-tested marketing strategies with consumer preferences and best practices to help you develop and deliver e-mails that your prospects and customers look forward to receiving. I explain how to apply basic business and marketing principles to your e-mail strategy, such as maximizing your revenue and coming up with meaningful objectives. I also explain how to use e-mail templates to design professional-looking marketing e-mails and how to come up with relevant e-mail content to put into your designs.

E-mail marketers are also subject to legal requirements, consumer mistrust, and Internet service providers (ISPs) blocking and filtering unwanted e-mails by the billions. This book shows you how to adhere to professional standards, improve your deliverability, and execute your e-mail marketing strategy with current laws in mind.

Because your prospects and customers have to share their e-mail address in order for you to deliver valuable e-mails, this book explains how to build a quality e-mail list of subscribers who reward your e-mail marketing efforts with immediate action and outstanding return on investment (ROI). I include tactics that you can use immediately to start building your list as well as tips for obtaining permission and getting your list subscribers to take action on your e-mails.

E-mail marketing doesn't conclude with the successful delivery of an e-mail, so I also explain how you can find out who is opening and clicking your e-mails. I include tips for using e-mail tracking reports and Web analytics to increase the number of your e-mail list subscribers who regularly make purchases and refer your business to their friends and colleagues. I also explain how you can use e-mail to improve search engine optimization, blogs, surveys, and other new technologies to deepen your customer relationships and extend your online presence.

About This Book

E-Mail Marketing For Dummies answers your questions about e-mail marketing and gives you tips and ideas for executing the various steps involved in a successful e-mail marketing campaign.

This book isn't written to impress technically savvy intellectuals. It's for business owners who have to make the most of every minute of every day. I include lots of bulleted text with concise descriptions and ideas for implementing each topic immediately.

The content in each chapter stands alone, so you don't have to read all the chapters in order. You can use this book like an entire series of books on the subject of e-mail marketing. You can scan through the table of contents and read about a single topic to refresh your memory or to get a few ideas before beginning a task, or you can read an entire chapter or a series of chapters to gain understanding and gather ideas for executing one or more parts of an entire e-mail campaign.

Conventions Used in This Book

To make this book easier to scan and internalize, I use the following conventions:

- Words in *italics* are used to point out industry terminology or words that have special definitions in the book. Sometimes, specific examples — such as suggested wording for calls to action — appear in italic.
- Web addresses and text you see onscreen appear in a different font, as in

  `www.HelpWithEmailMarketing.com`

What You Don't Have to Read

Sidebars, set off in special gray boxes, are included in this book to add clarity to complex concepts or to give anecdotal examples of the tips and ideas in the book. You don't have to read them to benefit from this book.

Foolish Assumptions

It's hard to imagine that anyone has managed to stay completely away from e-mail. However, to get the most out of this book I assume you already

- Have a working e-mail address
- Are responsible for (or are soon to be responsible for) marketing a small business
- Know how to use a computer and a mouse
- Have a Web site or a physical location (or you soon will)
- Have a product or service that people need or have an idea for a product or service that people need

How This Book Is Organized

E-Mail Marketing For Dummies is divided into five parts in chronological order according to the steps involved in developing and executing a successful e-mail marketing strategy.

Part I: Getting Started with E-Mail Marketing

Part I explains where e-mail fits into a small business marketing mix and describes the benefits and limitations of e-mail as a marketing tool. I give you insight into the consumer landscape including tips for understanding spam and complying with spam laws as well as maximizing the revenue you gener-ate from using e-mail. Part I also tells you about the benefits of using an E-Mail Service Provider (ESP) to help you manage the logistics of your strategy.

Part II: Mapping Out an E-Mail Marketing Strategy

Part II helps you to build a solid foundation for sending e-mails by telling you how to set objectives and how to build a quality e-mail list full of prospects and customers who will help you to meet your objectives. I explain how to set money-making objectives as well as timesaving objectives, and I tell you when and how often to send your e-mail campaigns. Here are also lots of great ideas for finding new e-mail list subscribers and keeping the ones you already have. I also tell you how to ask permission to send e-mail so that your e-mails are perceived as more professional and inviting.

Part III: Constructing an Effective Marketing E-Mail

Part III explains the nuts and bolts of designing and building a marketing e-mail. I tell you how to use layout and design elements to make your e-mails easy to read, and I tell you how to develop relevant content for your e-mails. I also explain the importance of making your content valuable and writing effective calls to action so your audience does something meaningful with your e-mails after receiving them. Part III also gives you lots of ideas for prompting your audience to open and read your e-mails.

Part IV: Delivering and Tracking Your E-Mails

Part IV is where your e-mail marketing strategy finds an enduring future. I explain how to use e-mail tracking reports to determine whether your e-mail strategy is working. I show you how to calculate important metrics, such as open rates and click-through rates. I also explain how to identify and minimize bounced and blocked e-mail and how to optimize your e-mails to sidestep some kinds of e-mail filters. The concluding chapter in Part IV explains how to use click-through data and Web analytics to increase your results and how to deepen your customer relationships and expand your online presence with e-mail surveys and other technology marketing endeavors such as search engine optimization and blogs.

Part V: The Part of Tens

In Part V, you find two lists each containing ten important bite-sized summaries of e-mail marketing information. The first list contains the ten e-mail marketing practices you should avoid, and the second list contains ten resources you should seek out.

Appendix A is an HTML primer that aids you in customizing your e-mails beyond the confines of a visual editor or designing through a user interface. Appendix B shows one small business' entire e-mail marketing portfolio and includes an example of each type of e-mail you should have in your e-mail marketing arsenal.

Icons Used in This Book

When you scan the contents of this book looking for tips, reminders, and ideas, you can look for the following icons in the margin to help you find important information fast:

This icon signifies a tip, idea, shortcut, or strategy that can save you time or trouble.

This icon signifies information that you should remember when taking certain actions.

This icon signifies important details that might cause your strategy to stumble or come to a halt if left unaddressed.

This icon signifies information that is technical in nature.

This icon signifies a strategy or process that either requires or is made much simpler by using an ESP. In Chapter 1, you can read about the benefits of using an ESP to help with your e-mail marketing.

Where to Go from Here

If you have a new business or if don't know a lot about marketing, you might want to start with Part I and read each chapter in order. If you're an experienced business owner and tech-savvy marketer with a large e-mail list, you can scan through each part's table of contents and read the chapters or topics in any order.

Either way, it's time to get started with building your repeat and referral business as well as deepening your relationships with your prospects and customers with e-mail marketing!

Part I
Getting Started with E-Mail Marketing

The 5th Wave   By Rich Tennant

"For 30 years I've put a hat and coat on to make sales calls and I'm not changing now just because I'm doing it by e-mail in my living room."

In this part . . .

*E*very marketing medium has its strengths and limitations, and e-mail is no exception. Part I helps you to
understand e-mail's place in the world of marketing so you
can launch your e-mail strategy in the right direction.

Chapter 1 gives an overview of some basic marketing principles and tells you in general terms how to apply marketing
principles to your e-mail strategy. This chapter also explains
the benefits of e-mail marketing and how to maximize those
benefits by using professional e-mail services.

Chapter 2 tells you how you can make money from your
e-mail marketing efforts and includes tips for lowering
costs as well as increasing revenue. Here are examples of
using e-mail to follow up with prospects and grow your
repeat business while lowering your costs.

Chapter 3 explains spam from the consumer's perspective
as well as from a legal and industry perspective. The chapter
includes information about the CAN-SPAM Act of 2003 and
tips for avoiding spam complaints from consumers.

Chapter 1

Adding E-Mail to a Successful Marketing Mix

*W*alking into a business where the first dollar of profit is framed victoriously on the wall always reminds me how important the first customer is to any small business. Your first customer represents validation of your business idea and proof that your products and services are valuable enough to cause someone to part with his money in order to obtain them.

The first dollar of profit is certainly cause for celebration. However, no matter how useful, important, unique, beneficial, or fitting your products or services are to consumers, no one will purchase them if you can't effectively demonstrate that their value exceeds their price.

Demonstrating your value takes a lot of communication as well as the application of sound marketing principles. E-mail, Web sites, business cards, signs, and postcards are all good ways to communicate your value to consumers, but some mediums are better than others for certain kinds of objectives, and all your marketing mediums have to work together to have the greatest impact.

In this chapter, I show you how to use e-mail in combination with other marketing mediums and how to apply basic marketing principles to your e-mail marketing strategy so your framed dollar of profit won't start to feel lonely.

Fitting E-Mail into Your Marketing Strategy

Including e-mail in your marketing mix isn't as simple as transferring more traditional message formats into electronic formats or abandoning more expensive mediums in favor of e-mail delivery. Maximizing your business' e-mail marketing potential involves two ongoing tasks:

- ✔ Analyzing the strengths and limitations of each medium in your marketing mix
- ✔ Developing messages that work harmoniously across multiple mediums to achieve your objectives

Determining which mediums are likely to work together to make a significant, positive impact on your business is a matter of some trial and error. At the same time, though, some mediums have obvious advantages for small businesses. E-mail is one such example because it's cost effective and because the returns on permission-based e-mail campaigns are generally outstanding.

According to the Direct Marketing Association (www.the-dma.org) economic impact study released in October 2006, e-mail marketing returned $57.25 for every dollar spent in 2005. The study also found that print catalogs generated $7.09 and non–e-mail Internet marketing generated $22.52 for each dollar spent on those marketing mediums.

Combining e-mail with another medium can improve the returns on both mediums. The next sections explain the benefits of combining e-mail and other mediums together, and include tips for using various combinations.

Sending commercial e-mail to complete strangers is illegal. To keep on the right side of the law, combine at least one other medium with e-mail in order to initiate relationships with prospective customers. For more information about the legalities of sending commercial e-mail, see Chapter 3.

Combining e-mail with other mediums

Delivering your messages by combining different mediums is an effective way to market your business, but you'll probably find it more affordable to lean heavily on a few communication mediums where delivering your message results in the highest return.

Using e-mail for targeted follow-up is one of the best ways to maximize your overall return on the marketing dollars you spend. Here's how you can employ a targeted follow-up:

1. Your business uses traditional marketing mediums to initiate contact with new prospects.

   For example, if you have a pizza place, you can position an employee holding a sign on a busy sidewalk to talk to potential customers.

2. You collect contact and interest information from the prospects who respond to your initial contacts.

   In exchange for a free slice of pizza, you ask potential customers for an e-mail address and what kind of coupons they'd be interested in receiving via e-mail.

3. You send e-mails containing personalized messages based on the information you collect.

   If your potential customer indicates an interest in chicken wings, you can send coupons for, um, chicken wings. You can also ask your customer to print the menu — that you cleverly included in the e-mail — and forward your offer to a friend.

Branding your message across all mediums

In marketing, you're likely to employ several mediums and messages over a period of days, weeks, months, and years to communicate everything necessary to attract and retain enough customers. Keeping the design elements and personality of your messages similar or identical over time — *branding* — reinforces each of your messages and makes each successive message more memorable to your audience.

Consumers are more likely to respond positively to your e-mail messages when they can identify your brand and when the content of each message feels familiar to them. Plan all your marketing messages as if they were one unit to ensure that each message contains design elements that become familiar to your audience when multiple messages are delivered.

Here are some branding ideas to help you give all your marketing messages a familiar look and feel:

✔ **Make your logo identifiable and readable in all types of print and digital formats, with color schemes that look good online and in print.**

In general, your logo and colors should look consistent on

- Signs
- Order forms
- E-mail sign-up forms
- Your Web site
- Receipts
- Business cards
- E-mails

✔ **Include your company name in all your marketing.**

Incorporate you name in

- E-mail From lines
- E-mail addresses
- Your e-mail signature
- Online directories
- Your blog

✔ **Format your messages consistently across mediums.**

When repeating messages in multiple mediums, make sure the following elements are formatted consistently in your e-mails:

- Fonts
- Layouts
- Images
- Headlines
- Contact information
- Calls to action

Make sure that you can also communicate your brand effectively by using words if you want to take advantage of words-only messaging opportunities, such as radio, podcasting, and text-only e-mail delivery. You can find tips for using effective wording in Chapter 8.

Applying Basic Marketing Principles to Your E-Mail Messages

Convincing consumers to part with their money to obtain your products or services usually involves communicating one of two basic messages:

- **Your products or services are unique and unfamiliar to consumers.**

  Your challenge is to educate consumers who are likely to need your products or services so they will buy from you.

- **Your products or services are easily identifiable and widely available.**

  Your challenge is to convince consumers that your business is the best choice among the competition.

Communicating a memorable message almost always takes multiple attempts to get consumers to respond. Effective marketing communications also require you to apply a fair amount of strategy and tactical thinking so that your messages stand out from all the other messages that consumers receive.

Applying basic marketing principles to your e-mail messages helps ensure that your marketing communications are in tune with your audience and your overall objectives. Although you can apply literally hundreds of marketing principles to the e-mail strategies and tactics throughout this book, begin building your message strategy with a few general principles in mind.

Marketing message strategy is an ongoing cycle of three basic steps:

1. Determine your message and the best audience for your message.

2. Deliver your message by using the medium that is best suited for your audience and your message.

3. Evaluate your results and apply your experience, as well as more refined marketing principles, to determine your next message.

   Figure 1-1 illustrates these three steps.

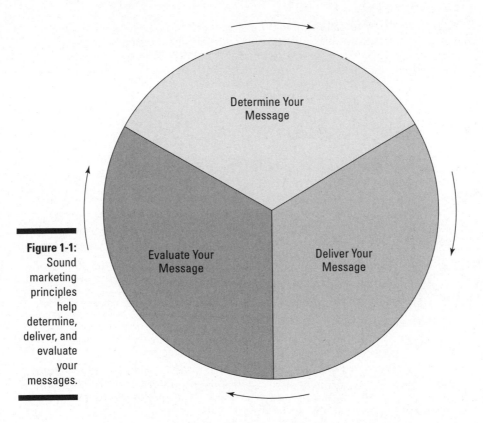

Figure 1-1:
Sound
marketing
principles
help
determine,
deliver, and
evaluate
your
messages.

The following sections discuss some basic marketing principles that help you determine and evaluate your e-mail messages and related content. Using marketing principles to determine each message and then evaluating each message allows you to begin with a sound message strategy and continue to refine your messages and your strategy over time. I cover e-mail delivery in Part IV of this book.

Determining what your e-mail messages should say

E-mail is a great marketing tool, but you can't simply communicate any e-mail message multiple times and expect the messages to result in sales. Make your e-mail messages as concise as possible; people usually scan e-mails rather than take the time to read every word. Clear and concise messages are by far the best choice for e-mail content, but your messages should include the following content at a minimum:

✔ **Your value proposition:** A *value proposition* is a statement that tells con-sumers why your products or services are worth paying for. A good value proposition shows consumers that your products or services solve a problem or fulfill a want or need better than anyone else can. Here are some examples of value propositions:

- *Don't put Rover in a cage for the holidays. Our pet-sitting services make your vacations worry-free and allow your pets to enjoy the holidays too — in the comfort of their own home.*

- *Want it tomorrow? Our free shipping is the fastest available.*

- *Just because a diamond is forever doesn't mean your payments have to be. Our home equity loans can help you pay off high interest debt and our service is more personal than the big banks.*

✔ **Information to support your value proposition:** Value propositions rarely entice someone to make an immediate purchase all by themselves. Most of the time, you'll need to support your value proposition with additional information to convince buyers to take action. You can include this sup-portive information along with your value proposition in one e-mail mes-sage, or you might need multiple support messages delivered over periods of time. Examples include

- Testimonials and facts

- Directions to your office, store, or Web site

- Incentives to help someone justify taking action

- Images and other design elements to reinforce the text

✔ **One or more calls to action:** A *call to action* is a statement that asks someone to take a specific type of action in a specific way. Calling for action is important because people tend to delete e-mails after they read them if they aren't told what to do next. For example, just because your phone number appears at the bottom of an e-mail doesn't mean that people will automatically pick up the phone and dial the number. You'll get better results if you ask your audience to phone you for a specific reason; of course, provide the phone number. However, an effective call to action doesn't necessarily entail asking for an immediate purchase decision. Sometimes, your prospective customers have to take many steps to end up with a store receipt their hand. Examples of calls to action could include

- *Call now and ask for a free consultation.*

- *Click this link to add this item to your shopping cart.*

- *Click this link to download the informational video.*

- *Save this message to your inbox today.*

- *Print this e-card and bring it with you for a free cup of coffee.*

You can read more about creating effective calls to action in Chapter 10.

Determining the most effective wording for your e-mails usually entails some testing combined with educated assumptions based on how your customer perceives your business and your products or services.

Here are some questions to ask yourself to help determine what your e-mail messages should say. As you answer each question, think in terms of what your customers find beneficial about your business instead of simply stating your own interests.

- ✔ What are the features of your products or services?
- ✔ How will the features of what you sell benefit your consumers?
- ✔ How you are different from your competition?
- ✔ Why are your differences worth paying for?
- ✔ Can you summarize your answers to the previous four questions in a paragraph? Try to use two lines of text or ten words or fewer.

If you aren't sure how your customers would answer these questions, rewrite the questions and ask a few of your customers to respond. You might be surprised by their answers!

Determining how your e-mail messages should look

Design elements, such as images and colors, are important parts of every e-mail message because they can reinforce the words that you use or cause your words to feel differently to the reader. Figure 1-2 shows a plain e-mail message before any design elements are applied to it.

Figure 1-2: This e-mail lacks the design elements necessary to reinforce the message.

```
We're Having a Vacation Sale!

Since there aren't any real holidays coming up we're inviting you to
create your own special holiday. Call it whatever you want, but make
sure you choose your special holiday and book it by the end of this
month because airfares are lower than ever right now and there are no
restrictions. There's never been a better time to take time off and
enjoy yourself with one of our special travel packages.
Choose a holiday below or call us to create your own!

Lighthouse Vacation
Imagine yourself surrounded by beautiful water and magnificent sunsets.
Choose this vacation by e-mailing us or calling today!

Beach Vacation
Our private beaches are perfect for relaxing or an aquatic adventure. Scuba diving,
deep sea fishing, and snorkeling are just a few of the activities you can enjoy.
Choose this vacation by e-mailing us or calling today!

Vacations must be booked by the end of the month to receive special airfare discounts.
Some date restrictions may apply. Ask about dates when you call or e-mail us.

Save 25%
Book your holiday vacation by the end of the month and you will save an additional
25% on a car rental. Offer Expires: at the end of the month
```

A text-only e-mail not only fails to reinforce and enhance the value proposition, but it's also difficult to scan and read. Even simple design elements can have a significant impact on the look and feel of an e-mail message. Figure 1-3 shows the same e-mail with simple added design elements that support and reinforce the message.

Figure 1-3: This e-mail includes design elements to enhance the message.

The formatted e-mail uses images, links, colors, borders, fonts, and effective layout to reinforce certain elements in the message and also makes the main idea of the message easier to grasp because of the holiday vacation theme.

Here are some questions you can ask yourself to help you determine how your e-mail messages should look.

- ✔ What emotions or circumstances cause people to think of your products or services?
- ✔ Which words, fonts, images, and colors communicate those emotions and circumstances?
- ✔ What other mediums are you using to deliver your messages?
- ✔ What limitations and advantages of each medium could affect the look and feel of your messages?

Chapters 8 and 9 cover design elements that you can add to your e-mails to effectively get your message across to your subscribers.

Targeting your e-mail messages

When you're excited about your business, thinking of almost everyone as a potential prospect is easy. You might indeed identify a large audience that needs your products or services, but plenty of people won't buy from you for one reason or another.

At the same time, pockets of opportunity for communicating your messages might exist that you haven't thought of. You can make your e-mail messages more effective by targeting prospects and customers who are most likely to make a purchase decision and also excluding people who are probably never going to buy. Here are some questions you can ask yourself to help determine to whom you should send your e-mail messages:

- ✔ Who is most likely to need your products or services?
- ✔ Who already buys other products or services that are similar or identical to yours?
- ✔ Who buys other products or services that could be perceived as substitutes for yours? Who buys products or services that compliment yours?
- ✔ Who has already purchased from you and when will they be ready to buy again? How many messages does it take to get someone to repeat versus attracting a new customer?

Developing e-mail content in accordance with consumer interaction

Your e-mail content should match how consumers tend to interact with the medium so that your audience can easily internalize and take action on your message. Consider the following comparison between using e-mail to deliver a message and using a billboard to deliver a message.

Imagine planning to put up a billboard next to the highway where people drive by at 65 miles per hour. You aren't likely to get good results if your billboard message includes two paragraphs of text along with an office phone number, cell phone number, fax number, e-mail address, and detailed directions to your office because no one driving by on the highway can internalize such a detailed message so quickly.

And some of the information on the billboard is also difficult for people to take action on even if the billboard's layout makes it easy for drivers to see. For example, drivers aren't likely to send an e-mail to an unfamiliar e-mail address in the body of the billboard message because (hopefully) the drivers aren't in front of their computers then.

People interact with e-mails in much the same way that they interact with billboards because people tend to hastily scan through the content of an e-mail to see whether anything is worth responding to or reading in more detail.

Be sure to use headlines, images, links, and text in ways that allow your audience to internalize your message as they scan.

In contrast, people take action on e-mails much differently than they do from billboards and other indirect mediums. People who see a billboard have to employ another medium (such as a phone or a computer) to make contact with the related business, but people can actively respond to e-mail messages by using the medium itself. For example, people can easily respond to an e-mail by

- Clicking a link in the body of the e-mail
- Downloading a file linked within the e-mail
- Forwarding the e-mail
- Replying to the e-mail
- Clicking a phone number in a mobile e-mail
- Printing the e-mail
- Saving the e-mail to their inbox

Evaluating your messages

Continuously keeping track of the effect your e-mail messages have can help you refine your strategy and make educated changes while you determine future messages.

Message evaluation begins by stating measurable objectives. It then continues while you track and measure your results to determine whether your objectives are achieved. Measurable goals could include the following:

- ✔ Increasing the number of Web site visitors by a certain amount
- ✔ Increasing the number of orders or purchases by a certain amount
- ✔ Receiving feedback and information on a specific issue
- ✔ Increasing event attendance by a certain number
- ✔ Changing opinions or perceptions over a set period of time
- ✔ Increasing the size of your contact database by a certain number

Tracking and measuring your message results can be a snap with an E-Mail Service Provider (ESP). (Read more about ESPs later in this chapter.) An ESP tells you exactly who opens your e-mail and who clicks the links in your e-mail message. Figure 1-4 shows a sample of an e-mail click-summary report.

Not all your e-mail evaluation has to be based on clicks, however. For example, you might ask people to phone you and request more information. Then, you can evaluate your message based on how many phone calls you receive and what people say when they call. Other methods of tracking and measurement include

- ✔ **Ask people to print your e-mail message to redeem an offer.** You can then count the number of customers who return a printed e-mail to your store or office.

- ✔ **Ask people to mention your message when e-mailing a reply.** You can track how many e-mails mention the message.

- ✔ **Ask people to fill out an online form.** You can analyze the data collected from the forms.

- ✔ **Ask people to forward your e-mail to friends and colleagues.** You can track how many new subscribers you receive as a result of the forwarded e-mails.

- ✔ **Track activity in the product lines and services mentioned in your message.** You can calculate the difference between the average level of activity and the change in activity.

Emails : Reports : Click-through Statistics

Click-through Statistics

Here you can compare the effectiveness of each link in this email by viewing the click-through statistic. For recent emails, you can click on the unique click-through number to see the contacts who clicked on a link.

You may save the contacts who clicked on this email as a new list - the new list will not be displayed on your Visitor Signup Form as a default. Contact click-through data is maintained for 90 days from the day of the email.

< Back   🖨 Printable Version

Email Name: New Workshop Calendar 3-06-07

Date Sent: 3/7/2007

Email Link	Unique Click-throughs	Click-through Distribution
http://colorado.constantcontact.com/	34	9.9%
http://colorado.constantcontact.com/learning-center/books/index.jsp	4	1.2%
http://colorado.constantcontact.com/regional/bio.jsp	8	2.3%
http://colorado.constantcontact.com/regional/bio.jsphttp://colorado.constantcontact.com/regional/bio.jsp	3	0.9%
http://colorado.constantcontact.com/regional/events.jsp?trumbaEmbed=view%3Devent%26eventid%3D59878132	52	15.2%
http://colorado.constantcontact.com/regional/events.jsp?trumbaEmbed=view%3Devent%26eventid%3D64116411	159	46.4%
http://colorado.constantcontact.com/services/index.jsp	4	1.2%
http://community.constantcontact.com/	2	0.6%
http://www.bouldersbdc.com/?site_id=167&id_sub=7726&page_id=4724&productgallery_id=1	77	22.4%
Total Click-throughs	343	100%

Save as List

Figure 1-4:
Use a click-summary report to find summary information for each click.

Courtesy of Constant Contact

Reaping the Benefits of E-Mail Marketing

E-mail might seem like a cost-effective way to deliver your marketing messages. For the most part, it is because you can send personalized, targeted, and interest-specific messages to a large number of people. The value of e-mail marketing doesn't end with the cost, however. E-mail marketing has certain advantages over other forms of direct marketing for your business and for the people who request and receive your e-mails.

Asking for immediate action

You won't have to wait around too long to determine whether an e-mail message was successful. According to Marketing Sherpa (www.marketingsherpa.com) 2007 E-mail Marketing Benchmark Guide, 80 percent of the e-mail you send is opened in the first 48 hours after delivery.

After an e-mail is opened, it doesn't take long for your audience to take immediate action because people can take action on an e-mail with one click of the mouse. Immediate actions include

- ✔ Opening and reading the e-mail
- ✔ Clicking a link
- ✔ Clicking a Reply button
- ✔ Forwarding
- ✔ Printing the e-mail
- ✔ Saving the e-mail

I show you how to ask for immediate action in Chapter 10.

Gathering feedback

E-mail is a two-way form of communication, and even commercial e-mail can be used to gather feedback and responses from your audience. People can easily reply to e-mails, and many consumers love to share their opinions when it's easy for them to do so. Feedback from e-mails comes in two basic categories:

- ✔ *Stated feedback* happens when someone
  - • Fills out an online form
  - • Fills out an online survey
  - • Sends a reply
- ✔ *Behavioral feedback* happens when you track
  - • Clicks on links
  - • E-mail open rates
  - • E-mails forwarded to friends

If you aren't receiving replies and feedback from your marketing e-mails, you probably aren't asking for them. I cover customer interaction in Chapter 13.

Generating awareness

When was the last time you mailed thousands of postcards, and your customers began crowding around copy machines trying to duplicate the postcard so they can stick stamps to them and forward the message to their friends? E-mail programs have a Forward button with which users can easily send a copy of your e-mail to one or more people in your recipient's address book. ESPs also provide a trackable forward link that you can insert in your e-mails so you can find out who is forwarding your e-mails.

Staying top-of-mind

If you send periodic e-mails with valuable content, people who aren't ready to buy right away are more likely to remember you and your business when they become ready to buy. If your content is valuable enough to save, your prospects and customers might even create an inbox on their desktop with your company name on it and start filing your e-mails for future reference. When they pull them out to read again, your message is communicated again. Here are some ways that e-mail can be used for top-of-mind awareness and future reference:

- ✔ Archive your e-mail newsletters on your Web site.
- ✔ Ask people to save your e-mails to a folder in their e-mail program.
- ✔ Ask people to print your e-mails and post them.
- ✔ Print your e-mails and place them in a flip book on your counter so you can refer back to recent offers and show samples of the value of your e-mail list.

Taking Advantage of E-Mail Service Providers

The days where you could send a single e-mail and blind-copy hundreds of other people are over. Spam filters, firewalls, junk folders, and consumer distrust are all reasons to turn to professionals for help with your e-mail strategy. *E-Mail Service Providers* (ESPs) are companies that provide one or more of the following commercial e-mail services:

- ✔ Improved e-mail deliverability
- ✔ Database and list management
- ✔ E-mail template design
- ✔ E-mail message and content creation
- ✔ Tracking reports
- ✔ Advice and consulting

ESPs allow you to accomplish much more with your e-mail marketing than you could on your own. Some ESPs even provide various levels of outsourcing for higher prices if you don't want to do your own e-mail marketing. Here are a few examples of the kinds of benefits that ESPs provide:

- ✔ **Give your business a professional look.** ESPs can help you create great-looking e-mail communications without programming knowledge. Most ESPs provide templates with consumer-friendly layouts to accommodate any type of message. Some ESPs provide template-creation wizards that allow you to control all your own design elements for a low cost, and some ESPs either include professional services to help you with semi-custom designs or allow you to completely outsource and customize your template designs. Here are some of the templates that ESPs usually provide:

  - Newsletters

  - Promotions

  - Announcements

  - Press releases

  - Event invitations

  - Greeting cards

  - Business letters

  Figure 1-5 shows an e-mail template that an ESP provides.

- ✔ **Keep your marketing legal.** ESPs are required to incorporate current e-mail laws in order for customers to easily comply. Reputable ESPs take compliance a step further than the basic legal requirements and adhere to more professional standards in line with consumer preferences. Examples of professional standards include the following:

  - Safe one-click unsubscribe links

  - Privacy statements

  - Physical address added to e-mails

  - Sending from a verified e-mail address

- ✔ **Help you with logistics and reporting.** ESPs can help you manage the data and feedback associated with executing your e-mail strategy. Here are some examples of ways in which ESPs can help you manage your information:

  - Storage and retrieval of subscriber information

  - Reports on deliverability

  - Automated handling of subscribe and unsubscribe requests

  - Tracking information on blocked and bounced e-mail

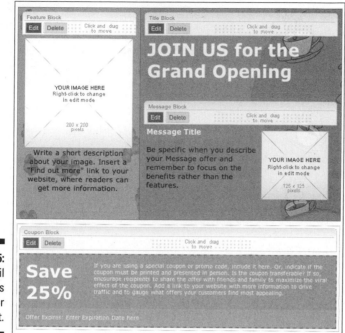

Courtesy of Constant Contact

Figure 1-5:
This e-mail
template is
ready for
content.

✔ **Help with content.** ESPs want you to be successful because if your
e-mail messages are effective, you will likely reward your ESP by being
a loyal customer. Many ESPs have resources available that will help you
develop your content and use best-practices. Examples include

• Online communities

• Webinars

• Tutorials

• Classroom-style training

• Consultation

✔ **Teach you best practices.** ESPs can give you valuable information on
consumer preferences that would be too expensive or impossible for
you to obtain on your own. ESPs send a lot of e-mails on behalf of their
customers, and they are good at staying up to date on consumer preferences and professional standards. Some ESPs are willing to share their
knowledge in order to make your e-mails more effective. Some things
you might learn include

• Best times and days to send

• How to improve your open rates

- How to avoid spam complaints
- What to do when e-mail is blocked or filtered
- How to design and layout your content

The following is a list of some of the leading ESPs in various niches:

- ✔ **Constant Contact (www.constantcontact.com):** Comprehensive service designed for small businesses offering an easy-to-use graphical user interface (GUI), simple list upload, and over 200 templates as well as an integrated e-mail/online survey product. Starts at $15 flat fee per month and includes unlimited free support and online training.

- ✔ **Microsoft Office 2007 (http://office.microsoft.com):** Offers template creation through Word and Publisher documents and includes a separate e-mail marketing service for bulk sending through Outlook. Watch out for CAN-SPAM compliance issues and minimal support options. Starts at $9.95 flat fee per month after purchasing and installing the Office Suite (MSRP is $399.99).

- ✔ **Vertical Response (www.verticalresponse.com):** Offers e-mail marketing and postcard marketing integration. Fees for e-mail marketing only are charged on a per e-mail sent basis starting at $15.00 per thousand with tiered discounts after the first 1,000 sent e-mails.

- ✔ **1 Shopping Cart (www.1shoppingcart.com):** Offers auto responders and other types of e-mail campaigns along with the ability to integrate opt-in mechanisms with an online shopping cart. Starts at $29 per month.

- ✔ **Exact Target (www.exacttarget.com):** Offers an e-mail marketing application with higher-level database integration and advanced features. Schedule a demo for pricing information. An annual contract may be required.

To conduct your own ESP investigation, search for *Email Marketing Solutions* online.

Chapter 2

Maximizing Revenue with E-Mail

*M*aking more money than you spend is at the foundation of every business opportunity. When the idea for your business first hit you, hopefully, you took the time to make a few calculations to determine whether your idea seemed capable of making a profit.

Although I'm sure that many successful small businesses start with little more than basic math, one very important calculation rarely finds its way into a business plan: the cost of acquiring enough customers for your business to survive.

Your future customers aren't going to come find you in your home office or start calling you the minute you hook up your mobile phone service. You have to find ways to tell people about your business, and you have to make sure that your communication efforts make more money than they cost.

E-mail is a cost-effective form of communication, but sending e-mail only because it's inexpensive is sort of like buying the latest and greatest computer so you can play solitaire. In this chapter, I show you how to capitalize on the power of e-mail to turn your customer acquisition costs into more opportunities for growth and reward.

Increasing Revenue with Repeat Customers

You don't have to be in business too long before you recognize that repeat customers are important. If you've been in business for a while, you might even know your repeat customers by name, and you get excited when you see them pulling up in their car or when their phone number appears on your caller ID.

Staying in front of your customers with valuable periodic e-mails is probably one of the best things you can do to drive loyalty, repeat sales, and referrals. Repeat customers are more likely than cold prospects — people who are totally unaware of your business — to make immediate purchases in response to a single message. Customers who are familiar with your business have history with you that makes up for a lot of the communications you would have to send to tell a cold prospect why your products or services are worth paying for.

The more familiar your customers are with your business, the fewer messages you need to send. Sometimes generating repeat business can be as simple as sending a payment reminder or an announcement that the newly updated products are available.

The next sections explain the value of repeat business and tell you how you can increase your revenue using e-mail to drive repeat customers to your business in the most profitable ways.

Understanding the value of repeat customers

Repeat customers are not only easier to obtain than first time customers, but it's also much more profitable to do business with repeat customers than with cold prospects. Figure 2-1 illustrates the value of repeat customers over time.

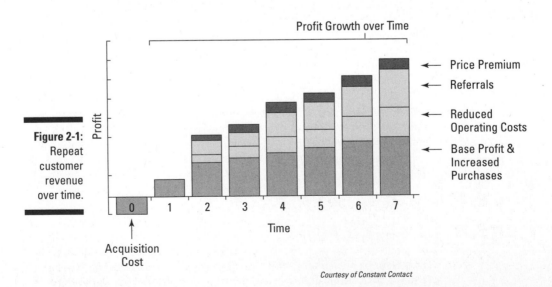

Figure 2-1: Repeat customer revenue over time.

Courtesy of Constant Contact

Here's how repeat customers can help your business grow:

✔ **Cost to obtain a customer:** Figure 2-1 shows a loss in Year 1 because a first-time customer usually represents a cost to your business instead of a profit. For example, suppose you open a restaurant and you want to sell 100 plates of food per day. Getting strangers to come for lunch takes a lot of communication. Here are some of the costs you might incur when getting the word out:

- A sign for the side of your building
- Ads in the newspaper and the phone directory
- Coupons in the mail
- Search engine optimization

After spending so much money on awareness, the first 100 people to buy lunch for $10 represents a loss to the business if you spend more than $1,000 on awareness. I cover lowering your customer acquisition costs in more detail later in this chapter.

✔ **Base profit:** Your *base profit* is the amount of money left over after you pay all your expenses. Base profit grows incrementally as the number of profitable purchases increase.

✔ **Profit from increased purchases:** Profits increase over and above base profits after your fixed costs are covered, and each additional purchase results in a lower percentage of revenue allocated to fixed costs. For example, say that your rent is $100 per month and that $10 from each purchase pays the rent. After ten purchases, your $10 represents additional profits. Repeat buyers also spend more money on the average purchase than first-time customers.

✔ **Profit from reduced operating costs:** When repeat customers grow more familiar with your business, they don't require as much hand-holding as new customers. For example, new customers might need to call tech support frequently to use your products effectively. After they become familiar with your products, though, you won't need to field as many phone calls to support repeat purchases.

✔ **Profit from referrals:** The more frequently your customers interact with your business and your products and services, the more likely they are to talk about their experiences with their peers. Referrals are a lot like repeat customers because when the referred customer trusts the source of the referral, you generally don't need to spend as much time or money convincing the referral to make a purchase.

✔ **Profit from price premiums:** Competing on price is a bane for some small businesses. Repeat customers who trust you and become comfortable with frequent purchases are not as willing as first-time customers to move their business to your competitors when your prices are a little higher. Higher prices shouldn't be used to reward loyalty, but you can use price premiums as a way to offset the costs of rewarding loyalty. Lots of repeat customers will pay more to have special privileges.

Sending multiple messages to drive revenue

Communicating with prospective customers is always somewhat of a numbers game because even your best prospects and repeat customers aren't ready to make an immediate purchase every time you contact them. A successfully delivered marketing message usually reaches people who fall in one of three categories:

- ✔ **Immediate purchasers:** The smallest slice represents immediate purchasers (see Figure 2-2). Building a marketing strategy based on a single message, or *one-time touch*, to go after cold prospects in hopes of immediate purchases usually results in a loss or a small return on investment (ROI). Sometimes, immediate purchases happen just because you delivered your message at the right place and at the right time. A single message that results in an immediate purchase usually means that the prospect has already done some research or is otherwise familiar with you or the products and services you sell.

  This type of immediate purchase is the exception, of course, and not the rule.

- ✔ **Interested prospects:** A second portion of the pie represents prospects who show interest but aren't ready to make a purchase immediately. Interested prospects are unlikely to return for these reasons:

  - Need time for more research or compare products

  - Waiting for money to become available

  - No trust built yet for you or your business

  - A similar recent purchase

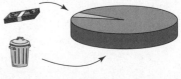

Prospects who show interest but aren't yet ready to buy are unlikely to remember a single message and turn to your business several weeks, months, or years later when they become ready to make an immediate purchase. Instead, they might end up becoming the immediate purchaser in response to someone else's message.

Figure 2-2:
An immediate purchaser represents the smallest slice of the pie.

One-time touch

Immediate Purchaser   Immediate Purchase

Interested (Buy Later)   Unlikely to Return
Not Now (Maybe Later)
No Interest

✔ **Uninterested people:** The rest of the pie represents people who aren't interested at all in your message. There will always be people who are not at all interested in your products or services for one reason or another. Even the best marketing strategies can't keep you from spending a portion of your time and money needlessly contacting people who will never buy from you.

You can turn interested prospects into immediate purchasers by following up on your messages. Periodic follow-up messages can also help to turn your immediate purchasers into repeat purchasers. Figure 2-3 shows how a follow-up message can garner you customers.

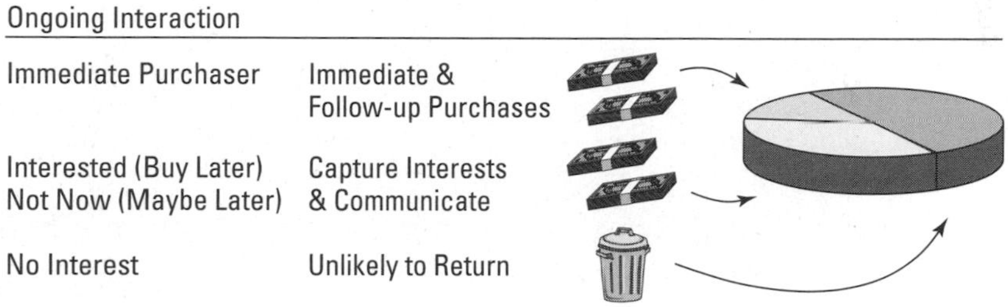

Figure 2-3:
A repeated marketing message increases immediate purchases over time.

Ongoing Interaction

Immediate Purchaser	Immediate & Follow-up Purchases
Interested (Buy Later) Not Now (Maybe Later)	Capture Interests & Communicate
No Interest	Unlikely to Return

Here's how the three categories of customers break down:

✔ **Immediate purchasers:** The second biggest slice now represents immediate purchases. Repeat messages help to build trust in you and your offers, and follow-up messages help your interested prospects with research and incentives to justify an immediate purchase.

✔ **Interested prospects:** Sending additional messages to customers who have already made an immediate purchase and probably aren't interested in buying again keeps your business top-of-mind when your recent customers are ready to buy again.

✔ **Uninterested people:** The third slice of the pie represents the prospects who are still not interested in your messages or your repeat messages. You might be tempted to continue sending messages to prospects who never seem interested, but you're better off focusing your marketing dollars on messages that target the most likely buyers. If your messages always result in an extraordinary lack of interest, you need to change your message or your audience.

Repeating the wrong message with the wrong frequency has the potential to drive your audience away. When you send follow-up messages, make sure your repeat messages employ the following sound marketing principles:

✔ **Make your messages personal.** People are less likely to open your e-mails if they don't recognize who it's from. Before you send a follow-up message, think about where the people on your e-mail list came from and then act accordingly. For example:

- • If you met each prospect on your list personally, send the e-mail using your name in the From line.

- • If you collected e-mails by using a form on your Web site, include your domain name in the From line.

Check with your E-Mail Service Provider (ESP) whether you can do an electronic mail-merge on your database so that you can personalize your e-mails with each recipient's first name.

✔ **Make your messages memorable.** Most marketing messages are easily forgotten by consumers. If you can't connect your e-mail messages to a prior relationship, your prospect might feel that your follow-up messages are junk mail. Your e-mails will generally be more memorable when you consistently remind your prospects that they know you. For example, send follow-ups in these situations:

- • Within 24 hours of the very first contact if you met the prospect in person

- • A welcome e-mail when your prospect signs up for your e-mail list online

✔ **Timing is everything.** Setting your audience's expectations and sending e-mail according to a frequency plan helps to ensure that your messages aren't overwhelming:

- • *Periodically remind all your prospects* how they came to be subscribed to your list and what they can expect to receive going forward.

- • *Don't let too much time go between communications.* Once monthly is a good minimum as long as your content is relevant.

- • *Remain consistent with your timing.* For example, if you choose to send an e-mail every Friday, make sure you always send it on Friday at the same time.

✔ **Make your e-mails valuable.** After you capture the attention and interest of your prospects, you generally have one or two chances to impress them before they decide whether they want more of your communications. Before you send follow-up e-mails, ask yourself what your prospect is likely to find valuable. Keep these points in mind:

- • Send only the information your prospect requested.

- • Keep your messages concise and easy to scan.

- Analyze your message feedback and make changes quickly to match your prospects' interests.
- Include information in your e-mails that is valuable to prospects even if they don't make an immediate purchase.

Saving time with e-mail follow-up

Another way how e-mail helps to drive revenue is by making follow-up more time efficient. For example, sending a monthly e-mail newsletter takes the same amount of time and effort whether you send it to 100, 1,000, or 10,000 people.

Adding prospective customers to your e-mail database over time can amount to a lot of additional follow-up and repeat messages that you would otherwise be unable to handle by using more traditional forms of communication.

Table 2-1 compares networking alone and networking with e-mail follow-up. The column on the left shows the monthly number of initial contacts made by meeting 20 people at each of 12 monthly networking events. The column on the right shows the total monthly follow-up contacts and cumulative total follow-up contacts made by sending a monthly e-mail.

Table 2-1		Networking Follow-Up Efficiency with E-Mail	
Networking Only		*Networking with E-Mail Follow Up*	
Month	*Initial Contacts*	*Follow-up E-Mails Sent*	*Cumulative E-Mail Contacts Made*
January	20	20	20
February	20	40	60
March	20	60	120
April	20	80	200
May	20	100	300
June	20	120	420
July	20	140	560
August	20	160	720
September	20	180	900

(continued)

Table 2-1 *(continued)*			
Networking Only		*Networking with E-Mail Follow Up*	
Month	*Initial Contacts*	*Follow-up E-Mails Sent*	*Cumulative E-Mail Contacts Made*
October	20	200	1,100
November	20	220	1,320
December	20	240	1,560
Totals	**240**	**1,560**	**1,560**

As a business owner, I hope you are in touch with more than 20 people per month, but even if you meet only 240 people a year, imagine the time you would save by sending e-mails instead of making 1,560 phone calls or sticking 1,560 stamps to stacks of postal mail.

If networking isn't a part of your marketing strategy, compare your initial contact methods with an e-mail strategy. For example, if you place an ad in the phone directory that generates 20 calls per month, make sure you ask those 20 callers for their e-mail addresses so you can follow up.

Lowering Your Costs

Following up on your messages will improve your chances for making more money over time, but only if your messages end up costing you less than the excess revenue your repeated messages generate. Your challenge is to figure out how to send follow-up messages without spending too much money.

Determining whether your repeat message strategy is too expensive isn't as simple as adding all your advertising expenses or sticking to an arbitrarily reasonable percentage of your revenue for your marketing expenses. The facts are that some repeat messages raise the cost of obtaining a new customer, and some repeat messages actually lower the cost of obtaining a new customer.

Spending more money to repeat your marketing messages to lower your costs might sound counterintuitive, but grasping the concept is important for you to make good choices about your marketing expenses. The next sections show you how to use repeated e-mail messages to lower the costs associated with gaining new customers.

Gaining a healthy perspective on your costs

When you own a small business, you can easily focus too much attention on cutting costs instead of making sure that every dollar you spend signifies more than a dollar in return. For example, you might not think that an increase in your electric bill is something to smile about. Say, though, that you own a jewelry store and you discover that a high-intensity light bulb uses more electricity but makes your jewelry sparkle more brilliantly, you might find yourself delighted to pay more for electricity. The light bulbs that cause the increase in your electric bill are responsible for more jewelry sales.

Viewing your costs in terms of their associated return is a great way to justify the costs that return profits and also minimize the costs that just drain your bank account. One of the reasons why e-mail is such a fantastic way to maximize revenue is because e-mail marketing is capable of high returns on each dollar spent sending e-mail.

Figuring out the cost to obtain a customer

The amount of money you need to spend to get a consumer who is totally unaware of your products or services to make a purchase is called an *acquisition cost.* Calculating the acquisition cost for each customer is important for two reasons:

- ✔ **The cost per customer helps to determine whether the same amount of profit could have been obtained for a lower cost.** For example, if you could obtain 120 customers by simply offering a $5 discount to each customer, spending $8.33 per customer to build a Web site isn't as profitable as offering a discount.

- ✔ **The cost per customer represents a benchmark for determining whether spending more money on marketing will be more profitable.** For example, if all your visitors to your Web site make an immediate purchase, it makes sense to spend more money to increase the number of visitors but only if you can drive more visitors in a cost-effective way.

Suppose you put up a Web site that costs $1,000. Every person who visits your Web site makes an immediate purchase, which results in a profit of $10. Thus, you need to make 100 sales to break even, as shown in this formula:

$1,000 (Web site cost) = $10 (profit per sale) × 100 (sales)

Now suppose that your Web site gets ten visitors per month for 12 months. Every visitor makes an immediate purchase, so your profit and loss statement for the year appears as follows:

(120 [total sales] × $10 [profit per sale]) – $1,000 (Web site cost) = $200 (total profit)

Making a profit is always better than a loss, but to get a true measure of your profit, you have to calculate the cost of acquiring 120 customers as well. Adding the cost of acquisition results in the following:

$1,000 (Web site cost) / 120 (total sales) = $8.33 (cost per customer)

Table 2-2 shows the original cost per sale generated by your Web site, and then demonstrates the effect of repeated e-mail marketing messages intended to drive more traffic to your Web site for conversion.

Table 2-2	Web Site Cost of Acquisition with E-Mail		
Original Cost per Sale	**Cost of 100,000 E-Mails**	**Added Sales**	**New Cost per Sale**
$8.33 (@120 sales)	$1,000	200	$6.25 ($2,000 / 320)
$6.25	$1,000	200	$5.77 ($3,000 / 520)
$5.77	$1,000	200	$5.55 ($4,000 / 720)
$5.55	$1,000	200	$5.43 ($5,000 / 920)

Of course, this strategy assumes that every time you send 100,000 e-mails, you drive 200 additional visitors to your Web site. Every additional e-mail campaign costs more money yet results in both more revenue and a more profitable and lower cost of acquisition.

Take a look at your Web sites for places where prospects are confronted with compelling reasons to make an immediate purchase decision. Examples might include

✔ Visiting your Web site or store

✔ Attending a seminar or workshop

✔ Personally experiencing your sales presentation

✔ Receiving your e-mails

✔ Trying your products and services

Lowering your acquisition costs through e-mail

Suppose you own a retail business where most of your sales are made through weekly group seminars in your store. Someone you met at a networking event comes to your seminar and makes a purchase, netting you one sale for your networking efforts. You also signed up 10 people of the 20 you met to your newsletter list. Figure 2-4 shows how effective your marketing dollars are.

Networking Event

20 business cards total
 10 weren't interested at all
 5 seemed interested
 4 weren't interested but maybe later
 1 immediate purchase

Cost of event, time, gas, handouts, etc. = $100
Total customers gained from the event = 1
 Cost of each customer gained = $100 ea

Profit from all purchases due to event = $100
 Total net profit from event = $0

Figure 2-4: Simple cost of acquisition calculation.

After one week, you send your first monthly e-mail to your new list subscribers, which gains you four additional purchases through your in-store seminars. Figure 2-5 shows how your previous calculations look after you update them with the new purchase information.

E-mail follow-up not only resulted in $400 in additional revenue, but it also resulted in lowering the acquisition cost of each customer you met at the networking event from $100 per customer to $20 per customer because you were able to obtain an additional four purchases by sending follow up e-mails.

Many businesses are bought and sold on the strength of their customer database. Possessing contact information and detailed information on buying behavior, purchasing patterns, and interests are assets that make your business valuable and your revenue and growth more predictable. You can build on your e-mail list while at the same time helping yourself maximize the return on all your assets. You can read more about building your e-mail list in Chapter 5.

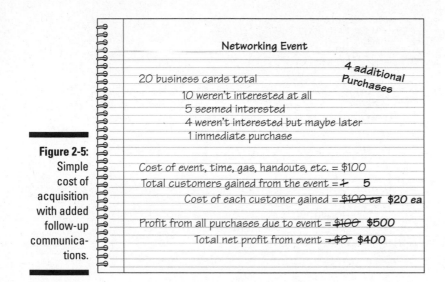

Networking Event

20 business cards total   *4 additional Purchases*

    10 weren't interested at all
    5 seemed interested
    4 weren't interested but maybe later
    1 immediate purchase

Cost of event, time, gas, handouts, etc. = $100
Total customers gained from the event = ~~1~~ 5
    Cost of each customer gained = ~~$100 ea~~ **$20 ea**

Profit from all purchases due to event = ~~$100~~ **$500**
    Total net profit from event = ~~$0~~ **$400**

Figure 2-5:
Simple
cost of
acquisition
with added
follow-up
communica-
tions.

Chapter 3

Becoming a Trusted Sender

- -

In This Chapter

▶ Understanding spam

▶ Minimizing spam complaints

▶ Familiarizing yourself with e-mail laws

▶ Enhancing your e-mail professionalism

▶ Choosing how often to send marketing messages

- -

*E*veryone who uses e-mail deals with spam on one level or another. According to a 2006 study by Epsilon Interactive (www.epsilon.com), consumers perceive 70 percent of the e-mail they receive as spam. Consumers receive so much spam that they're hesitant to open e-mails unless they know and trust the sender, and they are more than willing to report your e-mails as spam to their Internet service provider (ISP) if your e-mail doesn't appear trustworthy.

Every e-mail marketing strategy is subject to the possibility of consumer spam complaints, and numerous legal and professional standards apply to commercial e-mail. Consumers also expect marketing e-mails to come from a trusted source with just the right frequency and amount of content. Here are the three authoritative benchmarks for determining whether your commercial e-mails are regarded as spam:

✔ Legal standards, as outlined in the CAN-SPAM Act of 2003

✔ Professional standards, as outlined by consumer advocates and the e-mail marketing industry

✔ Consumer preferences, as dictated by consumers themselves

Adhering to e-mail professionalism keeps your e-mails legally compliant and improves your relationships with the people who receive and open your e-mails. In this chapter, I show you how to become a trusted e-mail sender, minimizing consumer spam complaints while maximizing the trust between your business and your existing and future e-mail list subscribers.

Minimizing Spam Complaints

Spam is also known as *unsolicited commercial e-mail.* Although numerous stories, analogies, and myths exist about the origin and meaning of the term *spam,* one thing is for sure — consumers don't like receiving it.

Even if your e-mail doesn't meet the legal definition of spam, consumers can easily report your e-mail as spam and thus impede your ability to send e-mail in the future. For example, Yahoo! customers can deem your e-mail as spam with a click of a button (see Figure 3-1). Most ISPs (including AOL, Yahoo!, and Hotmail) give their customers Spam buttons to use to block suspected spammers.

If your e-mails are perceived as spam by your audience and you receive too many spam complaints, ISPs will block your e-mail server from sending e-mails to their customers. It can take as few as two spam complaints per 1,000 e-mails to block your e-mail server temporarily, and higher percentages can result in your server being added to a permanent block list.

Readers click this button
to report e-mail as spam.

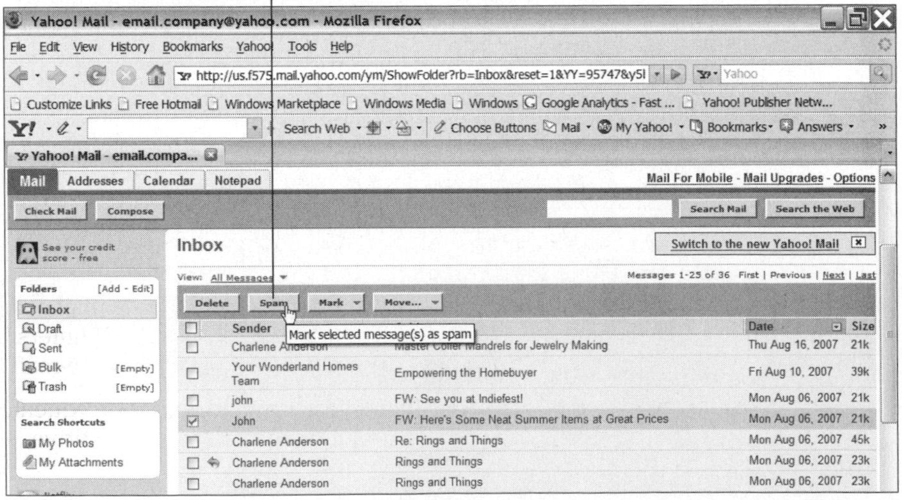

Figure 3-1:
Most ISPs
allow
customers
to report
e-mails as
spam.

Spam: Meat(like) or Monty Python mayhem?

According to the Hormel Foods Web site, the luncheon meat SPAM originated in 1936 when the company came up with the recipe. The company held a contest to help name the product and offered $100 as a prize for the winning name. The winner, Kenneth Daigneau, combined the letters *sp* from *spiced* and the letters *am* from *ham* to create the word SPAM — short for *spiced ham.*

In 1975, Monty Python's Flying Circus created the infamous comedy skit wherein Vikings sing, "Spam, spam, spam, spam . . ." in a restaurant that includes SPAM in every menu item.

Not long after the Monty Python skit hit the air, Internet users in Multi-User Dungeons (MUDs; multi-user computer games), bulletin boards, chat rooms, and Usenet (User Network) message boards began using the term *spam* to refer to annoying postings and unwanted messages. Ultimately, the term was also applied to unwanted e-mail messages. Today, consumers define spam on their own terms and log their complaints accordingly.

Because consumers have control over the Spam button, no e-mail marketing strategy is immune to complaints. Keeping your e-mails in line with the consumer preferences described in this section is the best way to ensure that your spam complaints remain below industry tolerances.

According to a 2006 holiday survey conducted by Return Path (www. returnpath.com), over one-third of consumers are willing to report the extra e-mails they receive during the holidays as spam, as shown in Figure 3-2.

To avoid having your e-mails reported as spam, you need to understand how consumers evaluate e-mails. When you think about whether your audience is likely to perceive your e-mail as spam, remember that spam is in the *I* of the receiver:

- ✔ *I* **don't want it.** Unwanted marketing e-mails are perceived as spam by most consumers, especially if they feel that they didn't authorize the sender to send it. Sometimes, consumers even start to perceive e-mails as spam after they receive them for months just because they no longer want them.

- ✔ *I* **can't verify it.** If consumers can't tell whether an e-mail came from a legitimate source, they perceive it as spam. Most consumers look at the From line in an e-mail header to determine whether an e-mail is familiar.

- ✔ *I* **think it's too frequent.** Consumers tend to perceive frequent e-mails as spam when they feel that the content is irrelevant, repetitive, or too long.

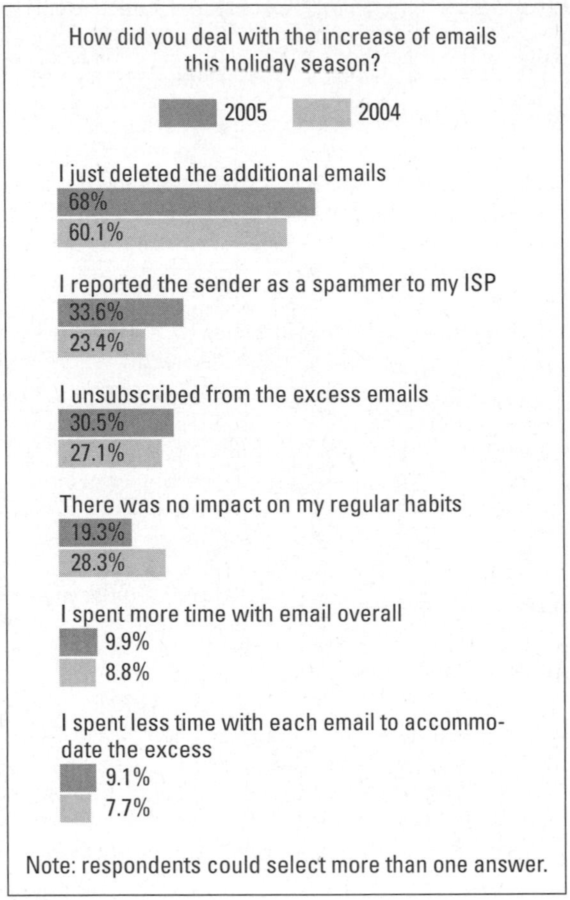

How did you deal with the increase of emails
this holiday season?

■ 2005   ■ 2004

I just deleted the additional emails
68%
60.1%

I reported the sender as a spammer to my ISP
33.6%
23.4%

I unsubscribed from the excess emails
30.5%
27.1%

There was no impact on my regular habits
19.3%
28.3%

I spent more time with email overall
9.9%
8.8%

I spent less time with each email to accommodate the excess
9.1%
7.7%

Note: respondents could select more than one answer.

Figure 3-2:
Many
consumers
will report
your e-mail
as spam if
they feel
they receive
too many.

Courtesy of Return Path

Even when consumers don't perceive your e-mail as spam, they might
be inclined to click the Spam button on your e-mail for one or more of the
following reasons:

✔ They can't figure out how to unsubscribe from your e-mail.

✔ They don't trust the unsubscribe link in your e-mail.

✔ They accidentally click the Spam button while sorting through their
e-mail inbox.

✔ They unintentionally include your e-mail while clicking the Spam button
on a large group of other spam e-mails.

Keeping spam complaints to a minimum is a matter of adhering to professional practices and consumer preferences over the course of your entire e-mail marketing strategy.

You can minimize your spam complaints over time by doing the following:

- ✔ **Ask for explicit permission to send e-mail when you collect e-mail addresses from prospects and customers to make sure that your customers want your e-mails.**

   You can read more about building a list with permission in Chapter 5.

- ✔ **Make your e-mail content valuable so your e-mail list subscribers continue to want your e-mails.**

   You can read more about creating value in your e-mails in Chapter 13.

- ✔ **Make your sign-up process memorable for your list subscribers and clearly identify your business in every e-mail's From line so your audience can verify the source of your e-mails.**

   Ideas for optimizing your e-mail From line appear in Chapter 7.

- ✔ **Use logos and colors in every e-mail that match your brand identity so that your audience recognizes your business.**

   You can read more about designing your e-mails and building brand awareness in Chapter 6.

- ✔ **Keep your e-mail frequency in line with your e-mail content and your e-mail list subscribers' expectations.**

   You can read more about the relationship between frequency and content later in this chapter.

- ✔ **Use an E-Mail Service Provider (ESP) that provides an unsubscribe link in every e-mail you send and allows your subscribers to access their profile to change their interests.**

   Figure 3-3 shows an example of an unsubscribe link and a link to access a user profile at the top of an e-mail.

- ✔ **Ask everyone who unsubscribes from your e-mail list to tell you why they don't want your e-mail.**

   You can then adjust your strategy accordingly.

- ✔ **Use an ESP that authenticates your e-mails.**

   You can read more about e-mail authentication in Chapter 12.

Figure 3-3:
Including an unsubscribe link and a link to change preferences at the top of your e-mail gives an alternative to clicking the spam button.

Courtesy of Wonderland Homes

Complying with Spam Laws

Spam is bothersome enough that lawmakers enacted the CAN-SPAM Act of 2003 to help prosecute spammers. The acronym comes from its official title, the Controlling the Assault of Non-Solicited Pornography and Marketing Act of 2003. Names aside, the law makes certain e-mail marketing practices illegal and gives legal definitions to many best practices.

The following sections summarize the basic tenets of the CAN-SPAM Act of 2003. You can read the CAN-SPAM Act for yourself at `www.ftc.gov/spam` to make sure that your own e-mails comply.

This section is intended to broaden your understanding of industry practices and should not be used to make decisions regarding your own compliance to the law. Contact your attorney if you need more information.

Determining which e-mails have to comply

The CAN-SPAM Act of 2003 applies to commercial electronic mail messages, which the law distinguishes from transactional or relationship messages. In general, the CAN-SPAM Act defines the two separate kinds of e-mail messages, as follows:

- ✔ A **commercial e-mail** is basically an e-mail containing an advertisement, promotion, or content from a business' Web site.

- ✔ A **transactional or relationship e-mail** is basically anything other than a commercial e-mail.

Although understanding that some e-mail messages fall outside the definition of commercial e-mail is important, it's equally important to understand that all e-mails sent in the name of your business can be construed by the recipient as commercial in nature. Best practice is to make sure that all your business-related e-mails are legally compliant.

Collecting e-mail addresses legally

The CAN-SPAM Act makes certain types of e-mail address collection illegal and requires permission from your e-mail list subscribers before you send certain types of content. (The CAN-SPAM Act uses the term *affirmative consent* instead of *permission*. You can read more about the best practices for permission in Chapter 5.)

Potentially illegal e-mail addresses collection methods aren't always easy to spot, so the best practice is to make sure that you have explicit permission from everyone on your list to send them e-mail. Here are some best practices for steering clear of potentially permission-less e-mail addresses:

- ✔ **Never purchase an e-mail list from a company that allows you to keep the e-mail addresses as a data file.**

    E-mail addresses kept in a data file are easily bought and sold, and e-mails addresses with explicit permission are too valuable to sell.

- ✔ **Never collect e-mail addresses from Web sites and other online directories.**

    I advise against this practice because you don't have affirmative consent from the owner.

- ✔ **Don't use an e-mail address collection service.**

    Unless such a service collects confirmed permission from every subscriber that it obtains.

✔ **Don't borrow an e-mail list from another business or send e-mail to an e-mail list.**

Those subscribers didn't explicitly opt-in to receive your e-mails.

✔ **Don't rent an e-mail list unless you are certain that the list rental company's practices are legally compliant.**

Most rental companies don't have permission-based lists. (You can read more about list rental in Chapter 5.)

Including required content in your e-mails

The CAN-SPAM Act requires you to include certain content in your e-mails. Include the following in your e-mails to stay CAN-SPAM–compliant:

✔ **Provide a way for your subscribers to opt-out of receiving future e-mails.**

You're required to remove anyone who unsubscribes from your e-mail list permanently within ten days of the unsubscribe request, and you can't add that person back without his explicit permission.

✔ **Make sure that your e-mail includes your physical address.**

If your business has multiple locations, include your main address or the physical address associated to each e-mail you send, as shown in Figure 3-4.

If you work from home and you don't want your home address in every e-mail, include your post office box address as long as the post office or box rental company associates the box to your legitimate business address.

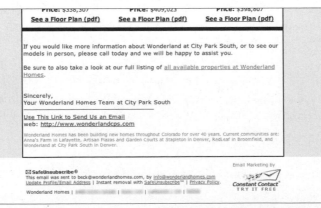

Figure 3-4:
Adding
a physical
address to
your e-mail
is required
under the
CAN-SPAM
act.

Courtesy of Wonderland Homes and Constant Contact

✔ **Make sure that your e-mail header information clearly identifies your business and does not mislead your audience in any way.**

Your e-mail header includes your From line, Subject line, and your e-mail address. Make that sure your e-mail's From line information clearly and honestly represents your business.

✔ **Make sure that your e-mail Subject line isn't misleading.**

Don't use your Subject line to trick your audience into opening your e-mail or to misrepresent the offer contained in your e-mail.

✔ **Make sure that your e-mail clearly states that the e-mail is a solicitation.**

The exception is when you have permission or affirmative consent from every individual on your list to send the solicitation. (Read more about permission in Chapter 5.)

✔ **Make sure that your e-mail complies with any applicable guidelines for sexually oriented material.**

If your e-mail contains such material, make sure your e-mail Subject line complies with the CAN-SPAM Act supplementary guidelines and also clearly states that the content of the e-mail is adult in nature without being explicit in the way you describe the content. You can access the supplementary guidelines on the Federal Trade Commission (FTC) Web site at www.ftc.gov/spam.

Enhancing Your E-Mail Professionalism

Understanding and adhering to the tenets of the CAN-SPAM Act is important, but you aren't going to impress too many consumers if your e-mails are just barely CAN-SPAM compliant.

ISPs and ESPs expect your e-mail marketing efforts to comply with professional industry standards. Executing your e-mail marketing strategy in line with professional standards helps to improve consumer confidence and differentiates legitimate e-mailers from spammers.

The following sections include tips for keeping up with consumer trends and the practices of the most reputable ESPs and ISPs. You can read more about e-mail professionalism at the Email Sender and Provider Coalition Web site at www.espcoalition.org.

Using full disclosure during e-mail address collection

The CAN-SPAM Act encourages you to have affirmative consent with your e-mail list subscribers to send them commercial e-mail, but the most professional practice is to use an extra measure of disclosure when asking for permission. Here are some ways how you can take affirmative consent to a more professional level:

✔ **Ask for explicit permission to send e-mail everywhere you collect e-mail addresses.**

Whether you exchange business cards with prospects in person or collect e-mail addresses through a form on your Web site, make sure you obtain explicit permission as part of the process. It's also a good idea to keep a record of your permission exchanges in case you're faced with a legal complaint in the future.

✔ **If you use e-mail list check boxes on Web site forms, keep each check box cleared (unchecked) as the default.**

For example, if you use your Web site's shipping form to collect e-mail addresses, require your shoppers to select a check box to add themselves to any non-transactional e-mail lists. Make sure that the check box also includes a description of the types of e-mails your shopper is signing up for.

✔ **Send a professional welcome letter e-mail to all new e-mail list subscribers.**

Make sure that the welcome letter e-mail arrives within 24 hours of the initial subscription request and also include privacy information and a description of the types and frequency of e-mails that the new subscriber receives. Figure 3-5 shows a welcome letter e-mail.

✔ **Send periodic permission reminders to confirm that your e-mail list subscribers are still interested in your e-mails.**

You can send a periodic business letter or include a few sentences at the top of your e-mails asking your subscribers to confirm their interests.

You can read more about building an e-mail list with permission in Chapter 5.

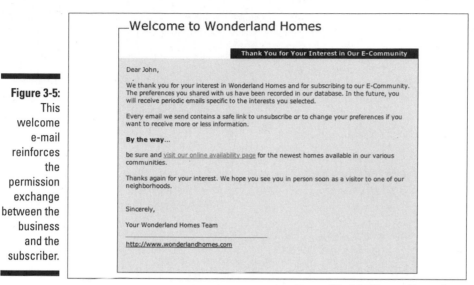

Courtesy of Wonderland Homes and Constant Contact

Figure 3-5:
This welcome e-mail reinforces the permission exchange between the business and the subscriber.

Allowing your audience to unsubscribe from receiving e-mails

The CAN-SPAM Act requires that you include a way to allow your audience to unsubscribe from receiving future e-mails from you, but the law doesn't specify which mechanisms are appropriate for processing unsubscribe requests. You can ask your subscribers to reply to your e-mails with their unsubscribe request and manually keep track of your unsubscribed prospects and customers, but this process can be tedious with larger lists.

The most professional practice, and the most automated, for processing unsubscribe requests is to use an ESP to automatically and permanently remove anyone who unsubscribes from all e-mail lists in one click. Figure 3-6 shows a one-click unsubscribe link in the footer of an e-mail.

Most reputable ESPs automatically insert a one-click unsubscribe link into your e-mails. When a subscriber clicks the link, the ESP automatically removes the subscriber or changes the status of the subscriber in the ESP's database to unsubscribed so that the subscriber stops receiving e-mails immediately.

Providing a one-click unsubscribe mechanism gives your potential e-mail list subscribers confidence when subscribing to your e-mail lists and encourages them to differentiate your e-mail from spammers who use dubious opt-out methods, if any.

Unsubscribe link

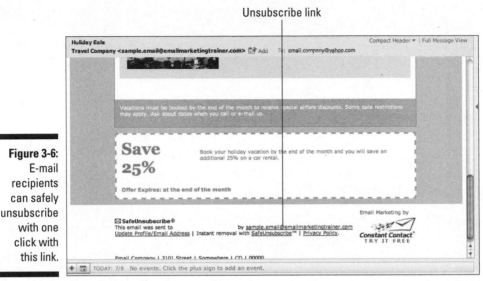

Figure 3-6:
E-mail
recipients
can safely
unsubscribe
with one
click with
this link.

Sending e-mail content in line with your audience's expectations

The CAN-SPAM Act doesn't specify what types of e-mail content to send to your e-mail list subscribers. The best practice is to send e-mail content that matches your audience's expectations or interests. Here are some tips for setting expectations for your potential e-mail list subscribers and for sending e-mail content that matches their expectations as well as their interests:

✔ **Include a description of your e-mail content and your typical frequency in your sign-up process.**

For example, if you send a monthly e-mail newsletter along with periodic promotions to your e-mail list, your e-mail list sign-up form might include a sentence that reads

Signing up allows you to receive our monthly e-mail newsletter as well as periodic special offers related to our newest products.

✔ **Send only the content that your e-mail list subscribers expect you to send.**

For example, if potential e-mail list subscribers share their e-mail address in order to receive a quote for your services, don't send them offers unless they gave you permission as part of requesting a quote.

> ✔ **Allow your e-mail list subscribers to choose their own interests.**
>
> If you send several distinct types of e-mail content — such as coupons and event invitations — give your e-mail list subscribers a list of categories to choose from when signing up. Make sure to give them a mechanism for changing their interests, such as a link to their profile, in every e-mail.

Deciding When and How Often to Send

Consumers tend to perceive e-mail that arrives too often as spam, so you need to figure out the frequency rate and timing of your e-mails. *Frequency* refers to the number of e-mails you send and the period of time in between each e-mail you send. Typical frequencies include

- ✔ Once
- ✔ Daily
- ✔ Weekly
- ✔ Bi-monthly, or every other week
- ✔ Monthly

Balancing the frequency of every e-mail message with the needs and expectations of your audience is more of an art than a science. According to a 2006 Epsilon Interactive consumer e-mail study, 73 percent of consumers will unsubscribe if they feel that a company sends e-mail too frequently.

Consumers are willing to receive e-mails with almost any frequency as long as the content of the message remains relevant and valuable to them. Keep your content relevant to your consumers, and they — most likely — will remain happy with your frequency.

For example, a stock broker could probably get away with sending an e-mail twice per day to his subscribers if the message contains a single line of text announcing the current price of important stocks. The same stock broker would probably run into trouble, however, if he used the same mailing frequency to send a promotional e-mail asking his customers to invest in various stocks because not everyone is likely to make investment decisions with that frequency.

Even though proper frequency depends on relevant content, you should recognize the factors that most consumers consider to value the frequency of your e-mails. Consumers generally judge your e-mail frequency depending on the following:

- ✔ The total number of e-mails
- ✔ The length of each e-mail
- ✔ How often you ask them to take action
- ✔ The relevance of the information you provide
- ✔ The timing

Determining how many e-mails to send

Determining the proper number of e-mails to send is a fine balance: Send too many e-mail messages, and you overwhelm your audience with too many e-mails. Conversely, send too few, and you can overwhelm your audience with too much content in each one.

The total number of e-mail messages that you send should match your consumer's need for your information — and not your need to send the information.

For example, a realtor might want to send dozens of e-mails over a period of weeks to people actively shopping for a home while sending only one e-mail per month to people who rent an apartment, with no immediate intentions of purchasing a home.

Estimating the total number of messages your audience expects usually depends on two factors:

- ✔ **The number of times your audience engages in a buying cycle**

   If your prospects or customers purchase your products or services once per week, sending 52 e-mails per year is probably a good place to start with your frequency. If your prospects or customers take months or even years to make purchase decisions, you can base the number of e-mails you send on the number of times that they are likely to talk about their purchases with their peers. For example, if you sell once-in-a-lifetime vacations, you might create an affinity club for past vacationers and keep your customers talking about their experience by sending invitations to members-only social reunions four times per year.

✓ **The amount of information your audience needs to make a purchase decision**

Some purchase decisions are easy for consumers to make, but others require much more consideration. If your audience requires a lot of information to justify a decision, the number of e-mails that you send should increase so you don't overwhelm your audience with too much content in a few e-mails. Instead, send several e-mails with a bit of content in each one.

Estimating how many e-mails you need to effectively deliver all of your information might be as simple as dividing your information into equal parts or as complex as delivering successively greater amounts of content as your audience becomes more engaged.

Although paying attention to the needs of your audience is always the best policy, sometimes your e-mail content dictates the appropriate number of messages to send. For example, the total number of e-mails you send might depend on

✓ **The amount of change in your content:** If your e-mails always have the same basic message, you don't need to send as many as if your content were always fresh and new.

✓ **The theme of your content:** If your e-mail includes frequency in the theme, you can match the number of e-mails you send to that theme. For example, if your subscribers sign up for a daily motivational quote, you need to send 365 e-mails for the year, but delivering an annual report requires only 1 e-mail per year.

Choosing the proper e-mail length

E-mails are generally more effective when you make them as concise as possible. Consumers who want to receive lengthy e-mail messages frequently are the exception rather than the rule. There is no such thing as the perfect e-mail message length that works best for everyone and every format. Frequency and length depend on your audience and the value of your content.

Until you become familiar enough with your audience to know how much content they will tolerate in each e-mail, adopt a less-is-more mentality. As a general rule, the longer the content, the less frequently your audience will tolerate getting your e-mails.

Although your audience will ultimately tell you when your messages are too long by unsubscribing or opening your e-mails less frequently, you can reduce the size of your individual e-mails and correctly match your frequency with your length by doing the following:

✔ **Break your content into parts and send a series of e-mails.**

Be sure to include links to all your content so interested readers don't feel like they're being deprived. Figure 3-7 shows an e-mail newsletter with links to additional information for more interested readers. (See Chapter 8 for more information about creating links to additional content.)

✔ **Use images to describe the value of your products or services.**

Images can replace long passages of text. For more information about proper image use, read Chapter 9.

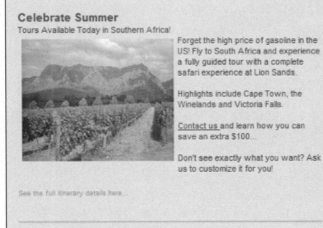

Figure 3-7: This e-mail allows readers to access more information through links.

Courtesy of Safari Ventures, Inc.

Using too many images or using large image files might make your e-mail download more slowly, and attaching images to your e-mails directly degrades your deliverability.

✔ **Use white space and design elements.**

You make your e-mails easier to scan and consumers can quickly find the information they value.

Figuring out how often to call for action

When your e-mails are always asking your audience for some type of action, chances are that the majority of your audience isn't ready for action with every frequency you choose. Calling for action is a balance: Some calls to action wear off if you send them too often, and others won't work unless you repeat them often enough.

You can call your audience to action with frequency:

✔ **Design your e-mail templates for action.**

Create an e-mail template exclusively for urgent messages while maintaining a look that is consistent with your brand. Then, reserve that template for only the most urgent messages you need to send. For example, you might use your urgent template for 4 of 12 monthly promotional messages.

✔ **Match your calls to action with your audience's preferences.**

Because different people take action for different reasons, you can change your calls to action to match the reasons why different people in your audience take action. For example, a golf and tennis shop might want to divide an e-mail list by golfers and tennis players so that they can send an invitation to a half-off sale that includes a free gift for walking in to the store. The e-mail sent to the golf list offers a free sleeve of golf balls, and the e-mail sent to the tennis list offers a free can of tennis balls. I cover collecting interest information from your list subscribers in more detail in Chapter 5.

✔ **Match the timing of your calls to action with your audience's behavior.**

Calling for action precisely when your audience is ready to take action is likely to result in the best response to your call. Because you can't tell exactly when your audience is ready to take action on every call to action, keep track of the types of behavior your audience exhibits to help you determine when you need to call for action and when you should send other types of messages. For example, an auto mechanic might keep track of customers who recently purchased new tires so they can receive more-frequent offers for alignments or tire rotations.

Setting e-mailing frequency by relevance

The more relevant and valuable you can make your information, the more likely your audience is to tolerate and request more frequent e-mails.

The relevance and value of your content is ultimately determined by your audience. To match your audience's desired frequency as it relates to relevant content, group your e-mail content together by expected frequency. For example, if you send a monthly newsletter, you might place your content that changes monthly (such as articles and offers) in the main column, but place content that changes less frequently (such as links to your Web site or upcoming events) in a side column, as shown in Figure 3-8.

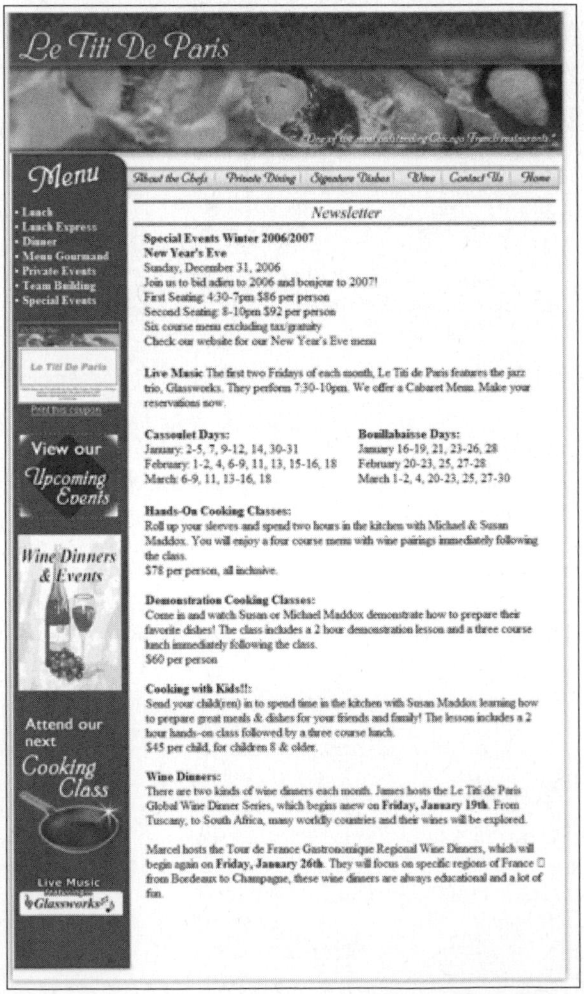

Figure 3-8:
A side column is useful for displaying static information in every e-mail.

Courtesy of Le Titi De Paris

Choosing the best day and time for delivery

Your audience is more likely to respond positively to your e-mails if you send them when folks are most likely to have time to read and take action on them. For example, if a large percentage of your e-mail list contains people's work e-mail addresses, you might want to avoid sending your e-mails early on Monday mornings when the people on your list are likely to walk into a full inbox and prioritize your e-mail to the bottom of their list.

You can determine the best days and times to send your e-mails when you do the following:

1. **Test for the best day.**

   Divide your list into equal parts and send the same e-mail on different days to determine which day receives the best response. For example, if you have 1,000 e-mail addresses, you can send 200 on each day of the week. Whichever day receives the best response can be your sending day going forward.

2. **Test for the best time of day.**

   After you test for the best day, you can then test for the best time of day. Divide your list and send the same e-mail at different times on the same day.

3. **Set up a master calendar for each list.**

   If you send more than one e-mail format, use a spreadsheet or a calendar so you can view your e-mails by frequency and format.

   Planning allows you to visualize your e-mail frequency and make adjustments so you don't inadvertently send too many e-mails too close together and overwhelm your audience. You can also use a calendar to help determine when to send e-mails that come up at the last minute.

Figure 3-9 shows an e-mail frequency planner that allows you to view your e-mail frequency plan for an entire year. You can download this frequency planner at www.emailtrainer.com.

Email Frequency Planner

List Name: _____

Formats	#/year	Frequency	Day	Time	Notes
Newsletters	24	2x per month	Tuesdays	9:30 AM	send to all lists
Promotions	15	every other month	Fridays	1:30 PM	additional promotions during end of year
Event Invitations	10	every other month	Wednesdays	9:30 AM	include next event in right column of each newsletter
Announcements	6	date driven	date driven	3:00 PM	
Press Releases	3	event driven	Thursdays	8:00 AM	send to press list only
Other Holiday Card	3	date driven	date driven	3:00 PM	
Other _____	0				

N = Newsletter; P = Promotion; E = Event Invitation; R=Event Reminder; A = Announcement; PR = Press Release

Tracking Totals: Total emails | Bounce Rate | Open Rate | Click Rate

Month	Entries	Bounce Rate	Open Rate	Click Rate
January	A(1) N(4) P(11) N(19)	%	%	%
February	N(4) E(8) PR(10) R(12) P(25)	%	%	%
March	N(4) P(11) N(19) A(25)	%	%	%
April	N(4) N(19) E(22) R(24) P(25)	%	%	%
May	N(4) P(11) N(19) A(25)	%	%	%
June	N(4) E(8) PR(10) R(12) N(19) P(25)	%	%	%
July	A(3) N(4) P(11) N(19) A(25)	%	%	%
August	N(4) N(19) E(22) R(24) P(25)	%	%	%
September	N(4) P(11) N(19) A(25)	%	%	%
October	N(4) E(8) PR(10) R(12) N(19) P(25) A(31)	%	%	%
November	N(4) N(19) A(23) P(25)	%	%	%
December	N(4) A(15) N(19) P(21) P(23) P(26)	%	%	%
Totals		%	%	%

Figure 3-9:
Use an e-mail frequency planner to track format and frequency.

Part II
Mapping Out an E-Mail Marketing Strategy

The 5th Wave   By Rich Tennant

"Oh, we're doing just great. Phillip and I are selling decorative jelly jars. I send e-mails and Phillip sort of controls the inventory."

In this part . . .

Measure twice; cut once. If you're a carpenter, those words are a reminder to carefully plan before taking any actions that are not easily reversed. If you're an e-mail marketer, careful planning includes developing sound objectives and building a quality list of e-mail addresses.

Chapter 4 shows you how to come up with sound objectives and how to think through an e-mail strategy in terms of your objectives. Here are tips for creating financial objectives as well as time-saving objectives. This chapter explains how to organize your e-mail content by objective.

Chapter 5 explains how to build a quality e-mail list and gather essential information in addition to e-mail addresses. The chapter also shows you where and how to collect e-mail addresses from prospects and customers and also explains how to obtain permission to send.

Chapter 4

Developing Objectives

*Y*ou might be surprised if I said that marketing mediums, such as television ads or postcards, can't truly do anything, but it's true. If you don't believe me, grab a stack of your business cards, set them on your desk, and then wait . . . a long time. Business cards — by themselves — can't do anything.

All kidding aside, using any marketing medium effectively requires you to do something intelligent with that medium. One of the most intelligent things you can do before you start sending e-mails as a marketing medium is to develop objectives to help guide your e-mail content and your actions down the road.

With a little thought and some advance planning, setting your objectives helps ensure that prospects and customers can also do something intelligent, and positive, with your e-mail marketing campaigns. This chapter tells you how to create sound marketing objectives so your e-mails can follow a roadmap that leads to accomplishing your goals.

Coming Up with Broad-Based Objectives

I bet that your number-one objective is to make money with your business. Of course, you probably have other reasons to run your business: freedom and flexibility with your time or maybe to keep you from languishing in a cubicle. Whatever the reason, your business has to make money.

Making money is a very broad-based objective. *Broad-based objectives* are goals that are stated apart from the supporting details necessary to achieve the goal. Keeping broad-based objectives in mind is a good way to keep your e-mail marketing strategy focused on the big picture. Broad-based objectives are more useful for making decisions, however, when you define them clearly so you can add the appropriate supporting details later.

Defining your objectives helps you to determine

- ✔ What types of content to put in your e-mails
- ✔ How many e-mails you need to send
- ✔ How often you need to send e-mails
- ✔ To whom to send your e-mails
- ✔ When to change or refine your strategy

The next sections help you state broad-based e-mail objectives in clear terms so you can use them to help identify the steps involved in accomplishing each objective.

Financially based objectives: I want more money

A small business owner in one of my seminars defined his broad-based objective of making money by saying, "Someday I'd like to add the word *profit* to my loss statement." If making a positive impact on your profit and loss statement is one of your broad-based objectives, e-mail can make a significant contribution to both sides of the ledger because e-mail can help you increase revenue and cut costs.

Stating your broad-based financial objectives clearly begins with understanding how e-mail causes your audience to respond financially in favor of your objectives. The next section explains how e-mail causes several types of financial responses and gives you examples of stated objectives for each cause.

Increase sales

E-mail has the ability to become the proximate cause of a sale, such as when someone clicks a link in your e-mail to make a direct purchase from your Web site as shown in Figure 4-1. E-mail can also help generate activity and inquiries that can lead to increased sales, such as when someone replies to an e-mail in order to request an appointment or additional information.

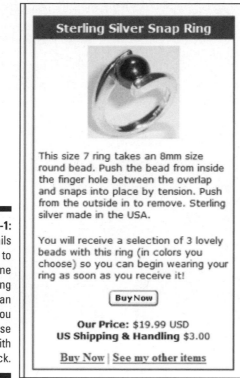

Sterling Silver Snap Ring

This size 7 ring takes an 8mm size round bead. Push the bead from inside the finger hole between the overlap and snaps into place by tension. Push from the outside in to remove. Sterling silver made in the USA.

You will receive a selection of 3 lovely beads with this ring (in colors you choose) so you can begin wearing your ring as soon as you receive it!

Buy Now

Our Price: $19.99 USD
US Shipping & Handling $3.00

Buy Now | See my other items

Courtesy of Anderson-Shea, Inc.

Figure 4-1:
E-mails linked to online shopping carts can help you increase sales with every click.

If your objective is to increase sales, you can state your broad-based objective in the following ways and craft your e-mail content with one of the stated objectives in mind (depending, of course, on your business):

- ✔ Drive foot traffic to your store
- ✔ Bring visitors to your Web site
- ✔ Increase event attendance
- ✔ Ask for referrals
- ✔ Generate phone or e-mail orders

Increase repeat business

Potentially, sales not only increase when you reach more prospective customers with your message but also when you motivate and prompt current customers to make repeat purchases.

E-mail is a great way to make repeat purchases more convenient and efficient because you can link your audience directly to an online purchase process. Time and convenience are powerful motivators to increase the number of customers who make frequent and regular repeat purchases.

If your objective is to increase repeat business, you can state your objective in the following ways and craft your e-mail content with one of the following stated objectives in mind:

- ✔ Stay at the front of your customers' minds.
- ✔ Attract prospects to convenient purchase links and options.
- ✔ Reward repeat customers with incentives based on repeat sales as shown in Figure 4-2.

Figure 4-2:
This e-mail rewards repeat customers and gives an extra incentive for timely action.

Courtesy of Costa Azul Adventure Resort. Photo by Preston Hall.

Shorten a sales cycle

Your *sales cycle* is how long someone takes to become interested and actually make the purchase. For example, if you own an automobile dealership the sales cycle is how long someone takes to recognize their need for a new car, research models, visit showrooms, test drive models, negotiate price, and finally purchase the vehicle.

Your sales cycle also applies to prospects. Your *prospecting sales cycle* is how long someone takes to make a purchase after they become aware of your products or services.

Use e-mail to help shorten your sales cycle by sending prospective customers the following types of information:

- ✔ Information to help justify a decision
- ✔ Reminders to take action
- ✔ Incentives to take immediate action (see Figure 4-3)

Figure 4-3:
Giving your prospects and customers incentives to take immediate action helps to shorten the sales cycle.

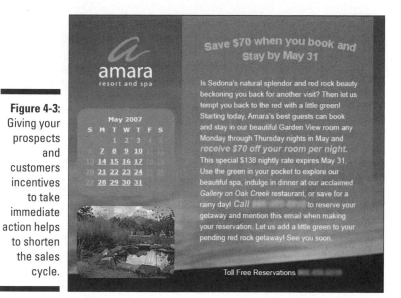

Courtesy of Amara Resort and Spa

If your objective is to shorten your sales cycle, you can state your objective in the following ways and craft your e-mail content with one of the following stated objectives in mind:

- ✔ Drive prospects to helpful or persuasive information.
- ✔ Provide reminders to act at various sales cycle stages.
- ✔ Announce incentives to reward completed purchases.

Lower your costs

Keeping your costs under control while staying productive is always a challenge. E-mail is a cost-effective tool because e-mail is affordable to deliver and lowers costs by saving paper, printing, and labor costs. (You can read more about lowering your costs with e-mail in Chapter 2.)

If your objective is to shorten your sales cycle, you can state your objective in the following ways and lower your costs when you set up your e-mail campaigns with one of the following stated objectives in mind:

✔ Automate appointment reminders.

✔ Deliver information electronically instead of in print.

✔ Use e-mail instead of, or in conjunction with, phone calls for customer follow-up.

Time-based objectives: I want more time

If you have a healthy respect for the value of time, using e-mail marketing can help make the time you spend on your business more efficient. Here are some time-based objectives to consider adopting.

Automate tasks

Some processes are worth the efforts of time-intensive interaction, but others should be automated so you can spend more time selling or recharging your batteries away from your business. If your objective is to automate tasks, you can state your objective in one of the following ways and increase automation with any of these stated objectives in mind:

✔ Direct prospects and customers to online information.

✔ Use auto responders for some types of follow-up.

✔ Schedule several e-mail campaigns to run automatically in advance.

Reduce administrative tasks

Running a business takes a lot of administration, and managing administrative tasks can take time away from selling and interacting with customers and prospects. If your objective is to reduce administrative tasks, you can state your objective in one of the following ways to help you focus on lightening your administrative burden:

✔ Include a link in every e-mail to an online form that allows customers and prospects to keep their contact information up to date.

✔ Use e-mail templates to save time designing messages.

    ✔ Automate list management and reporting with an E-Mail Service
       Provider (ESP).

Interact efficiently with customers

Staying connected with customers and making them feel that you care about
them can be time-intensive if all your customer interaction happens in person.
On the other hand, automating customer interaction can make your customers
feel like they aren't being treated personally.

Efficient customer interaction works when you establish a healthy balance
between personal interaction and electronic communication. If your objective
is to interact efficiently with customers, you can state your objective in one
of the following ways and use e-mail to improve your interaction efficiency:

    ✔ Ask customers to use surveys and feedback forms.

    ✔ Use e-mails to confirm purchases.

    ✔ Use e-mail newsletter content to answer common questions.

    ✔ Link customers to online resources for support.

Narrowing Your Objectives in Six Steps

Narrowly defined objectives are far more useful than broad-based objectives
for making decisions about delivering specific e-mail content. After you define
broad-based objectives (as I describe in the first part of this chapter), the next
step is to restate them in more meaningful ways and match them with specific
tasks.

You can narrow your broad-based objective by taking six steps:

1. Figure out your ultimate goal.

2. Decide who your customers are.

3. Consider how you want a customer to take action.

4. Communicate your objective.

5. Decide where you want to accomplish your objective.

6. Time your objective.

The following fictitious story walks you through the process of narrowly
defining an objective by using the six suggested steps. After you read all the
examples and get the basic idea, you can apply these steps to your own
objectives or come up with your own set of steps.

Flip and her partner, Flop, decided to open a pancake restaurant because they loved pancakes, people, and the idea of selling 20 cents worth of flour and eggs for $1.25. Flip takes care of the marketing decisions, while Flop is busy in the kitchen. Generally speaking, business is good.

Flip wants to make more money so that Flop can hire some extra help and take more time off. At a recent business meeting, Flip and Flop decide that they would like to get more people to eat at their restaurant. Flip agrees to do some thinking and return to the next business meeting with some specific action items for reaching their new objective.

Step 1: Set the ultimate goal of your objective

Before you start narrowing your broad-based objective, write it down for a starting point. You can use a pad of paper, a white board, or a computer. After each step that follows, write a new objective to replace the preceding broad-based objective using the example as a guide.

1. Set and refine the ultimate goal

Flip already learned the hard way that some objectives seem worthwhile for a moment but then fail to move her business closer to her ultimate goals.

Flip decided that she wanted to drive more traffic to her Web site so that visitors would make online pancake party reservations. When her Web site traffic went up but sales didn't increase, she decided to hold off on the company party.

This taught her that Web site traffic alone doesn't necessarily get more people to make online pancake party reservations. She has since made sure to include details about making online pancake party reservations in her Web site objectives so that her e-mail content supports both driving the traffic and asking visitors to make a reservation. Flip decides that this experience is useful for helping to refine her current objective.

Now, Flip wants to get more people to eat at her restaurant. However, what she really wants is for more people to visit *to sell more pancakes* — because pancakes have the best margins.

Here's how Flip restates her original objective in light of her ultimate objective:

- ✔ **Original objective:** I want to get more people to eat at my restaurant.
- ✔ **Restated objective:** I want to get more people to eat at my restaurant *so that I can sell more pancakes.*

Now restate your original broad-based objective using Flip's restated objective as a guide. At this point your objective has a clearer focus, but it's not ready for action.

Step 2: Decide whom you want to respond to your objective

Some objectives go unachieved simply because your audience isn't willing or able to help you accomplish the objective. Understanding the appropriate audience helps you to create e-mail content that speaks to specific interests and needs within a particular group.

---

2. Define your target audience

Flip noticed over the years that the business people who eat at Flip's on their way to work usually come alone and occupy a table of four by themselves. She has also noticed that Flip's sells the most pancakes when families with teenagers visit the restaurant. Flip thinks that she really wants families with teenagers to respond to help her meet her objective.

Here's how Flip restates her previous objective to help her attract more families:

> ✔ **Objective from the previous step:** I want to get more people to eat at my restaurant so that I can sell more pancakes.
>
> ✔ **Restated objective:** I want to get more *families with teenagers* to eat at my restaurant so that I can sell more pancakes.

Restating your objective with your audience in mind should get you thinking about what kind of language to use in your e-mails and how to design the look and feel so your audience identifies with your content. (You can read more about designing your e-mails in Chapter 6.)

Step 3: Determine why someone takes action on your objective

Consumers make purchasing decisions only because they want to or feel they have to. Your audience won't help you reach your objective unless you demonstrate why your audience wants or needs to act on your content. Stating your objective with your audience's motivations in mind helps your objective, and your content, to focus on giving real value to your audience. (You can read more about creating valuable content in Chapter 8.)

3. Zero in on your offer

Flip is beginning to get excited about selling more pancakes to families, and now she needs to figure out why families with teenagers would bother to drive past the other breakfast spots in town to eat at Flip's. Flip decides that the next few times a family with teenagers comes in to eat, she will buy their breakfast in exchange for a few minutes of their time answering questions about Flip's pancakes. Her surveys reveal that families with teenagers come to Flip's because the coffee is the best in town and because the pancakes are reasonably priced, which makes Flip's an economic choice for families with hungry teenagers.

Flip decides that her objective should be restated to reinforce the fact that her target customers want her to keep her prices low and the quality of her coffee high.

Here's how Flip restates her previous objective to give families with teenagers a reason to buy more pancakes:

- ✔ **Objective from the previous step:** I want to get more families with teenagers to eat at my restaurant so that I can sell more pancakes.
- ✔ **Restated objective:** I want to *offer free coffee with any pancake purchase* to get more families with teenagers to eat at my restaurant so that I can sell more pancakes.

At this point, your restated objective represents an overall strategy, but it still lacks a definition of the specific tactics involved in accomplishing the original broad-based objective.

Step 4: See how people find out about your objective

Obviously you're reading this book because you want people to find out about your objectives by reading one of your e-mails. It's a good idea, however, to state your objective in a way that clearly defines how you plan to collect and use the e-mail addresses belonging to the audience you identified in Step 2.

4. Start spreading the word

Flip can't wait to start spreading the word about her new free coffee offer, and she's beginning to wonder how she will reach enough parents so they will want to visit the restaurant with their teenagers. Flip has been sending an e-mail newsletter once per month and has a list of 250 customers.

Flip decides that she can start collecting more e-mail addresses belonging to families with teenagers by sponsoring a booth at the county fair and by asking her wait staff to exchange free cups of coffee for e-mail addresses when families visit the restaurant. She also decides that she has enough e-mail addresses to start promoting her coffee offer right away to her current customers.

Flip believes that her teenage customers have friends who are teenagers, too, so she wants to make sure the parents of her customers' friends also know about her coffee offer. Flip decides that e-mail can help her with that objective.

Here's how Flip restates her previous objective to include how her audience will find out about her new offer:

- ✔ **Objective from the preceding step:** I want to offer free coffee with any pancake purchase to get more families with teenagers to eat at my restaurant so that I can sell more pancakes.

- ✔ **Restated objective:** I want to offer free coffee with any pancake purchase *by sending an e-mail to my customer list* to get more families with teenagers to eat at my restaurant so that I can sell more pancakes.

- ✔ **New sub-objective:** I want to get families with teenagers to forward my free coffee offer to their friends.

At this point, your objective hints at one or more tactics that allow you to take specific actions, but your objective still needs two more refinements before it's ready to guide your actions through all the steps involved in an e-mail campaign.

Step 5: Set where your objective will be accomplished

A transaction needs a place to happen, and you need to guide your audience to the place that is most likely to result in the accomplishment of your objective. Stating your objective with a place in mind helps to guide your messaging so that your audience understands where to go and how to get there.

5. Refine the offer

Flip's has a spacious dining room with booths and tables, a breakfast bar for take-out service, a drive-up lane, and a Web site to sell Flip's t-shirts and coffee mugs. Flip doesn't think the drive-up lane is a good place to hand out steaming hot cups of free coffee, and she knows that families typically don't use the drive-up lane unless someone is on his way somewhere alone. Flip decides that the best chance of accomplishing her objective is to draw families into the dining room.

Here's how Flip restates her previous objective to keep her focused on where her objective will be accomplished:

- ✔ **Objective from the preceding step:** I want to offer free coffee with any pancake purchase by sending an e-mail to my customer list to get more families with teenagers to eat at my restaurant so that I can sell more pancakes.

- ✔ **Restated objective:** I want to offer free coffee with any pancake purchase by sending an e-mail to my customer list to get more families with teenagers to eat at my restaurant so that I can sell more pancakes *in the dining room.*

- ✔ **Sub-objective from the preceding step:** I want to get families with teenagers to forward my free coffee offer to their friends.

Stating your objective with a place in mind not only helps you to clarify the steps your customers take, it also helps you to create offers that drive your audience toward the most likely or profitable place for conversion. For example, if the most profitable place to sell your products happens to be in a group demonstration, you might create a bigger incentive for attending a group demonstration than for making an individual appointment.

Step 6: Predict when your audience will respond to your objective

Stating your objectives to include timing helps you to create a sending schedule and stay focused on it during the creation of multiple e-mails. You can read more about proper frequency and timing in Chapter 3.

6. Set an e-mail timing strategy

Flip takes a look at her address book and notices that about half of her e-mail list contains work addresses and that the other half contains personal addresses. Flip knows that families with teenagers almost never have time to eat pancakes during the week, so she expects that her coffee offer will result in a lot of weekend sales.

She knows that if she sends her e-mails on Monday or Tuesday, people usually forget about her message by the weekend. Flip decides to send her coffee offer e-mails to her business list on Friday right after lunch as well as to her personal list on Thursday mornings just to give people a little extra time to check their personal e-mail.

Flip also decides that weekly e-mails are too frequent for most of her repeat customers, so she decides to divide each of her lists into four equal parts and send weekly e-mails while rotating the list so that each list member gets one e-mail every four weeks. She also hopes that breaking up her communications will spread out her visitors so that the traffic into the restaurant is nice and steady instead of overcrowded. Flip thinks that she has narrowed her objective down to a very useful guide for creating her first e-mail.

Here's how Flip decides to state the final objective:

- ✔ **Objective from the preceding step:** I want to offer free coffee with any pancake purchase by sending an e-mail to my customer list to get more families with teenagers to eat at my restaurant so that I can sell more pancakes in the dining room.

- ✔ **Final restated objective:** I want to offer free coffee with any pancake purchase by sending a *weekly* e-mail to one-fourth of my customer list *on Thursdays and Fridays* to get more families with teenagers to eat at my restaurant so that I can sell more pancakes in the dining room.

- ✔ **Sub-objective from the preceding step:** I want to get families with teenagers to forward my free coffee offer to their friends.

Figure 4-4 shows how Flip's fictitious e-mail campaign turned out.

Stating and restating objectives in certain terms can be a lot of work, but the results are well worth the effort. The more closely your e-mail content resembles your objectives, the more your audience is able to clearly identify the purpose of your e-mail and act toward the accomplishment of your objective without distraction.

Figure 4-4:
Flip's
Pancake
House
e-mail
campaign.

Organizing Your E-Mail Content into Themes Based on Objectives

Stating clear objectives gives you a platform for creating e-mail content that accomplishes your objectives. Running a small business involves frequently setting new objectives and developing new e-mail content in line with those objectives. When your time is limited, you might be tempted to create e-mail content that fits your schedule better than your objectives.

One of the most important reasons to use specific objectives to guide the creation of your e-mail content is to keep you from bombarding your customers and prospects with all your information.

Sending all the information you can think of to everyone and then hoping that someone finds something interesting in your e-mails is *spraying and praying,* and it's no way to reward all your hard work. Avoid using the following e-mail strategies to prevent spraying and praying:

- ✔ Newsletters with mixtures of themes, multiple unrelated articles, and numerous calls to action

- ✔ Promotions featuring multiple contrasting products along with non-promotional content

- ✔ Announcements pertaining to a select group of contacts but sent to everyone

- ✔ Procedural e-mails including excessive or confusing promotional messages

While you develop e-mail content, think about how your audience will perceive your intentions. If you want your audience to help you accomplish your objectives, your audience needs to know why you are sending them e-mail and what you are asking them to do. Because you can't just tell your audience to buy something (um, because you are trying to buy another beach house in Hawaii), you have to translate your objectives into themes that clue your audience in on your objectives without explicitly telling them what you are trying to accomplish.

E-mail messages make more sense to your prospects and customers when the content you create and deliver is tied together under familiar themes. A *theme* is the main idea of your entire e-mail campaign. Themes are not the same as formats. *Format* refers to the classification and configuration of an e-mail.

Most objectives can be grouped into one of four familiar themes:

- ✔ Promotional
- ✔ Information
- ✔ Procedural
- ✔ Relational

E-mails can sometimes include content with multiple themes, but in such cases, it's usually best to have one main theme and several related themes grouped together visually under the main theme. Grouping content visually is covered in Chapter 6.

Promotional themes

When the main objective of your e-mail is to persuade your audience to take a specific action or to ask for a specific purchase decision, make sure your e-mail includes only content that supports and relates to a promotional theme.

For example, if your e-mail's main objective is to ask your audience to purchase a specific product, including an invitation to a related product seminar would follow your theme. Comparatively, including an invitation to an unrelated event would detract from your theme. Examples of content you might include in an e-mail with a promotional theme include

- ✔ Product images and descriptions
- ✔ Coupons
- ✔ Testimonials
- ✔ Headlines and links that call for action

   ✔ Links to information that supports the main call to action

   ✔ Directions on how to take action

Figure 4-5 shows an e-mail that promotes products.

Figure 4-5:
An e-mail
with a
promotional
theme.

Courtesy of Constant Contact

Informational themes

When the main objective of your e-mail is to inform your audience to help them form an opinion, include only that content which supports and relates to an informational theme.

Informational themes differ from promotional themes: Informational themes rarely include a specific call to action other than reading the message content. For example, a newsletter with an informational theme might have three articles about the benefits of clean air. The following types of content are information in nature:

   ✔ News articles

   ✔ Stories and narratives

   ✔ Opinions and viewpoints

   ✔ Announcements with no specific call to action

   ✔ Event calendars

   ✔ Frequently asked questions (FAQs)

Figure 4-6 shows an e-mail with news articles.

Procedural themes

When the main objective of your e-mail is to give official instructions or explain processes, include content that supports and relates to a procedural theme. Procedural messages are like informational messages in that they rarely call for specific action outside of reading the content in the e-mail. Examples of content you might include in an e-mail with a procedural theme include

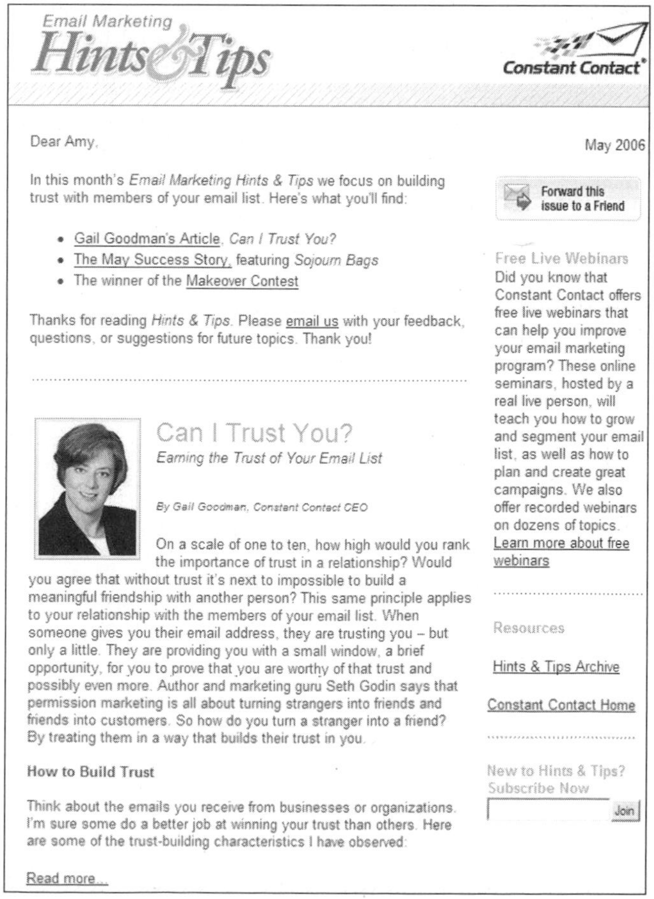

Figure 4-6: An e-mail with an informational theme.

Courtesy of Constant Contact

✔ Text welcoming a new customer or list subscriber

✔ Notifications and official statements

✔ Footer text explaining a shipping or privacy policy

✔ Disclosures and warranties

Figure 4-7 shows an e-mail that includes a notification.

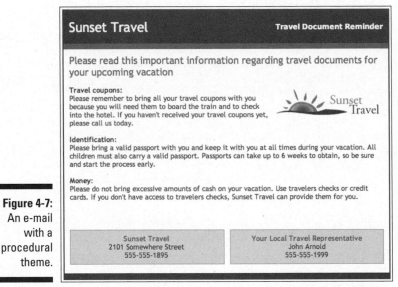

Figure 4-7:
An e-mail
with a
procedural
theme.

Courtesy of Constant Contact

Relational themes

When the main objective of your e-mail is to build or deepen personal relationships, your e-mail should include only content that supports and relates to a relational theme. *Relational themes* are typically one-way communications with no call to action. Examples of content you might include in an e-mail with a relational theme include

✔ Greetings and acknowledgments

✔ News or stories about personal experiences

✔ Customer recognition messages

Figure 4-8 shows an e-mail with a customer recognition message.

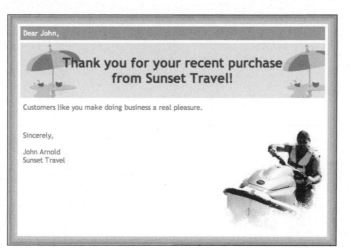

Figure 4-8:
An e-mail with a relational theme.

Courtesy of Constant Contact

Multiple themes

When your objectives tell you to include multiple themes in one e-mail format, be extra careful to ensure that your themes share an obvious main theme in some way.

Figure 4-9 shows a multi-themed newsletter. This newsletter is sent to dues-paying members of a chamber of commerce and contains

- **Promotional:** An offer to prompt the audience to complete a membership renewal.
- **Informational:** An announcement containing a conference agenda.
- **Relational:** An offer to attend a networking event.

To include multiple themes in your e-mails, I recommend doing the following:

- State the main theme clearly at the beginning.
- Group sub-themes together with layout and design elements, such as headings and white space.
- If you can't find a main theme to tie themes, use two separate e-mail formats and send the messages separately under their own themes. For example, a golf club sale might work in conjunction with information about a new store location under a moving sale theme, whereas new location information combined with informative golfing tips might be too distinct to include under a common theme.

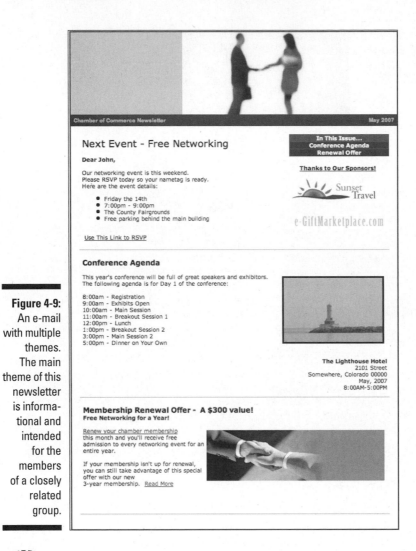

Figure 4-9:
An e-mail
with multiple
themes.
The main
theme of this
newsletter
is informa-
tional and
intended
for the
members
of a closely
related
group.

Make sure that all sub-themes are relevant to your audience. If not, divide your e-mail list into groups by theme and send targeted messages that interest each group under their own themes.

Staying Focused on Your Objectives

Losing sight of your objectives usually happens when your timeline slips or when you don't seem to be progressing toward the achievement of your objectives. In such cases, you can easily become focused on making changes to your objectives to agree with your e-mail content instead of altering your e-mail content to more closely resemble your objectives.

Before making changes to your objectives, make sure that you give your e-mail a fair chance to do its job. Delivering effective e-mail content inherently has a lot of variables that you can't control, such as changes in your audience's attitudes and unforeseen reactions to your content or frequency. Predicting exactly how long it takes to reach an objective isn't an exact science, either. Sometimes it takes weeks or even months to see substantial positive results from an e-mail strategy — especially if e-mail is new to your marketing mix and your audience isn't used to receiving e-mails from you.

The following sections help ensure your objectives and your e-mail content both have a fair chance to prove themselves.

Write down your objectives

Objectives don't need to be set in stone, but writing them down — in a note-book, in a calendar, or on a whiteboard — helps you see them in a concrete way. Writing your objectives also helps schedule content delivery and helps you to memorize your objectives so you can use them to guide the actions you take when you're away from your notepad. Here are some tips for writing your objectives:

✔ **Keep a calendar of planned e-mail marketing campaigns.**

You don't want to hurt your objectives by mistiming important communications or sending too many communications too closely together.

✔ **Refer to your objectives often.**

Make sure that your e-mail marketing decisions closely resemble the original objectives over time.

✔ **Track your progress.**

Make sure that you're moving closer to your objectives by measuring quantifiable data such as the increase in sales, number of Web site visitors, or hours of free time. Don't rely solely on hunches. (You can read more about tracking your e-mails in Chapter 11.)

✔ **Plan your next step before you reach an objective.**

You can avoid being tempted to send random communications or leave your contacts in electronic silence between objectives.

Stick to your objectives

Sometimes, failing to reach your objectives is just a matter of giving up too early or getting distracted and not regaining your focus. Testing and fine-tuning content and objectives takes time and attention to details. Paying attention to all the fine details of your marketing strategy takes a certain amount of dedication and time blocking. Here are some tips for pressing on when you feel confident that your objectives are sound and your attention is slipping.

✔ **Share your objectives with someone you trust.**

Add this person to your e-mail list so she can let you know when your content seems to drift away from your original intentions.

✔ **Periodically revisit your objectives.**

Review your progress by analyzing the responses to your e-mails to make sure your e-mails are moving you in the right directions. (You can read more about e-mail analysis in Chapter 11.)

✔ **If you need to overhaul your e-mail content, make small changes.**

That way, you won't shock your contacts with totally new message formats and themes.

✔ **Consider outsourcing your e-mail strategy to a professional.**

When you don't have the time to stick to your objectives, get help! You can find outsourcing recommendations at www.emailtrainer.com.

Build from your objectives

Reaching your objectives isn't an effort solely dependent on your e-mail strategy. Your whole business has to operate in harmony with your objectives, or your e-mail strategy could be rendered ineffective. For example, if your e-mail strategy is to drive traffic to your Web site so that people will register for an event, your Web site should be built with the same objectives in mind. Objectives help to make e-mail marketing decisions, but make sure your other activities support your objectives as well. Here are some tips for making sure your business operations share the same objectives:

✔ See all outgoing marketing and sales messages as a whole unit and also time your communications to support one another.

✔ Make sure your employees and other business partners are aware of your objectives so that they can act accordingly when dealing with customers, suppliers, and the public.

✔ Delegate smaller objectives that help to reach larger or ongoing objectives.

Chapter 5

Building a Quality E-Mail List

Collecting e-mail addresses isn't an easy task. Some people are so bothered by unsolicited e-mails that they're willing to share almost anything else with you before they will share their e-mail address. Others might give you their e-mail address, but when the e-mails they receive from you don't meet their expectations, they resort to unsubscribing or marking the e-mails as spam, even if they are loyal customers.

Fortunately, an e-mail list needn't be large to be effective. The best e-mail lists are those that contain the names of loyal repeat customers, referral sources who respect others' privacy, and interested prospects who know you and your business well enough to recognize your e-mails.

This chapter guides you through some of the best tactics for building a permission-based e-mail list with a high number of quality subscribers. This chapter summarizes how and where to collect information, what information to collect, and how to obtain permission to send. A quality list helps ensure that your e-mail messages are received by the people who are most likely to respond with repeat and referral business.

Where and How to Collect Contact Information

The quality of your e-mail list depends greatly on where and how you collect the information in the first place as well as where and how you store and manage the data. The best way to ensure that you collect quality information is to obtain information and permission directly from the person who owns the information in the first place — namely, your prospects and customers.

Your challenge is to provide multiple opportunities and incentives for prospects and customers to share their information as well as to manage the resulting data effectively and efficiently.

Many businesses have been bought and sold based on the strength of the contact information they possess. Quality list data stored in a useful format is a goldmine for targeting your e-mail marketing messages and converting prospects and customers into steady streams of repeat and referral sales.

Preparing your e-mail database

Sending e-mails to your list requires your list data to be stored in a useful electronic format, so take care to enter your data into a database while you collect. Building and maintaining an electronic database allows you to

- ✔ Organize and view your list data easily.
- ✔ Sort your list data into categories to send targeted e-mails.
- ✔ Process and keep track of unsubscribed contacts.
- ✔ Query your list to extract useful information and reports.

You don't need a highly sophisticated database for effective e-mail marketing although additional database features can improve your ability to target your contacts with specific messages. Keep in mind that databases with a lot of complex features are more expensive than simpler applications. Make sure any fancy functionality in your database is capable of returning more than a dollar for every dollar you spend to gain that function.

If you're not sure which database is going to give you the best results, start with a basic database application or with your E-Mail Service Provider (ESP) database utility. You can always upgrade later when your e-mail marketing strategy outgrows your initial functionality. Make sure the database you choose can easily transfer data to or synchronize data with your ESP. Most ESPs allow you to either import or synchronize data with the following database applications:

✔ Outlook and Outlook Express

✔ Excel

✔ QuickBooks

✔ ACT!

✔ Goldmine

✔ Access

✔ Eudora

✔ Mac Mail and Address Book

Whether you use a well-known database application or a customized solution, most databases can export data in one or more compatible formats. Ask your ESP for a list of supported formats and then check the export feature on your database to see whether you have a match.

I don't recommend storing your data in an ESP database system alone unless the service allows you to access the data belonging to unsubscribed contacts. Just because someone unsubscribes from receiving future e-mails doesn't mean that he or she isn't a good customer or prospect. Phone numbers, mailing addresses, and behavioral information become even more useful when someone has unsubscribed from your e-mail list.

After your database application is ready to accept information, decide where and how to allow your prospective subscribers to sign up for your e-mail list. The name of the game is *collect where you connect.* Everywhere you come into human contact, you should be ready to obtain contact information and permission. The more personal your approach to collection, the more useful and valuable your list will become. The following sections list some tactics for collecting contact information online, in person, and in print.

If you already have a database of prospective e-mail list subscribers, or if you have a lot of contact information from various sources waiting to be entered into a single database, flip ahead to the "Inheriting a list: Getting permission after the fact" section before adding those contacts to your e-mail list.

Collecting information online

Placing a sign-up link in every online presence possible is a great way to collect information with explicit permission. A *sign-up link* is a text box, button, or text that usually links to a sign-up form or confirmation page that allows your subscriber to enter and submit additional information and preferences. Figure 5-1 shows three different types of signups.

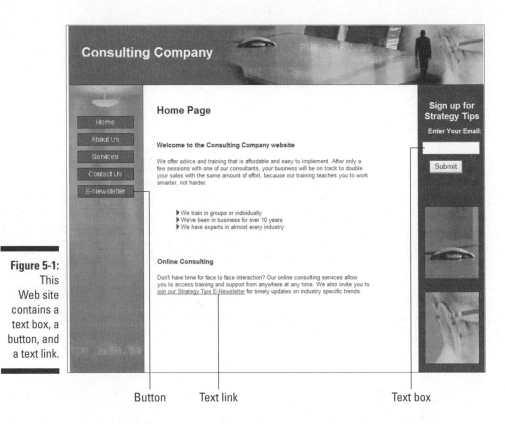

Button   Text link   Text box

Figure 5-1: This Web site contains a text box, a button, and a text link.

Some means of putting sign-up requests on a site include

✔ **Text boxes:** These allow your subscribers to enter information without clicking-through to an additional sign-up form. Text boxes can ask for an e-mail address, or they can contain several fields making up an entire form.

✔ **Buttons:** These are graphical representations of a link that takes the subscriber to a form to complete and submit. Buttons can be images with text inside, flashing boxes, icons, or other creative graphics.

A sign-up button should stand out, but you don't want to draw too much attention away from the content of your Web site for visitors who are already subscribers.

✔ **Text links:** These are short headlines of plain text linked to a sign-up form. Text links are ideal if you want to add an option to subscribe within the context of other information or if you would like to put a line of text in your e-mail signature.

✔ **Check boxes:** These are usually employed on multiuse forms to save additional steps. For example, someone who is making an online purchase already has to fill in her name and address, so adding a sign-up check box to the shipping form is a great way to gain permission to use the information for shipping the item and sending future e-mails. Figure 5-2 shows a shipping form with a simple check box within the text.

If you use check boxes, leave the box unchecked (cleared) as the default setting because you don't want people who overlook the box to become disgruntled when they receive future e-mails and feel that they were added to your list without their permission.

Whether you employ forms, buttons, text links, or any other element, try experimenting with different placement ideas. You can place a sign-up link almost anywhere HTML is possible. Try adding a sign-up link to the following locations:

- ✔ On every page of your Web site
- ✔ In your e-mail signature, as shown in Figure 5-3
- ✔ On your blog or personal Web site
- ✔ In banner ads and online advertising
- ✔ On other Web sites (with permission)
- ✔ In noncompeting businesses' e-mails (with permission)
- ✔ In online directories

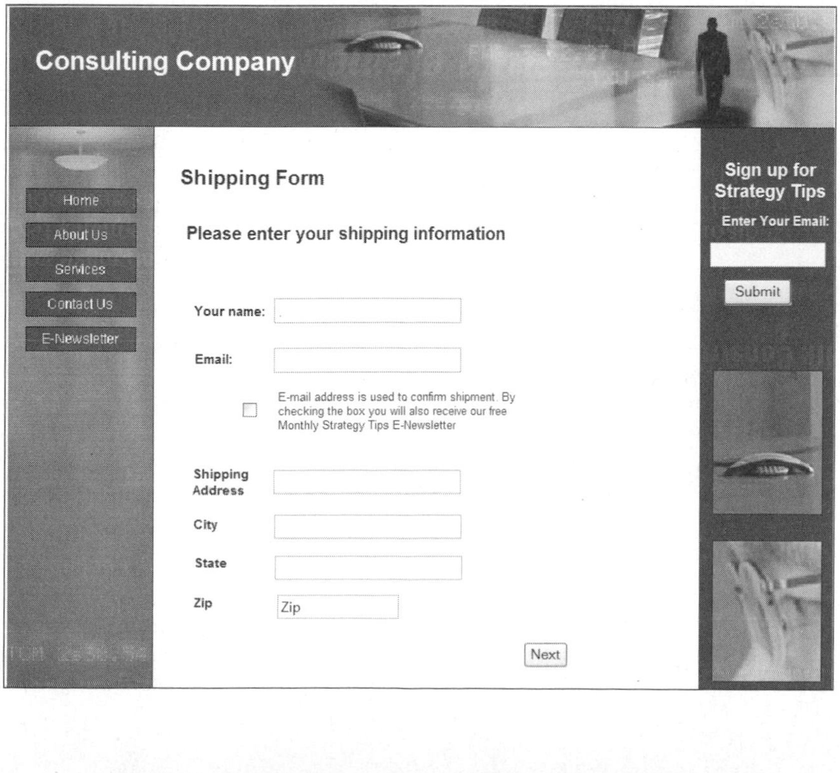

Figure 5-2:
This shipping form includes a simple check box with text.

Consulting Company

Home
About Us
Services
Contact Us
E-Newsletter

Shipping Form

Please enter your shipping information

Your name:

Email:

☐ E-mail address is used to confirm shipment. By checking the box you will also receive our free Monthly Strategy Tips E-Newsletter

Shipping Address

City

State

Zip   Zip

Next

Sign up for Strategy Tips

Enter Your Email:

Submit

Figure 5-3:
Place a
sign-up link
in your
e-mail
signature.

Regards,

Peter Smith
Owner, La Italia

Free lunch when you
Join Our E-Mail List

Collecting information in person

According to the Ten Foot Rule, whenever anyone is within ten feet of you, ask her for her contact information. A warm body or a verbal conversation can equate to a captive audience for communicating the benefits of joining your e-mail list.

Always ask for permission when you collect information in person. Here are some ways to connect and collect without being intrusive:

- ✔ **Swap business cards.**

  Ask whether that person's preferred e-mail address is on the card.

- ✔ **Place a guest book on the counter in your store or office.**

  Keep a guest book in your car so you can ask people anywhere to sign it.

- ✔ **Place a basket for business cards on your table at trade shows and events.**

  Make sure to place a sign on the basket that states your intent to send e-mails.

- ✔ **Train your employees to take down customer information.**

  Ask anyone who answers the phone in your business to ask for e-mail addresses and permission when customers and prospects call.

Collecting information through print

Adding sign-up information to direct mail and print advertising is a great way to help maximize your advertising dollars. You can use print to drive people to your Web site or store, you can ask them to fill out a paper form and return it, or you can ask them to send you an e-mail requesting to join the list.

Here are some ideas for using print to drive people to a sign-up process:

- ✔ **Send a postcard offering an incentive to return the card to the store (such as a free gift or an entry into a drawing) with the recipient's e-mail address filled into a space on the card.**

  Be sure to explain your intended usage and also ask permission in the text.

- ✔ **Position your sign-up incentive to add value to your print offer.**

  For example, you could print, *Free child's haircut with subscription to our preferred customer e-mail list.*

- ✔ **Add your sign-up incentive to the back of your business cards.**

  For example, a discount dollar-store's business card could include, *Our e-mail list members save 10% more! Join online, in person, or by phone.*

- ✔ **Purchase an intuitive domain name and place it in your print advertising to promote signups.**

  In the preceding example, the discount dollar store could purchase a domain such as www.JoinMyEmailList.com and point it to the sign-up form on the company Web site.

 As you begin to formulate a strategy for collecting information, make sure that you write down your tactics and objectives. Having consistent messaging everywhere you connect is best. Namely, if you don't plan your entire strategy, you might find yourself mixing messages and confusing your prospective subscribers. Too, it will be difficult to diagnose your results if you have too many variables in your messaging and placement.

Deciding What Information to Collect

The two things you need to collect are only an e-mail address and permission to send someone a professional e-mail. Generally speaking, enlisting subscribers is easier if you ask for as little information as possible. You'll improve your results in the long run, however, if you make plans to gather increasing amounts of information over time — such as interests and personal information — as you interact with customers and prospects.

I cover the different kinds of permissions later in this chapter in the "Asking for Permission" section. In the following sections, you can find out what kind of information you can collect beyond the e-mail address to build a list.

Gathering essential information

Essential information includes an e-mail address plus any information that the customer or prospect expects you to know in order to send them information personally and professionally. Essential information comes in two categories:

✔ **Professional:** This is information that your prospects and customers want you to know in order to send relevant business information. Examples can include

- Preferred e-mail address

- Product lines or services of interest

- ZIP code (if you conduct events or have multiple locations)

✔ **Personal:** This is information that you need in order to treat the prospect or customer as a human being with a name and feelings and needs. Examples include

- First name

- Opinions and preferences

Figure 5-4 shows a sign-up form that asks for both professional and personal information.

Figure 5-4:
This sign-up form asks for professional and personal information.

Professional information   Personal information

When is essential information essential?

How your prospects and customers view essential information is likely to depend upon how personally you interact with your prospects and customers at the beginning of a relationship. People are also more comfortable sharing information when they understand how you will use the information.

For example, an online retailer could be viewed as intruding when asking a site visitor for a physical address before he or she is ready to make a purchase. After the site visitor decides to check out with an item in the shopping cart, collecting a physical address becomes necessary in order to ship the item.

You don't have to obtain all essential information upon the first contact with a prospect or customer. As long as you have a good permission-based e-mail address, you can ask for more information in future e-mails by sending short, relevant surveys, and by using other contact methods as more trust develops in the relationship. Collecting information using surveys is discussed in Chapter 13.

Getting to know your list members better

Believe it or not, most of your prospects aren't interested in everything that you decide to send in the context of an e-mail strategy. As you collect contact information and permission, consider asking your prospective subscribers to share their interests. Using interest information allows you to sort your e-mail lists into categories and send information relevant to that category.

Asking your prospective subscribers open-ended questions about their interests can prove frustrating because people tend to be unique in their approach to questions about preferences. Some people share their true feelings, but others are inclined to tell you what you want to hear. Sometimes, people also share information that you can't possibly use or information that requires too many categories to efficiently manage. Instead of open-ended questions, come up with some basic list categories and ask your prospective subscribers to self-identify when signing up. Here's an example of an open-ended question and a category-specific question:

- ✔ **Open-ended question:** "Why do you dine with us?"

- ✔ **Revised category-specific question:** "Which answer best describes why you dine with us?"

  - Money-saving offers

  - New menu items

  - Winc recommendations

  - Live music and special events

When you're thinking of questions to ask your prospective list subscribers, the answers should be useful for targeting future e-mails. For example, asking people whether they're interested in golf might prove valuable if you plan on sending invitations to a golf tournament fundraiser or if your business sells travel packages that include golf vacations.

Here's a sampling of possible list categories and underlying lists that you can ask your subscribers to join so you can sort your communications by general interest:

- ✔ **Communication type:** Instead of sending all your marketing e-mails to everyone on your list, ask your subscribers to choose the information that they would like to receive — and then stick to it. You can always ask subscribers to update their preferences if you want to start sending more information at a later time. List titles could include

    - Monthly newsletter

    - Discounts and special offers

    - New product announcements

    - Parties and event invitations

    - Press releases

    - Tech support and product tips

    - Service interval reminders

    - Last-minute appointment specials

- ✔ **Demographic interests:** Asking for *demographic* information — such as age or income — can prove difficult because people are concerned about privacy, and they generally aren't as willing to share demographic information unless they know why you need it and how you use it. To get the information you need, though, try combining demographic and interest questions together as one category so that you can make inferences without having to be too direct. Here's a sample of possible list titles for specific types of businesses:

    - Spare-no-expense travel destinations

    - Singles-only event invitations

    - Golfing with kids younger than 12

    - Entertaining with limited space

    - Gardening on a budget

- ✔ **Preferred customer interests:** Some people will tell you what interests them only when they feel that they will get preferential treatment as a result. Try positioning interest information so that the reward is receiving the information. List ideas include

- Priority, reserved event tickets
- Members-only discounts
- First-to-know product announcements
- Early bird access to product-specific sales

Figure 5-5 shows a registration form that allows the reader to indicate a variety of interests.

Don't give your subscribers too many choices too early. Ask them to adjust their interests over time and collect information as you interact. You can also collect interest information without asking your subscribers by tracking their click behavior. For more about e-mail tracking, see Part V.

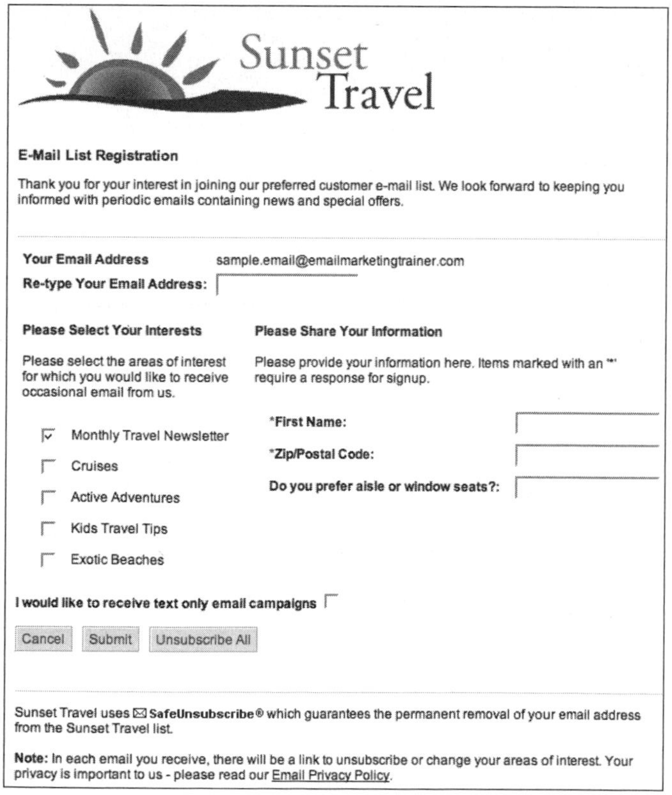

Sunset Travel

E-Mail List Registration

Thank you for your interest in joining our preferred customer e-mail list. We look forward to keeping you informed with periodic emails containing news and special offers.

Your Email Address sample.email@emailmarketingtrainer.com

Re-type Your Email Address:

Please Select Your Interests

Please select the areas of interest for which you would like to receive occasional email from us.

- [x] Monthly Travel Newsletter
- [ ] Cruises
- [ ] Active Adventures
- [ ] Kids Travel Tips
- [ ] Exotic Beaches

Please Share Your Information

Please provide your information here. Items marked with an "*" require a response for signup.

***First Name:**

***Zip/Postal Code:**

Do you prefer aisle or window seats?:

I would like to receive text only email campaigns

Cancel | Submit | Unsubscribe All

Sunset Travel uses SafeUnsubscribe® which guarantees the permanent removal of your email address from the Sunset Travel list.

Note: In each email you receive, there will be a link to unsubscribe or change your areas of interest. Your privacy is important to us - please read our Email Privacy Policy.

Figure 5-5: This sign-up form shows a selection of interest categories.

Creating a media mailing list

Most media entities accept press releases via e-mail and will post additional e-mail addresses for communicating newsworthy information person to person. If you're planning to send press releases, be sure to keep your media list separate from your customer list so that you can restrict media personnel to newsworthy press release e-mails only. Permission, privacy, and professionalism matter just as much to the media as it does to the consumer, so kindly contact your media professionals and ask them to be included on your press release list before you start sending.

Gathering behavioral interests

Collecting behavioral interests allows you to add insight to general interests and other information. You can collect behavioral interests by making assumptions based on frequent customer questions or by observing how prospects, subscribers, or customers behave in the context of your business relations.

 Keeping behavioral interests private is a good idea because the subjects of your behavioral studies might not self-identify with the label that you place on them. For example, you might label someone as a discount shopper because she uses a lot of coupons, but she might think the label makes her less important than other customers. Segmenting your subscribers into private lists using behavioral observation also allows you to send more relevant information without involving subscribers in a time-consuming process.

Here is a sampling of private list categories that can prove useful for sorting lists by behavioral interest. You might want to rename them, depending on how you are asking for the information:

- **Coupon users:** Some people buy some things only when your products or services are on sale or when they can save money over a competing product. Coupon users are more likely to respond to promotions with associated discounts and freebies, so it pays to be able to identify these folks.

- **Repeat buyers:** If you can identify when certain subscribers are likely to be thinking about a purchase, you can sort them by date of last purchase and send your message when they're likely to be interested in a purchase. For example, a hair salon might note a trend that customers think about their next haircut every 30 days. For a scenario like this, your coupon should arrive around the end of that 30-day period. Here's an example with a little longer time frame: If your business offers oil changes, try sending a promotion every three months. However, if your customers adhere to a longer buying cycle (such as customers who buy a new car every three to four years), don't wait that long to send them an e-mail because you don't want them to forget you.

- ✔ **Very Important Customers (VICs):** A VIC list can include big spenders, frequent shoppers, referral sources, or people who give you valuable feedback about your business. VICs should be pampered, thanked, and welcomed — treated like royalty.

- ✔ **Advocates:** Hopefully, you have some customers (besides Mom and Dad) who just love your business. Or maybe people on your list love helping others, so they're willing to spread the word to help your business grow. Segmenting advocates into a separate list allows you to send them gifts and incentives that no one else receives.

- ✔ **Customers and prospects:** The nature of a business relationship often changes after a person has parted with some of his money, and the nature of your communications might need to change as well. For example, after someone makes a first decision to buy, you can probably stop sending her links to online brochures or directions to your store — unless, of course, the purpose of your e-mail is to ask the customer to forward such information.

Offering Incentives to Increase Signups

Because your e-mail list is an asset — hopefully containing e-mail addresses belonging to loyal customers who spend more money as well as referral sources who love to tell others about you — offering an incentive in exchange for an e-mail subscription is really the least you can do to thank and reward your most valuable contacts.

Not all incentives are all-liked

After you determine where and when to ask for e-mail addresses and permission, decide how to ask. For example, if you offer subscribers a link to Join the E-Mail Blast, those people who don't want a blast or don't know exactly what they are likely to receive will pass on the opportunity to subscribe.

Find out what motivates your prospects and customers before determining an incentive. For example, some people will join an e-mail list in exchange for a discount on all future purchases. On the other hand, some people associate discounts with words like *cheap, discontinued, last year's model,* or *out of style.*

If your customers aren't motivated by discounts, consider employing a more creative strategy, such as a VIC club, where e-mail subscribers are the first to know about the latest high-tech products available at a prestigious price.

Offering incentives for joining your e-mail list can reward your business in at least two ways:

- ✔ **Increased signups:** The number of people willing to share their contact information with you is likely to increase if they feel that they're getting something of value in return.
- ✔ **Increased loyalty:** An incentive rewards your subscribers and can cause loyalty, repeat business, and referrals to increase.

Giving subscribers immediate incentives

Some incentives, such as ongoing discounts, can be an inherent part of being on the list — and are, therefore, immediate upon the subscription. Immediate incentives abound and could include

- ✔ Discounts or reward points on every purchase
- ✔ VIP access to special events, front row seats, and so on
- ✔ Access to members-only information
- ✔ Free trials, gifts, or additional services

Giving subscribers future incentives

Some incentives are not immediate but are instead forthcoming for members of the list. For example, imagine a clothing store that has a 48-hour sale twice per year, and only e-mail list subscribers are invited to save 50 percent if they order within the 48-hour period.

If e-mail list subscribers are the only customers invited to the event, the invitation is the incentive, but it isn't immediate because the subscriber has to wait for an invitation to take advantage of the incentive.

Because the sale happens only twice per year, the store could send other e-mails between the sales with other offers and information. Imminent incentives are limited only by your own creativity and could include the following promotions:

- ✔ Early shopping hours during the holidays
- ✔ Invitations to periodic private events, as shown in Figure 5-6
- ✔ Random rewards, such as prize drawings

Courtesy of Aicon Gallery New York, Design by Jill Litfin, 2007

Figure 5-6:
Invite your list subscribers to special events to make their subscription more valuable.

If you can't think of an incentive to offer your e-mail list subscribers or if the intrinsic value of the content in your e-mails is the incentive, use your messaging to be as clear as possible about expectations in place of an incentive.

For example, asking potential subscribers to *Sign up for Friday Quick Tips* tells them what to expect. Comparatively, asking a subscriber simply to *Sign up for Our E-Mail List* is too generic and might cause prospective subscribers to hesitate — or, worse, disappoint subscribers when their expectations are not met.

Permission and privacy as incentives

Adding a privacy and permission policy to your data collection forms as well as clearly stating your intended usage up front helps put people more at ease when sharing information. Even if no one reads your privacy and permission policy, the fact that a link to privacy information appears is often reassuring.

Remember that people who share an e-mail address always do so with personal expectations in mind, and sometimes those expectations are hard to determine. As a best practice, make sure that your privacy and permission policy benefits your subscriber more than your business. Keep your privacy and permission statements short, using information in accordance with people's expectations at the time of information exchange.

Asking for Permission

Collecting information without asking for permission can cause prospective subscribers to hesitate — or worse, they could perceive you as a spammer who abuses their privacy. Obtaining permission also ensures that your list starts out in compliance with the current CAN-SPAM laws.

The CAN-SPAM act of 2003 makes certain methods of e-mail address collection illegal and defines the types of business relationships you need in order to send commercial and transactional e-mails. You can read more about the current CAN-SPAM laws in Chapter 3.

Taking some time to formulate a professional permission strategy before embarking on e-mail collection tactics can reward your overall e-mail strategy with loyal subscribers who love to open, read, and take action on the e-mails you send.

Deciding on a permission level

When formulating your permission strategy, put yourself in the prospective subscriber's shoes so that you can assess the level of permission necessary to meet individual expectations.

Each type of permission is a two-way notion. You should be able to attest to each subscriber's level of consent, and your subscriber should feel that he did indeed authorize you to send him e-mail. This type of two-way permission comes in three basic levels, each with a higher level of demonstrated consensus: implied, explicit, and confirmed.

Level 1: Implied permission

Implied permission happens when someone shares her e-mail address with you in the course of normal business communications. The transaction implies that the purpose of giving you the e-mail address is to receive e-mails from you in reply. This level of permission is not recommended as a best practice even though it's sometimes suitable in the recipient's view. (I describe why this is not a best practice in a bit.)

An example of implied permission is a prospective customer who fills out an online form to obtain a quote for your services. The form includes an e-mail address field. The prospect shares her e-mail address within the form, expecting that you will use that e-mail address to send the quote. If you send the quote and then begin sending weekly promotions without disclosing the fact that sharing an e-mail address on the quote form results in additional e-mails, however, you run the risk that your new subscriber will feel violated.

The main reason why implied permission is not considered one of e-mail professionalism's best practices is that it is doesn't take much extra effort to move from implicit permission to a higher standard. In the previous example, the business owner could easily add a link to his or her permission policy under the e-mail address field. Or, he could insert text that reads

> *By sharing your e-mail address, you will receive your quote via e-mail along with concise weekly product updates of which you can safely unsubscribe at any time.*

Level 2: Explicit permission

Explicit permission happens when you include text or language disclosing how you plan to use the prospective subscriber's e-mail address. For example, an explicit subscriber might be a Web site visitor who clicks a link that reads *Sign up to receive our weekly e-newsletter* and then clicks another link on the following page to submit additional information that he types into an online form. Explicit permission also happens when prospective subscribers contact you and explicitly ask to be added to your e-mail list.

Explicit permission doesn't have to be a lengthy or complicated process, but the benefits of obtaining explicit permission are worth having a straightforward process. Here are some examples of explicit permission that you can adapt to your own subscriber situations:

- **Verbal:** When someone shares his e-mail address by handing you a business card or dictates an e-mail address to you during a phone conversation, you could query, "Is it alright if I send you my weekly event invitation e-mail?"

- **Written:** If a prospective subscriber sends a single e-mail to you and you want to add him to your e-mail list, you could reply to the e-mail and ask, "By the way, may I add your e-mail address to my list so that you can receive my monthly e-newsletter?"

- **Physical:** Some subscribers physically add their e-mail address to a guest book or sign up via a paper form. If you have such an arrangement, you could post a professional-looking plaque or sign next to the guest book or sign-up form that states *Thank you for giving us permission to send you our weekly e-mail coupons by signing our guest book. We promise never to share your e-mail address with anyone outside the company without your permission.*

- **Incidental:** Sometimes, you can ask for explicit permission in the context of a transaction related to your e-mail information. For example, you might want to give online shoppers the ability to receive cross-promotions by selecting a check box during the check-out process. The text describing the check box could read, *Select this check box to receive periodic promotions that enhance the value of your purchase.* Just be sure that the default setting on the check box is unchecked (clear), or else it is no longer an example of explicit permission.

No matter what the method of accepting permission, you should always take your prospective subscriber's circumstances into account. Even explicit permission can result in spam complaints or negative emotions if your subscriber doesn't remember subscribing or doesn't recognize the e-mails you send after subscribing. Here are some ideas for reinforcing permission:

- ✔ **Say thanks.** Send a welcome letter immediately after the subscriber joins the list.

- ✔ **Send e-mail reminders.** Insert a paragraph of text at the top of every e-mail reminding the recipient how you obtained their e-mail address.

- ✔ **Reinforce branding.** Include your logo and colors on your sign-up form and make sure that future e-mails match your brand. (Read more about this in Chapter 6.)

- ✔ **Reinforce familiarity.** Make sure that every e-mail's From line is memorable and familiar. (Read more on this in Chapter 7.)

- ✔ **Send a reminder letter.** Send a permission reminder letter periodically that tells your subscribers exactly how you obtained their e-mail address and gives them links for updating their preferences and unsubscribing.

Level 3: Confirmed permission

Confirmed permission happens when someone implicitly or explicitly subscribes to your e-mail list, and you respond to the subscriber with an e-mail requiring the subscriber to confirm his interest by reading your intended usage and then clicking a confirmation link. If the subscriber doesn't confirm, his e-mail address is not added to your list, even if he explicitly filled out and submitted a form or physically signed your guest book. Figure 5-7 shows an example of a confirmation e-mail.

Don't mix your list messages

I consulted with a restaurant owner once who also owned a travel agency. He decided to place sign-up cards on each table in his restaurant so that his restaurant patrons could sign up for his travel newsletter. Lots of restaurant patrons filled out the cards, but they were confused when they began receiving a travel newsletter because they thought they were signing up to receive e-mails from the restaurant.

To ensure that permission is viewed as explicit on both sides of the information exchange, be as clear as possible in your messaging and context. For example, don't send coupons when your subscriber signed up in order to win a prize, unless you clearly state your intentions. When your context and messaging are as clear as possible and you still notice subscriber confusion, consider using an even-higher level of permission.

Courtesy of Constant Contact

Figure 5-7:
A prospec-
tive
subscriber
must
click an
additional
link for
confirmed
permission.

Although confirmed permission is the most professional form of permission, it is also the most difficult for subscribers to understand. Therefore, confirmed permission is not always suitable. Generally speaking, confirmed permission should be used when you want to be *absolutely sure* that your subscribers want your e-mail.

Confirmed permission is the appropriate level if

- ✔ You send sensitive information.
- ✔ Your subscribers tend to forget signing up.
- ✔ You want to have a physical record of the subscriber's authorization to send e-mail.

Confirmation e-mails generally have low response rates, so if you're using explicit permission to build your list, you might lose subscribers who really want to be on the list but fail to read the confirmation e-mail and click the required link. The trade-off, however, is that your confirmed subscribers are more likely to receive and open your e-mails.

Inheriting a list: Getting permission after the fact

Sometimes, you might find yourself in possession of an e-mail list with questionable — or even no — permission. This often happens when you obtained your list in one of (or more of, but not limited to) the following scenarios:

- ✔ You purchased an existing business and inherited an e-mail list without knowing the source of the e-mail addresses on the list.

- ✔ Your list contains e-mail addresses collected over a long time period, and you can't identify each type of associated permission.

- ✔ You purchased a list or built your list with low permission standards before you read this chapter — and now you're wondering whether your list is useless.

Sending e-mails to a permission-less list might violate the current CAN-SPAM laws and is likely to result in a high number of spam complaints from recipients.

Follow these steps to determine the permission status of an inherited list with questionable permission:

1. **Sort your list by source. If the source doesn't imply a two-way business relationship and the recipient likely won't recognize your e-mail address, discard the e-mail address or set aside the contact info to ask for permission.**

   Sources can include order forms, business cards, e-mail correspondence, guest books, or purchased lists. Inherited lists rarely detail the source as a field in a database or a note on the back of a business card, so you need to determine the source by matching each record to other clues.

   For example, if your list is contained in a customer relationship management system database, you might be able to export all the customers who made a purchase — and assume that names were obtained as the result of a business transaction.

   Always discard purchased lists because purchased lists are almost never permission-based to begin with. (See "Building a List with List Brokers" later in this chapter for more information about purchased lists.)

2. **Sort your list by date. Discard any addresses belonging to customers who haven't made a purchase in over a year.**

   E-mail addresses belonging to customers who made purchases in years past and haven't returned are unlikely to appreciate your e-mails. Older e-mail addresses should be kept only if the person who owns the e-mail address is a recognizable current customer.

3. **Check your list visually. Discard any addresses that begin with ambiguous names or that are part of a distribution list.**

   Ambiguous names include `Webmaster@` or `Info@`. *Distribution lists* (single e-mail addresses that forward the e-mail to multiple addresses behind the scenes) are impossible to tell whether the underlying e-mail addresses are permission-based.

4. **Sort the rest of your list by category.**

   At this point, consider using different messaging, depending on your relationship to the person who owns the e-mail address. If the e-mail address belongs to a prospect, you might want to proceed more cautiously than if the e-mail address belongs to a person who has purchased a product several times.

5. **Confirm permission to send e-mail.**

   If, and only if, an e-mail list passes the preceding four tests and you're certain that the people who own the e-mail addresses on your list will recognize your business and your relationship to them personally, you should contact them to confirm permission.

   - *If you have a small list:* Confirmation can be verified with a phone call or an e-mail containing a confirmation link.

   - *If you aren't able to contact people personally:* Send a professionally written confirmation e-mail.

Verifying permission for an old, outdated, or questionable list can prove frustrating even if you follow these steps because people change their e-mail addresses from time to time, and because your database might not include the information you need to effectively sort through an inherited list.

If the aforementioned steps seem highly labor-intensive or prove to be impossible — or if you can't make a determination because of the organizational state of your database — you should probably bite the bullet and discard the list or attempt to reestablish permission with the people on your inherited list without sending e-mail.

If your list contains additional contact information other than the e-mail address, consider using direct mail, phone calls, and other advertising to drive the prospects through an explicit sign-up process on your Web site or in a physical location.

 While you're contacting customers on an inherited list, take the time to highlight some of the valuable incentives for subscribing to your e-mail list and build some customer momentum along the way. You also use those contacts to test your print messaging and see what kinds of incentives and mediums people are likely to respond to before you integrate the tactics for collecting contact information in the next section.

Protecting your e-mail list

A quality list of permission-based e-mail subscribers segmented by interest and behavior is something to be proud of. Lists and data are assets and represent a significant competitive advantage to your business.

When it comes to e-mail data, protecting your asset is as important as building it in the first place. Don't violate the trust of your e-mail list subscribers by sharing their e-mail addressees with others who don't have permission to send to your list. Don't abuse your e-mail list subscribers by sending information they didn't ask for or by using their permission as a platform for selling lots of unrelenting banner ads in the body of your e-mail newsletters.

As a general rule, don't do anything with your e-mail list data that is not explicitly agreed to and expected by your subscribers. For more information about privacy issues and on becoming a trusted sender, read Chapter 3.

Building a List with List Brokers

List brokers are marketing companies that collect and sell contact information. If you decide to build a list with the help of a list broker, you should recognize the significant differences between obtaining a list of physical addresses or phone numbers and obtaining e-mail addresses.

Purchasing a list of physical addresses or phone numbers is a relatively simple process. Typically, a list broker allows you to purchase a small list based on matching data in a larger list to your specifications. Hopefully, the list broker also excludes phone numbers listed on do-not-call registries and physical addresses belonging to people who opted-out of receiving postal mail.

When you contact a reputable list broker to obtain e-mail addresses, the process is not as simple as selecting demographic information and paying to receive a data file because the e-mail addresses on a brokered list must, by law, be permission based.

The process of obtaining e-mail addresses from any list broker is full of potential pitfalls because consumers get annoyed by unsolicited mail. If the broker you choose doesn't understand or adhere to permission laws and trends in the consumer landscape, sending e-mail to the list you obtain can damage your image and your future ability to send e-mail.

Because the consumer ultimately decides what "unwanted" e-mail looks like, you can do everything right and end up with negative results. Furthermore, most ESPs discourage or disallow rented lists and almost never allow purchased lists.

As of this writing, I recommend that you obtain e-mail addresses by using the collect-where-you-connect methods that I discuss earlier in this chapter. If you still feel it's best to proceed with the services of a list broker, however, read on and proceed with caution.

Sticking to quality

Confirmed-permission lists are the only viable option for sending e-mails through list brokers. Confirmed-permission lists can be quite expensive because they are more difficult to obtain and because they contain e-mail addresses belonging to people who (at least for the moment) are interested in receiving specific types of information. You can expect to pay between 10 and 30 cents per e-mail address to send a single e-mail to a confirmed-permission list.

Confirmed-permission lists vary in quality, so remember to ask any broker some tough questions about the process used to obtain permission. The acid test of quality for a confirmed-permission list is whether the subscriber remembers opting in and also whether members of the list expect an e-mail from you as a result.

Make sure to clarify the following information and use the responses to judge the likelihood of a memorable experience for the list subscriber:

- ✔ **Where and how the e-mail addresses were obtained:** Make sure that any online forms used to obtain the e-mail addresses asked for explicit permission to share the e-mail address as opposed to stating usage in a separate permission policy. (You can read about explicit permission earlier in this chapter.) If permission was given by selecting a check box, make sure that the subscriber had to select the check box to subscribe as opposed to leaving a pre-checked box as-is.

- ✔ **When permission was confirmed:** List subscribers might not remember opting-in if permission was confirmed at the onset of the subscription and time has passed between the initial confirmation and the e-mail you intend to send. Ask the list broker to provide the opt-in date with any sample list or count.

- ✔ **How interests are selected:** Some list brokers make assumptions about their subscribers' interests based on where the information is collected as opposed to brokers who actually ask subscribers to select or state their interests. For example, someone who fills out a survey and indicates that they love live jazz music is a more valuable list subscriber than someone who purchases a jazz CD from a music Web site and fails to share whether the purchase is a gift or motivated by another interest. Make sure that interest information was supplied by the subscriber before paying an additional fee for an interest-based list.

Renting to own

Because quality confirmed-permission lists are so valuable, beware of supposed confirmed-permission lists for sale as a data file. Quality confirmed-permission lists are always rented out because the e-mail addresses are too valuable to sell.

As you might guess, list rental means that the list broker will never give you the e-mail addresses used to send your e-mail. Instead, you supply content to the list broker, and the list broker formats and sends your e-mail to the list.

Because list rental buys only one sending opportunity, I recommend that you include a sign-up link in your brokered e-mail. Simply asking the recipients to *Buy It Now* is asking for a small percentage of responses.

Including a sign-up link asking recipients to subscribe to your personal e-mail list can make it possible to own the information from people who are interested but who aren't ready to buy the moment they receive your brokered e-mail. If the list broker doesn't allow a subscription link in the e-mail, make sure that any links in your brokered e-mail lead to a *landing page* that includes your sign-up box, button, or link.

If you can capture sales and information by using a rented list, make sure that your e-mails continue to meet or exceed all possible professional standards to help keep subscribers interested and happy to be on the list after they have confirmed.

For more information about e-mail professionalism standards and best practices, visit the Email Sender and Provider Coalition Web site at www. espcoalition.org and click the Resources link.

Part III

Constructing an Effective Marketing E-Mail

The 5th Wave   By Rich Tennant

"Sales are up since we introduced e-mail marketing. Still, I think I'm going to miss our old sales incentive methods."

In this part. . . .

When you build a marketing e-mail, you're putting a face on your objectives, strategy, and business. Your success depends heavily on the strength of your e-mail content and how well you use design elements to give your content a professional look and a readable layout.

Chapter 6 tells you how to design your e-mails to look professional and match your content. Here are also tips for making your e-mails easy to scan and for branding your e-mails to give your business a desirable identity.

Chapter 7 helps you come up with From lines that your subscribers can recognize and Subject lines that will make subscribers want to open your e-mails right away. Chapter 8 shows you the different types of text content you can include in your e-mails as well as tips for creating the content and placing it into your e-mail designs. Sometimes, a picture conveys exactly what you want to say, so Chapter 9 helps you insert images into your e-mails. Chapter 10 explains how to make your e-mail content valuable and how to get your audience to take action when receiving your e-mails.

Chapter 6

Designing Your E-Mails

*D*eciding how to design and layout your e-mail content is possibly the most important step in executing your e-mail marketing strategy. Designing your e-mail content entails choosing a format, such as a newsletter or event invitation, that matches your message and placing your content in visually appealing arrangements.

E-mail design is important because consumers tend to scan e-mails instead of reading them in their entirety. If your e-mails aren't easy to scan, no one will pay attention long enough to grasp your message or take action.

In addition to making your e-mails easy to scan, good e-mail designs enhance your business image by giving your e-mails a consistent and professional brand identity. Brand identity makes your e-mails more inviting and recognizable to your audience and tells your audience that your e-mail comes from a trust worthy and familiar source.

In this chapter, I show you how to organize and design your e-mail content so that your audience can easily scan and understand your message. I also cover branding your e-mails to enhance your business image and identity.

Designing your e-mails to maximize scanability and identity requires HTML. If you aren't an HTML programmer, check out any e-mail templates that your E-Mail Service Provider (ESP) provides. E-mail templates allow you to start with a familiar e-mail format, such as a newsletter or promotion, and then customize the format with your own layout and design elements before inserting your content.

Determining the Proper Format for Your E-Mail Campaigns

Consumers expect the format of your e-mail campaign to deliver certain types of information, so matching your e-mail content to the proper format helps to build your audience's trust in the content of your e-mails.

When I talk about *format,* I mean the *classification* (category or type) and *configuration* (layout or arrangement) of your e-mail.

Familiar formats include

✔ Newsletters with one, two, or three columns

✔ Promotions with one or more offers in one or more columns

✔ Event invitations and calendars in a variety of layouts

✔ Announcements and greetings in a single column

Choosing the proper format is also important because each format visually communicates the main idea of your e-mail content before your audience even begins to read it.

Deciding which format to use entails matching your e-mail content to the format that best suits your audience's expectations for the content. For example, most consumers expect e-mail newsletter formats to contain informative content, and consumers expect e-mail promotional formats to contain content asking them to consider a purchase decision or another type of commitment. (I cover e-mail content creation in Chapter 8.)

Because consumers tend to give e-mail messages only a few seconds to make a point, the e-mail format that you choose for your content should help convey your message's main intentions. Matching content to the proper format allows your audience to get the main idea of your message sooner and helps the reader decide how best to interact with the message. For example, someone who receives an e-mail message in a newsletter format might not be inclined to read the entire message immediately, but someone who receives an e-mail message formatted as an announcement might feel a sense of urgency to read the whole message right away.

An easy way to utilize various e-mail formats is to use an e-mail template for each format. An *e-mail template* is an HTML mock-up of an e-mail with design elements that you can customize and populate with your own text, images, and links. Unless you're a terrific HTML programmer, you need to have e-mail templates designed for you by an HTML designer or obtain them through a template-design service.

Most ESPs provide e-mail templates that you can customize for your purposes, and some ESPs provide various levels of customized template creation and content insertion services. Figure 6-1 shows templates that one ESP provides.

The next sections describe four basic e-mail formats that are familiar to consumers and useful for business communications. Each format is also common to many e-mail template designers and ESPs.

Figure 6-1: This ESP allows you to choose from a variety of customizable e-mail templates in all kinds of formats.

Courtesy of Constant Contact

Deciding on a newsletter format

Newsletters are e-mails containing information that interests a particular group such as the members of an organization or the customers of a certain store.

People don't read e-mail newsletters the same way they read paper newsletters, so don't be too quick to cut and paste your paper newsletter content into an e-mail newsletter template. Consumers are more likely to read newsletters when you summarize larger bodies of content and provide links to a Web site where additional content resides in HTML or in Portable Document Format (PDF).

E-mail newsletters are popular formats because they can deliver multiple messages and more creative types of content than other formats allow. Examples of e-mail newsletter content include

- ✔ Communications to members of an organization
- ✔ Advice and opinion columns
- ✔ Stories and musings
- ✔ Product support articles
- ✔ Event calendar highlights
- ✔ Excerpts and summaries of larger bodies of information

Figure 6-2 shows an e-mail newsletter template. Newsletters typically have multiple columns so you can organize different groups of content by priority. (You can read more about prioritizing your content with columns in the upcoming section, "Using columns to organize your content.")

Choose an e-mail newsletter format when your e-mail content meets the following situations:

- ✔ Contains multiple headlines and messages targeted to one or more audiences
- ✔ Contains multiple calls to action with multiple themes
- ✔ Requires a consistent look and feel to tie multiple messages
- ✔ Contains more informative content than promotional content
- ✔ Delivered on a regularly scheduled basis in order to keep your audience informed

Courtesy of Constant Contact

Figure 6-2:
Use an
e-mail
newsletter
template
when your
content is
mostly
informative
and needs
to be
organized
into
columns.

Choosing a promotional format

E-mail promotions ask your audience to take specific actions, usually in the form of a purchase decision or a personal commitment.

Promotional e-mail templates involve a wide variety of designs and layouts, so keep the images, text, headlines, and links focused on your main call to action. Be sure to keep the content related to the promotion.

Examples of e-mail promotional content include

✔ Sales and discounts that call for an immediate purchase or an immediate commitment to a decision

✔ Descriptions and images of products and services with links to more information

✔ Limited time offers requiring immediate action

✔ Step-by-step directions for taking action on the e-mail content

✔ Testimonials and facts to help readers justify a purchase decision

Figure 6-3 shows a promotional e-mail template for featuring multiple, related products. You should choose an e-mail promotional format when your content contains the following:

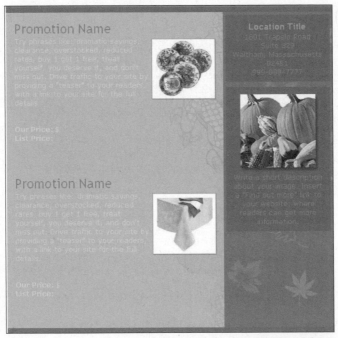

Figure 6-3:
Example of a promotional e-mail template.

Courtesy of Constant Contact

- ✔ A single main idea or message asking for a purchase decision or a personal commitment
- ✔ A single call or multiple calls to action tied by a similar theme
- ✔ Design elements that reinforce the items or actions that your message is promoting
- ✔ More promotional information than informative
- ✔ Delivery on a routine or event-driven basis in order to drive sales

Selecting an event invitation format

E-mail invitations focus on a single event or a group of related events and should contain a single call to action in the form of confirming or declining attendance.

E-mail is one of the best ways to deliver event invitations because people tend to respond to e-mail invitations more quickly than they respond to invitations delivered via postal mail.

Examples of e-mail invitation content include invitations to

- ✔ Attend customer appreciation events
- ✔ Attend seminars and workshops
- ✔ Public appearances
- ✔ Meetings and networking events

Figure 6-4 shows an e-mail event invitation template suitable for a customer appreciation event or a celebration. An e-mail invitation format is the way to go when your content includes

- ✔ A single invitation message or multiple, related invitation messages
- ✔ A single call to action focused on confirming attendance to an event
- ✔ Design elements to reinforce the event information
- ✔ One primary objective — to increase event attendance
- ✔ Delivery on an event-driven basis in order to motivate people to attend your events

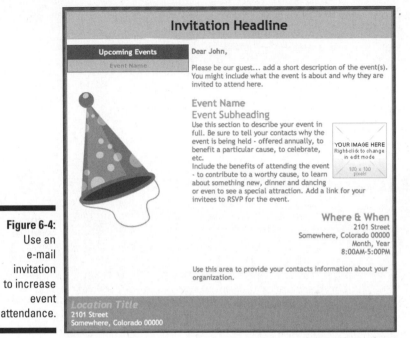

Figure 6-4:
Use an
e-mail
invitation
to increase
event
attendance.

Courtesy of Constant Contact

Going with an announcement format

E-mail announcement formats are useful when your e-mail message doesn't need to call for a specific type of action on the part of your audience. Some e-mail announcement formats make your e-mail seem urgent, like when you're sending a special bulletin. Other e-mail announcement formats can convey a message without any urgency, like when you're sending a Thank You card. Examples of e-mail announcement content include

- ✔ Press releases
- ✔ Holiday greetings and annual recognitions
- ✔ Official notices and statements
- ✔ News bulletins

Figure 6-5 shows an e-mail announcement template suitable for an official notice. Choose an e-mail announcement format when your content contains the following:

- ✔ A concise single message with little or no supporting information
- ✔ An absence of a specific call to action in the body of the e-mail, or the call to action simply asks the audience to read the message

✔ Design elements that enhance the main idea or headline in your message

✔ An entirely nonpromotional nature

✔ Delivery on a specific date or on an event-driven basis in order for your message to make sense

Figure 6-5:
Use an
e-mail
announce-
ment for
single
messages
with no
specific call
to action.

Courtesy of Constant Contact

The ABCs of E-Mail Layout

Consumers tend to focus their attention on your e-mail content by using the layout in the e-mail as a guide for their eyes. E-mail marketing experts often use e-mail heat maps to determine which areas of an e-mail are likely to draw the most attention. An e-mail *heat map* is an image generated by a special device that tracks eye movement when someone looks at an e-mail. You can see several examples of e-mail heat maps at `www.eyetools.com`.

Heat maps use different colors and shading to illustrate which parts of an e-mail draw the most attention. Data gathered by using heat maps and testing various e-mail designs helps to shed light on the e-mail designs and layouts that are most likely to get your content noticed.

The following sections show how to position your e-mail content to draw attention while keeping your audience focused on your main message.

Adding visual anchors

Visual anchors are design elements or text elements that draw attention to your content. Visual anchor designs are limited only by your creativity and the layout of your e-mail template. Figure 6-6 shows an e-mail with visual anchors throughout the body of the e-mail.

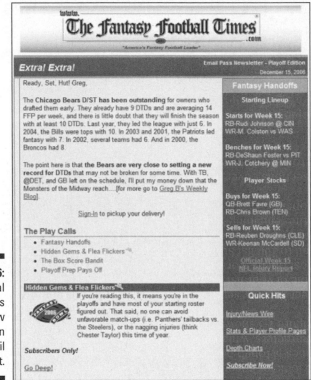

Figure 6-6:
Use visual
anchors
to draw
attention
to e-mail
content.

Courtesy of The Fantasy Football Times

Most ESPs allow you to create visual anchors from an e-mail template as a base.

Here are some visual anchors and how they draw attention to your content:

✔ **Headlines:** Headlines draw attention to themselves followed by the content immediately below the headline. Headlines attract the most attention when you differentiate your headlines from surrounding text using a different font, color, or style of text. Examples include

- *Block* (appear in front of a background color different from the main background color), as shown in Figure 6-7

- *Bold* (appear darker or heavier than the surrounding text)

- *Border* (appear inside a boxed outline)

- *Graphic* (images of text with special design elements)

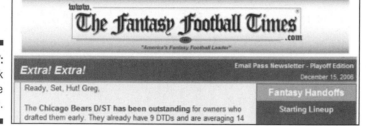

Figure 6-7:
A block
headline
graphic.

✔ **Images and graphics:** Images and graphics draw attention to themselves followed by adjacent text either to the left, right, or below the image. Image examples include

- *Portrait* (taller than wide)

- *Landscaped* (wider than tall), as shown on the right in Figure 6-8

- *Top-bar* (appear at the top of an e-mail and span the entire width of the page)

- *Background* (appear behind text)

- *Bordered,* as shown on the left in Figure 6-8

Figure 6-8:
A border
graphic.

✔ **Text links:** Embedded in a larger body of text, links draw attention to themselves followed by surrounding text. Stand-alone links draw attention only to themselves. Link examples include

- *Stand-alone* (apart from the text in a paragraph)

- *Content* (part of the text in a paragraph)

- *Grouped* (appear as lists), as shown in Figure 6-9

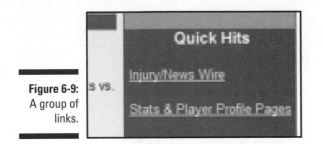

Figure 6-9:
A group of links.

✔ **Lines and borders:** Horizontal lines and borders draw attention to content above the line or border. Vertical lines and borders draw attention to content on the left or right depending on the strength of the visual anchors on either side of the line or border. Boxed borders draw attention to the content within the boxed border beginning with the upper left of the box. Line and border examples include

- *Horizontal* (divide content into top and bottom), as shown in Figure 6-10

- *Vertical* (divide content left and right)

- *Boxed* (divide the content contained in the box from surrounding content)

Figure 6-10:
A horizontal border.

Positioning your visual anchors and related content

A good way to visualize your content positioning is to mentally divide each of your e-mail templates into quadrants and then position your visual anchors and related content according to the order in which consumers tend to focus their attention on each quadrant.

Figure 6-11 shows how the majority of consumers scan e-mails. Most consumers begin reading in the upper left and then continue in one of two directions, depending on the strength of the visual anchors in the adjacent quadrants: across the page (the figure on the left) or down the page (the figure on the right).

Figure 6-11:
Most consumers focus on the upper left and then scan across the page (left) or down the page (right).

Because the upper left tends to get the most attention from consumers, position your most important visual anchors and related content there in your e-mail template.

And although you don't have to use an e-mail template to divide your content into quadrants visually, you should use a template to emphasize important content in the upper left. Here are some examples of positioning e-mail content in the upper-left quadrant:

✔ **Display your brand.**

Your audience is more likely to read your e-mail when they recognize the source of the e-mail. Make sure that your business name, logo, and other brand-identifying design elements appear somewhere in the upper left.

✔ **Begin your e-mail message with a main headline.**

A main headline doesn't have to reside completely within the upper left, but main headlines get more attention if they begin there.

✔ **Include your e-mail's main call to action.**

If your e-mail contains valuable offers, make sure your main offer is contained — or at least referenced — in the upper left. If your e-mail's main intent is to get your audience to read a specific section of your e-mail that contains your main call to action along with supporting information, make sure you use the upper left to prompt your audience where to look.

✔ **Place the strongest visual anchors.**

Visual anchors — such as icons, bullets, and graphics — can reinforce your audience's perception of your most important content. Strong visual anchors used in the upper left help minimize how long your audience spends trying to figure out what content is important enough to read. Figure 6-12 shows how an arrow, as a visual anchor, reinforces information. (Read more about visual anchors earlier in this chapter.)

✔ **Limit the size of images.**

Images draw attention, but if you include an image in your e-mail that takes up most of the upper-left quadrant, your audience might miss the text associated with that image. If you decide to use an image in the upper left, use one small enough to allow the inclusion of the first few words of a text headline. You can read more details about images in Chapter 9.

✔ **Show your audience where to look next.**

If your e-mail includes important content in different quadrants, use navigation links and directions in the upper left to help your audience navigate the e-mail. For example, the e-mail's upper-left quadrant might contain a table of contents with navigation links. (I cover navigation ideas in more detail later in this chapter.)

Figure 6-12:
Use an arrow as a visual anchor to emphasize content.

Courtesy of Constant Contact

Using columns to organize your content

Positioning visual anchors in quadrants is a fine way to attract attention to multiple groups of content, but unless you organize your visual anchors and related content into patterns, your audience won't be able to effectively prioritize the additional content that your visual anchors are trying to emphasize.

Using columns to organize your visual anchors and related content allows your audience to locate different groups of content as they scan through your e-mail. Choosing a column-based layout depends on two factors:

✔ **How many groupings of related content your e-mail contains:**
Grouping your e-mail content into categories before you choose a column-based layout is a good way to determine how many columns you're likely to need as well as where to place your visual anchors in relation to your content. For example, if your e-mail contains but one

type of article or offer, you probably need only one column to organize the related headlines, images, text, and links. Comparatively, if your e-mail contains multiple types of articles, offers, and calls to action (the case with most e-mail newsletter formats), you probably need two or more columns to help visually organize groups of related content. Content groupings include

- Articles of similar size with similar layouts
- Multiple events and other lists
- Promotions and offers with similar layouts
- Groups of closely related links, such as a group of Web site links
- Groups of similar announcements, such as recent news headlines
- Testimonials and quotes relating to the same offer
- Advertisements and graphics that stand alone

✔ **Which content grouping is most important for your audience to see:** After you mentally group your related content, you can choose a column-based layout that emphasizes your most important groupings while de-emphasizing less important groupings. You don't need a separate column for each content grouping, but I recommend keeping your most important content grouped in a single column. For example, if your e-mail has three product promotions and lots of other related content, you might place the product promotions in one main column and the rest of your related content in a smaller side column with one headline for each content grouping.

Most ESPs provide e-mail templates with lots of column-based layouts, and HTML designers and some ESPs can assist you in creating more customized column-based layouts.

Single column

Single column layouts are the best choice when your e-mail only has one grouping of content. For example, if you're sending an e-mail with several closely related offers or articles, you can arrange the offers or articles to appear in order of priority in one column. Single column layouts are a good choice for

✔ Single promotions

✔ Business letters

✔ Single event invitations

✔ Press releases

✔ Cards and announcements

Here are some tips for using a single column layout:

- **Begin your main headline in the upper-left quadrant.**

  Beginning a headline in the upper-left quadrant of a single column layout draws attention to the headline before the content in the body of the e-mail. See Figure 6-13.

- **Include your main call to action in the main headline or in a sub-heading that begins in the upper-left quadrant.**

  You can still repeat your call to action later in the column.

- **Use white space, borders, and images.**

  They keep your text content from bunching together.

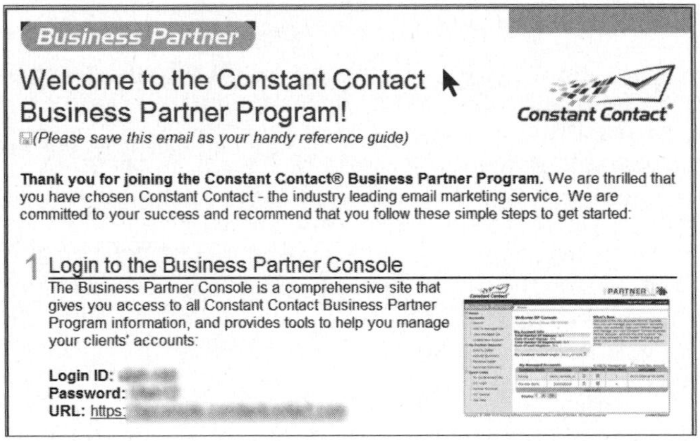

Figure 6-13: Draw attention to the headline before the content in the body of the e-mail.

Courtesy of Constant Contact

Two columns, equal width

Using two same-width columns is appropriate when you have two groupings of content that are equally important or when you have one grouping of content with two variations. For example, if you send an e-mail event invitation describing two events, using two same-width columns can help emphasize both events while giving only slight priority to the event in the left column. (Remember that people tend to first start reading from the left.)

Equal two-column layouts are a good choice for

- Double promotions
- Double event invitations
- A pair of announcements
- Two articles of equal importance
- Similar information intended for two audiences

TECHNICAL STUFF

Creating columns in HTML

Columns are actually HTML tables containing rows with two or more cells side by side. An HTML table starts with the use of a beginning table tag `<TABLE>`. Each column in the table is created by using a beginning row tag `<TR>` and then adding your content between beginning and ending cell tags `<TD>` and `</TD>`. After you add all the content for each cell or column, the row is closed using a closing row tag `</TR>` and the table is closed using a closing table tag `</TABLE>`.

Here's an example of a simple HTML structure that creates two columns of equal width:

```
<TABLE>
    <TR>
        <TD>content in column one</TD>
        <TD>content in column two</TD>
    </TR>
</TABLE>
```

Adding additional HTML to this basic structure allows you to define column widths, borders, background colors, and margins for each column. Using en e-mail template eliminates the need for learning how to build the HTML behind the template from scratch, but it's a good idea to be able to recognize basic HTML elements in case you need to make small adjustments. You can find a listing of basic HTML tags and sample documents at `www.w3schools.com`.

Here are some tips for using an equal, two-column layout:

✔ **Use the same layout for both.**

For example, if the left column starts with a headline and has an image on the right side of the column, make sure the right column starts with a headline and has an image on the right side of the column. Figure 6-14 shows two columns that both have an image at the top and the text below.

✔ **Use borders and white space to separate each column.**

You don't want your content to appear to run together in any way. Figure 6-14 shows how each column is delineated by a border and white space.

✔ **Place a single row that spans the entire width of both columns above your two equal columns.**

You can include your branding and a main headline to help tie both columns together under one main theme or you can include text to summarize your columns. Figure 6-14 shows how to tie together your columns with a row across the top.

White space separates
the two columns.

Both columns use the same layout.

Top row ties the columns together.

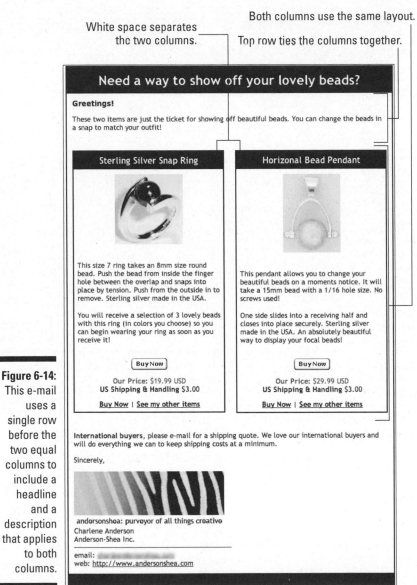

Figure 6-14:
This e-mail
uses a
single row
before the
two equal
columns to
include a
headline
and a
description
that applies
to both
columns.

Courtesy of Anderson-Shea, Inc.

Two columns of unequal width

Using two columns of unequal width is appropriate when you have content with varying degrees of importance. For example, using two columns of unequal widths are a good choice for

✔ Newsletters

✔ Promotions with lots of supporting content

✔ Event invitations with lots of related details

✔ Procedural e-mails with lists of related links

Here are some tips for using a layout of two columns of unequal width:

✔ **Summarize larger bodies of information into lists in your narrow column.**

For example, if the more-narrow column includes a list of upcoming events related to the offer in your main column, use an event title and a date as a link to more information instead of describing each event in detail. Narrow columns are perfect for lists of

- Links
- Archived articles
- Upcoming products
- Sponsors
- Step-by-step instructions
- Your contact information

✔ **Identify groups of related content with short headlines in the narrow column, as shown in Figure 6-15.**

For example, if the narrow column contains a list of navigation links as a table of contents, include a headline reading something like Quick Links or Find It Fast. Other short headline groupings could include

- Web Links
- Next Events
- Our Sponsors
- Contact Us
- Coming Soon
- Testimonials

Courtesy of Yang's Fitness Center & Martial Arts

Figure 6-15: This e-mail places related content under headings in the right column.

✔ **Place your most important content in the left column.**

> When you want to emphasize the content in the narrow column, place it on the left because a narrow column beginning in the upper left and continuing down the page is likely to draw your audience down the page as well. When you want to emphasize the content in the wider column, place it on the left. Your audience is more likely to scan all the way across a wider column when it begins in the upper left.

Rows of multiple columns

Using three or more columns in a row to follow a single column is a good way to emphasize related content equally. Rows of multiple columns are a good choice for

✔ Promotions with three or more images

✔ Event invitations with three or more locations

✔ Offers with three or more calls to action

Three or more columns running the entire length of an e-mail make an e-mail more difficult to scan.

Here's how you can use rows of multiple columns:

✔ **Repeat a similar message with slight alterations.**

> For example, you might use three columns to highlight directions to three different store locations or to display three images of the same product with varying degrees of options.

✔ **Use the same design and layout.**

When you use a row of multiple columns, make sure that all columns line up visually. Make each column equal length and width, and have all images and text line up like a grid, as shown in Figure 6-16.

✔ **Include a link.**

Because multiple columns aren't likely wide enough to contain all your information, include links to more information in each column. For example, if your columns contain an image of a product, link your image to more information about that product or include a text link that reads

```
View more details
```

and

```
Add to cart
```

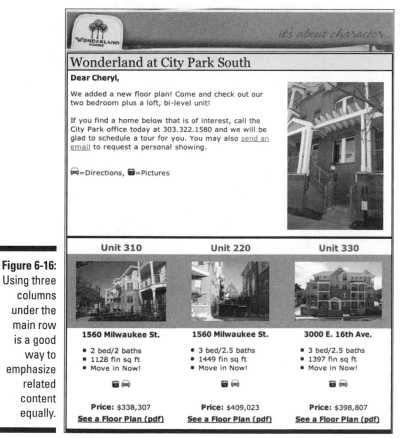

Figure 6-16: Using three columns under the main row is a good way to emphasize related content equally.

Courtesy of Wonderland Homes

A combination of column layouts

Figure 6-17 shows an example of an e-mail with a combination of column layouts. Multiple columns are effective when you need to include groups of related content with varying levels of importance. For example, to emphasize summarized information in the upper left of your e-mail and then emphasize several groups of longer content in a single column, use two columns in the top two quadrants of your e-mail followed by a single main column in the bottom two. Multiple column combinations are a good choice for

✔ Newsletters with one main article as well as less-important articles

✔ Promotions with related details of varying lengths

✔ Newsletters and promotions with multiple types of summarized information

Figure 6-17: Use different column layouts to accommodate multiple groups of content with varying lengths.

Courtesy of Constant Contact

Here are some tips for using a combination of column layouts:

✔ **Use a main headline for each column.**

For example, one column headline might read This Week's Headlines and another column might read Recent Headlines.

✔ **Coordinate your column background colors.**

When you have more than two columns, minimize the number of colors you use to differentiate your columns to prevent audience distraction. Using the same color for each column makes your content seem equally important, whereas changing the color for one or more columns might cause one column's content to stand out more or less.

✔ **Ask your audience to save your e-mail.**

Most people won't read an e-mail with multiple columns and lots of content. Use a main call to action to ask your audience to save your e-mail so they can refer back to it as they have time to read it.

A single e-mail should include only content that is closely related. If your content groupings can't be tied under one main theme, divide your content into separate e-mails instead of separate columns.

Making the Most of the Preview Pane

A *preview pane* is a window in an e-mail program that allows the user to see a small section of the e-mail without opening the entire e-mail. An increasing number of e-mail programs allow users to use a preview pane so that they can view portions of an e-mail before opening it or without opening the e-mail at all. Figure 6-18 shows a typical preview pane.

The preview pane area is some of the most valuable real estate in e-mail marketing because users can see some of your e-mail content in the preview pane before they decide to open your e-mail. Too, the preview pane can display much more information than your e-mail's header can.

Designing your e-mail content to maximize the preview pane will increase your open rate and prompt your users to read portions of your e-mails in more detail before deciding to read more or take immediate action on the calls to action within your e-mails.

Working around image blocking

Even though preview panes are useful to e-mail users, they also present challenges to e-mail senders. One of those challenges is that most e-mail programs automatically block images in the preview pane protect their users from viewing unwanted images. Figure 6-19 shows an e-mail in the preview pane with images blocked.

Figure 6-18:
This average-sized preview pane shows the top portion of an e-mail.

Preview pane

The blocked images in a preview pane display only when the user chooses to display the images in the e-mail. When images are blocked, most consumers rely on From lines and Subject lines to decide whether to download the images, which still makes the header information in your e-mail vitally important.

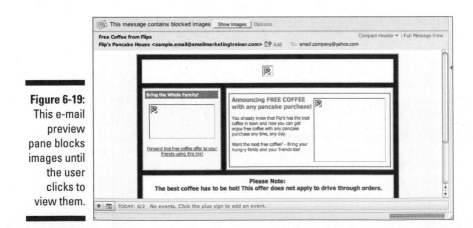

Figure 6-19:
This e-mail preview pane blocks images until the user clicks to view them.

You can, however, effectively lay out the content displayed in a typical preview pane to make sure your audience recognizes you and your business. Here are some tips for getting the most from a preview pane:

✔ **Avoid placing large images at the top of your e-mails.**

Your audience's preview pane may appear blank if an image at the top of your e-mail is as large as the average preview pane. Instead of using large images across the top of your e-mail, use a smaller image and include text above, below, or to one side of the image.

✔ **Include titles and captions with images.**

Using text above and below your images helps your audience to determine whether to view the images.

✔ **Use image descriptions in your HTML image references.**

An image description — also known as *alt text* — is a line of HTML code that tells an HTML reader to display text when images aren't displayed, as shown in Figure 6-20. Alt text also displays in some e-mail browsers when a user places a mouse over an image without clicking. Alt text appears in HTML within an image tag in quotes after `alt=` as follows:

```
<img src="http://www.emailtrainer.com/samplefolder/imagename.gif
          width="100" height="87" border="0" alt="Image Description"
          align="right">
```

Most ESPs allow you to insert an image description when you upload an image without requiring you to know any HTML code.

✔ **Add text at the top of your e-mail to ask your audience to add your From address to their address book.**

Most e-mail applications automatically show images when the sender's e-mail address is in the recipient's address book or contacts list. For example, the top of your e-mail could read

To ensure that images display properly in this e-mail, add newsletter@sunset-travel-news.com to your address book today.

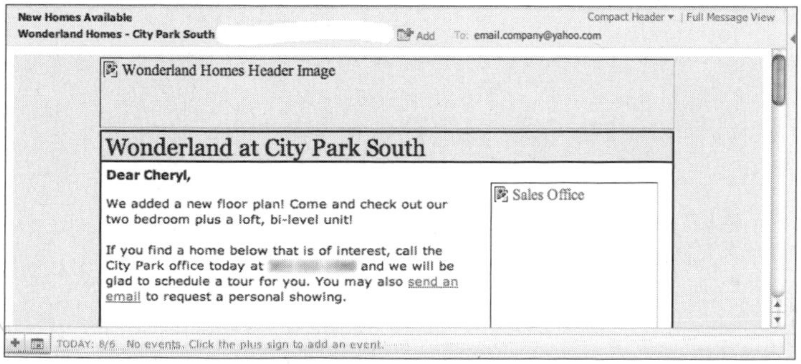

Figure 6-20:
Alt text displays in some e-mail applications in place of blocked images.

Courtesy of Wonderland Homes

Arranging content to appear in the preview pane

Designing your e-mails to maximize the content in the preview pane involves placing text and design elements at the top of your e-mails in strategic configurations. The most effective preview pane e-mails are those that fit entirely in the preview pane, but when your e-mails have to deliver more than an extremely minimal amount of content, the following tips can help your audience to internalize the content in the preview pane and scroll beyond.

- ✓ **Insert a short sentence of plain text at the top of your e-mails that tells your audience who you are and what your e-mail contains.**

  If you use a permission reminder at the top of your e-mails, briefly highlight the contents of your e-mail in the permission text.

- ✓ **Make sure your e-mail is no wider than 600 pixels.**

  Most e-mail programs match the screen resolution of the user's computer, and e-mails wider than 600 pixels might exclude some of your content.

  If you are using an e-mail template, it's probably already 600 pixels by design, but you can check your e-mail template's style sheet or table width tag if you're unsure about the overall width of your e-mail.

- ✓ **Place a headline directly under an image that spans the width of the e-mail.**

  It highlights the content in your e-mail that appears below the preview pane.

- ✓ **Include a table of contents (TOC) in your e-mail.**

  Add your TOC in a row near the top of your e-mail or in a side column in the e-mail. If you use a TOC in a column, make sure it appears at the top of your e-mail.

- ✓ **Use the same colors for borders, backgrounds, and other non-image design elements.**

  You can reinforce your brand consistently when you send e-mails with various formats.

- ✓ **Avoid using text at the top of your e-mails that fails to hint at the details that appear below the preview pane.**

  For example, an e-mail newsletter that has the date, issue number, and month at the top of the e-mail fails to describe the content of the e-mail newsletter in detail.

Branding Your E-Mails to Enhance Your Image

Branding is the use of graphic design elements to give your business a consistent and unique identity while forming a mental image of your business' personality. Examples include

- ✔ Graphics and logos unique to your business
- ✔ Text and fonts that differentiate your business
- ✔ Colors used consistently to give your business an identity

Branding your e-mails helps your audience to immediately recognize and differentiate your e-mails from the unfamiliar e-mails they receive. Keeping your e-mail branding consistent over time allows your audience to become familiar with you and your e-mails as they receive multiple e-mails from you.

The following sections show how you can brand your e-mails to match your identity and the expectations of your audience.

Branding your e-mails with colors and design elements requires using HTML. If you don't know HTML, look to your ESP. Most ESPs allow you to customize your e-mail templates with your branding elements. If you aren't using an ESP to send your e-mails, an HTML designer can help you create a custom look and feel for your e-mail templates.

Matching your e-mails to your brand

All your business communications should contain consistent branding elements, and your e-mails are no exception. Matching every e-mail to your brand gives your audience confidence and makes your business more memorable every time your audience clicks to access your Web site or walks into your store and sees the same branding elements.

You can design your e-mails to match your brand in the following ways:

- ✔ **Include your logo in your e-mails, as shown in Figure 6-21.**

   Position your logo in the upper left or top center of your e-mail where readers are most likely to see it.

   Using a company logo along with identifiable design elements brands your e-mail and reinforces your company's image.

Figure 6-21:
Use a
company
logo.

Courtesy of Avalon Photography

✔ **Use the colors from your logo in your e-mails.**

If your logo has multiple colors, pull the colors from your logo and use them for the borders, backgrounds, and fonts in your e-mails. If your logo use only one color, you can use a graphic design program to create a palate of colors that work well with the color in your logo. You can find a list of helpful color-matching tools at www.emailtrainer.com

✔ **Use the colors from your Web site in your e-mails.**

When readers click from your e-mail to your Web site, they might hesitate if your Web site looks different from your e-mail. When you design your e-mails, use the colors in your Web site in a similar fashion. For example, if your Web site uses a gray background with black text, use the same colors for those elements in your e-mails.

✔ **Match your Web site offers with your e-mail offers.**

If your e-mail includes an offer with a specific design, make sure that your Web site uses the same design elements in the offer if you're directing people to your Web site to complete a purchase or to read more information about the offer in your e-mail.

✔ **Match your print communications to your e-mails.**

If you're sending direct mail or printing ads to follow up or reinforce your e-mail messages, make sure that your print communications match your e-mails as well as the rest of your communications.

✔ **Use fonts that match your brand in your e-mails.**

Consistent fonts add to the overall look and feel of your e-mails as well as adding emotion behind the text. Keep your fonts consistent in all your communications and use the same fonts for similar visual anchors. For example, if your e-mail contains three articles with three headlines in one column, use the same font for each headline in the column.

The benefits of font consistency are negated if you use too many differ-ent kinds of fonts in one e-mail. Stick with two or three different fonts in each e-mail to avoid heaping visual distractions on your audience.

✔ **Make sure your e-mails reflect your business' personality.**

Design elements that match your brand can still spell a mismatch with your brand if your e-mails aren't written with your business' personality in mind. Show your e-mails to a few trustworthy friends or advisors and ask them to tell you whether your writing style is a good match for your image. If you aren't a good writer, consider using a copywriter to help you maintain your image using the text of your articles and offers. Tell your copywriter whether you want the text in your e-mail to make your business seem

- Serious or humorous

- Professional or casual

- Formal or friendly

- Exclusive or universal

- Urgent or customary

- Insistent or politely persuasive

Maintaining brand consistency with multiple e-mail formats

If you use multiple formats and each format doesn't match your brand with enough consistency, your audience might not recognize every e-mail you send. At the same time, if your audience can't tell the difference between your formats, you lose your ability to effectively communicate the appropri-ate amount of urgency in each of your e-mail formats. For example, if your readers recognize your e-mail as a lengthy newsletter format, they might be inclined to read it later. If your audience recognizes your e-mail as an event invitation, they might be inclined to take immediate action by responding with a reservation.

The best way to brand multiple e-mail formats is to match your brand iden-tity in each format while keeping your e-mails just different enough for people to know that each e-mail is unique. Figures 6-22 and 6-23 show two distinct e-mail formats with similar brand identity.

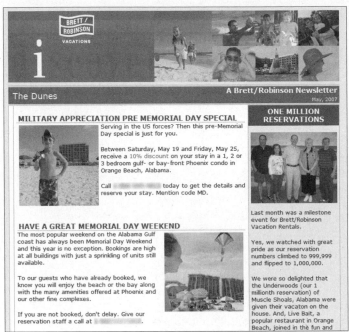

Figure 6-22:
This e-mail is branded to identify the business and reinforce its newsletter content.

Courtesy of Brett/Robinson Vacations

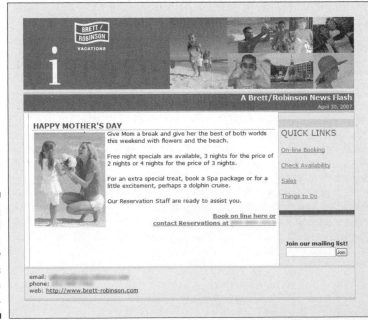

Figure 6-23:
This e-mail is branded to identify the business and offer a news flash.

Courtesy of Brett/Robinson Vacations

Making the difference just noticeable

If you look at a 1950s Coca-Cola bottle and a Coca-Cola bottle today, you'll notice a significant difference. Big companies like Coca-Cola continuously research their branding elements keep them up to date with consumer preferences. Still, Coca-Cola wouldn't dare to change the branding on its cans and bottles too rapidly, or consumers might have a hard time identifying them on the store shelves. Marketing experts use a concept known as *the just-* *noticeable difference* to change brand identities over time: that is, you change the brand just enough to be noticeable but not enough to be unrecognizable. If you need to change your e-mail branding elements, such as when your Web site gets a new face lift, make sure you change your branding elements slowly over time so your audience still recognizes your e-mails while the changes are taking place.

Here are some ways you can brand multiple e-mail formats with consistency while giving each format a unique identity:

- ✔ Use the same top-bar image with slightly different colors for each format.
- ✔ Change the colors in your logo slightly for each format.
- ✔ Use slightly different colors for backgrounds and borders in each format.
- ✔ Use graphical text to create a unique title for the top of each format.

Chapter 7

Creating From and Subject Lines That Get Noticed

*O*ne of the best ways to maximize the response to your e-mails over time is to place familiar and motivating information into every e-mail header. The *header* is the portion of your e-mail that contains the following:

✔ A From line

✔ A From address

✔ A Subject line

✔ Messages and code inserted by e-mail programs

In this chapter, I show you how to create an e-mail header that makes your e-mails more familiar to your audience and prompts your audience to open your e-mails.

Getting Acquainted with E-Mail Headers

Individual e-mail programs display portions of your e-mail's header information so users can sort and prioritize their e-mails and decide whether to view and open each e-mail. Figure 7-1 shows how Yahoo! Mail displays headers. When used appropriately, your header information helps your audience to identify you as a trustworthy sender and also helps to determine whether your e-mails are worthy of immediate attention.

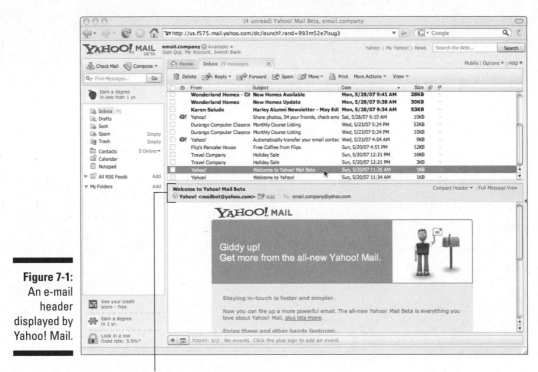

E-mail header

Although you can't control all the information in your e-mail headers, you can control three important pieces of information that are most useful to your audience and to the deliverability of your e-mails:

- **From line:** Your *From line* is a line of text that tells the recipient of your e-mail whom the e-mail is from. Most e-mail applications and E-Mail Service Providers allow you to add a line of text to the header of your e-mail to identify yourself.

- **From address:** Your *From address* is the e-mail address that is associated with you as the sender of the e-mail. Some e-mail programs display your From e-mail address along with your From line, but others display one or the other.

- **Your e-mail server's From address:** A *server address*, also known as an *Internet Protocol (IP) address,* is a unique number that identifies the server you use to send your e-mail. Most Internet service providers (ISPs) look at your e-mail server address in your header to see whether your server is recognized as a sender of legitimate commercial e-mail or whether your server has been reported as sending unsolicited e-mails. If you send e-mail from your own e-mail server or if your e-mail hosting company sends your e-mails from a server that is unfamiliar to the major ISPs, you can change the servers you send your e-mails from by switching to an ESP. You can read more about sender reputation in Chapter 12.

Filling Out the From Line

According to a 2006 consumer study by Epsilon Interactive (`www.epsilon.com`), approximately 65 percent of consumers use the From line in your header to determine whether to open your e-mail.

Altering your From line helps to ensure that most e-mail programs display enough information for your audience to identify and trust you as the source of your e-mails. Changing your From line is usually a matter of typing sender information in your e-mail application's account options, as shown in Figure 7-2.

ESPs allow you to create unique header information for each specific e-mail campaign during the campaign creation process.

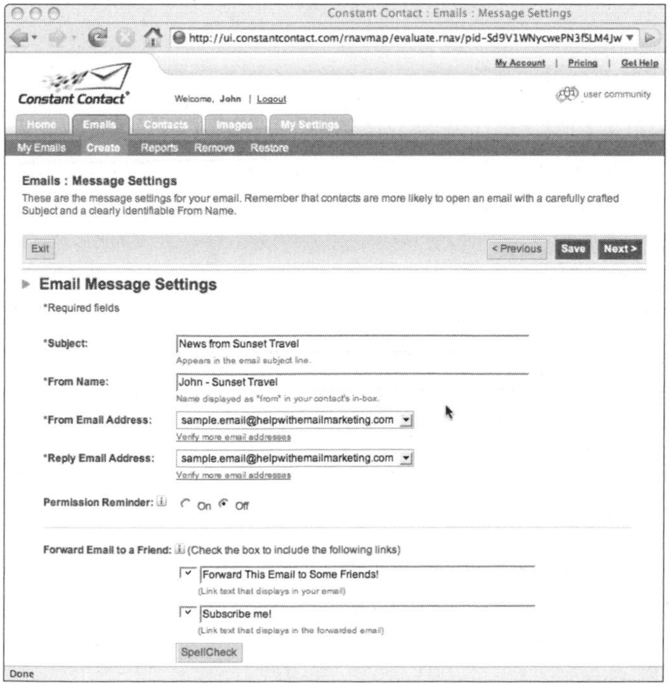

Figure 7-2:
This ESP interface allows you to create header information.

Courtesy of Constant Contact

Does this header look familiar?

E-mail applications usually display only the portions the e-mail header that are useful to their users. An entire e-mail header actually contains code and data that help e-mail applications to identify, sort, and deliver e-mails. E-mail programs also use the entire header to filter and block certain senders, so using an ESP with a good reputation and close relationships with ISPs and e-mail programs ensures that your e-mail header is familiar and identified as friendly to the programs that consumers use to read their e-mail.

Here's an example of an entire e-mail header. The portions that most e-mail applications display to their users by default are in bold print:

```
Microsoft Mail Internet Headers Version 2.0
Received: from edgemail1.roving.com ([192.168.254.99]) by svrmail.roving.com with
          Microsoft SMTPSVC(6.0.3790.1830);
Thu, 24 May 2007 15:07:10 -0400
Received: from ccm06.constantcontact.com (ccm06.constantcontact.com [63.251.135.98])by
          edgemail1.roving.com (Postfix) with ESMTP id 968167C0001 for <test-
          email@constantcontact.com>; Thu, 24 May 2007 15:07:13 -0400 (EDT) Received:
          from ws019 (unknown [10.250.0.101]) by ccm06.constantcontact.com (Postfix)
          with ESMTP id 5FD3211AEC0 for <test-email@constantcontact.com>; Thu, 24 May
          2007 15:07:13 -0400 (EDT)
Message-ID: <2002007742.1180033638314.JavaMail.prodadmin@ws019>
Date: Thu, 24 May 2007 15:07:18 -0400 (EDT)
From: Zak <zb.baron@constantcontact.com>
Reply-To: zb.baron@constantcontact.com
To: test_email@constantcontact.com
Subject: FW: Volunteers Needed For Sat. June 2nd
Mime-Version: 1.0
Content-Type: multipart/alternative;boundary="
----
=_Part_381273_1572255422.1180033638314"
X-Mailer: Roving Constant Contact 0 (http://www.constantcontact.com)
X-Lumos-SenderID: 1101539495996
Return-Path: ccbounce+zbbaron=constantcontact.com@in.constantcontact.com
X-OriginalArrivalTime: 24 May 2007 19:07:10.0436 (UTC) FILETIME=[BAE54A40:01C79E36]
------
=_Part_381273_1572255422.1180033638314
Content-Type: text/plain; charset=iso-8859-1
Content-Transfer-Encoding: 7bit
------
=_Part_381273_1572255422.1180033638314
Content-Type: text/html; charset=iso-8859-1
Content-Transfer-Encoding: quoted-printable
------
=_Part_381273_1572255422.1180033638314--
```

Ask yourself how your audience is most likely to recognize you and then craft your From line to include that information.

Including the following information in your headers keeps your e-mails familiar to your audience:

- ✔ **Your name:** If you're the only employee for your business or if your audience is most likely to identify with you personally rather than your business name, use your name.

- ✔ **The name of your business:** If your audience is likely to recognize the name of your business but won't necessarily know you by name, use your business name. If your business commonly uses initials instead of spelling out the entire business name, make sure that your audience recognizes the abbreviation. For example, if your business is Acme Balloon Consultants, Inc., don't place ABCI in your From line unless you are sure your audience can identify you by your initials.

- ✔ **Your name and your business name:** If you're a personal representative of a larger, well-known business or franchise, use your name along with your business name. For example, you might use your first name followed by your business name, as in

  > Steve – Sunset Travel

- ✔ **Representative name:** If you have multiple representatives in your business whom your customers and prospects know by name, divide your e-mail addresses into separate lists by representative and use the most familiar representative's name for each e-mail list.

- ✔ **Your location:** If you're part of a large franchise or have multiple locations and your audience isn't likely to recognize the names of individuals within your organization, use geography. For example, you might use your business name followed by the city, as in

  > Sunset Travel, Denver

- ✔ **Your Web site domain:** If your audience is more likely to recognize your Web site domain name over your name or your business name, use your Web site domain name. If your domain uses an abbreviation, initials, or an alternate spelling of your entire business name, you might still want to use your business' full name in the From line for brand clarity.

Current CAN-SPAM laws prohibit you from misrepresenting your From line. Make sure the information in your From line honestly represents you and your business. For example, if you're a member of the local Chamber of Commerce, don't send the other Chamber members e-mail using the name of the Chamber in the From line. For more information about professional standards and the CAN-SPAM laws, see Chapter 3.

Using Your E-Mail Address for Identity

In addition to making sure your From line identifies you and your business, you can create an e-mail address that serves as your From address. Doing so ensures that

✔ All the From information displayed in your e-mail's header is familiar to your audience.

✔ Your header provides useful information for the portion of your audience who can view only your From address.

Because the e-mail address you send from isn't necessarily tied to the server address your e-mail is sent from, you can use almost any From address in combination with almost any server address. Your ESP does the work to match your chosen From address with a server address.

Don't send e-mail marketing messages with a personal e-mail address generated by an ISP (such as AOL, Yahoo!, Hotmail, and so on) because such e-mail addresses don't include enough information to identify you and your business as the sender.

I recommend creating an e-mail address that identifies who you are and what you're sending. Here are some examples:

✔ **If you're sending a newsletter and your audience recognizes your personal name:** Send your e-mail newsletter by using

    newsletter@yourname.com

✔ **If you're sending coupons and your audience recognizes your business name:** Send your e-mail coupons by using

    coupons@yourbusinessname.com

✔ **If you're sending an event invitation and your audience recognizes a personal representative as well as your business name:** Send your e-mail invitation by using

    event_invitation@repname.businessname.com

✔ **If you're sending an announcement and your audience recognizes your Web site's domain name:** Send your e-mail announcement by using

    announcement@yourdomain.com

Current CAN-SPAM laws prohibit you from misrepresenting your From address. Make sure you use a real, working e-mail address as your From address. Reputable ESPs require you to send e-mails from a verified e-mail address to ensure your e-mails are CAN-SPAM compliant.

Writing a Subject Line

Your e-mail *Subject line* is a line of text that gives your audience a hint at the content in your e-mail. According to a 2006 Epsilon Interactive study (www.epsilon.com), approximately 31 percent of consumers use the Subject line to determine whether to open your e-mail.

The most effective Subject lines are those that prompt your audience to open your e-mails to look for specific information. Consistently coming up with good Subject lines is tough because most e-mail programs display only the first 30 to 50 characters, which gives you a limited amount of text to get your point across. Figure 7-3 shows how Microsoft Outlook displays Subject lines.

Test your Subject lines by sending the same e-mail with different Subject lines to a small sample of your list to determine whether a Subject line is going to result in the most opens. For example, if you have a list of 1,000 subscribers, send your e-mail to 100 list subscribers with one Subject line and to a different 100 list subscribers with another Subject line. Wait a day or two and send your e-mail to the remaining 800 with the Subject line that received the highest number of opens.

The following sections cover how to create short Subject lines that prompt your audience to open your e-mails.

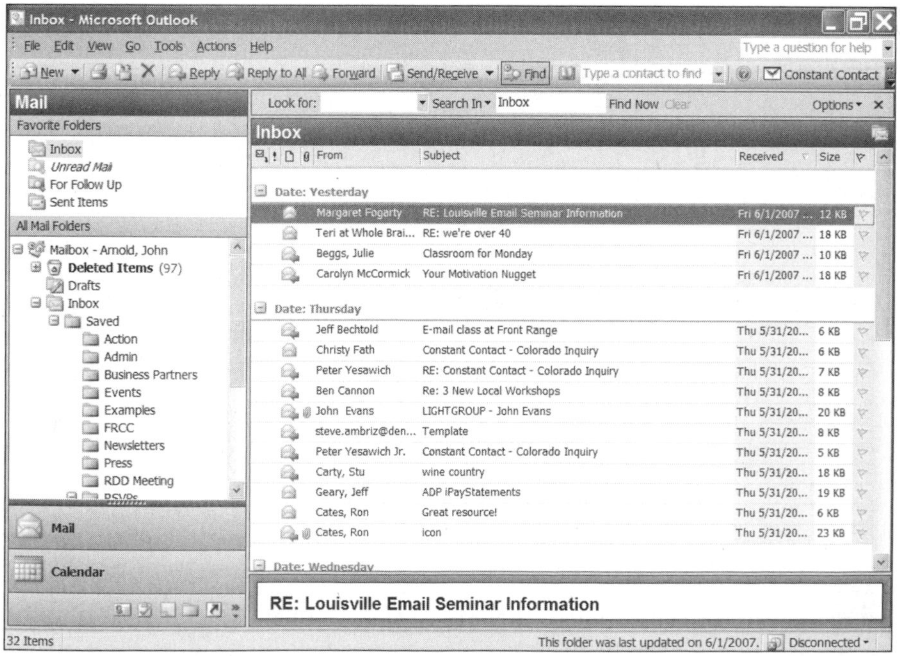

Figure 7-3:
E-mail
Subject
lines
displayed by
Microsoft
Outlook.

Highlighting the immediate benefit

Save the information highlighting the benefits of your products or services for the body of your e-mail and use the Subject line to tell your audience why to open your e-mail immediately. Stating the immediate benefit of opening the e-mail creates a sense of urgency and tells your audience that your e-mail is important.

Creating a sense of urgency with your text helps to increase viewer opens, but urgency can easily wear off if your Subject lines make urgent statements without hinting at the content in your e-mail. For example, Subject lines such as `Only 10 left` or `Sale ends soon` don't communicate the main subject of your e-mail — and are urgent only when they are used infrequently.

The following examples show how you can create urgency while still hinting at the main idea of the message. In each example pair, the first is a Subject line without urgency, and its mate is a revised Subject line with added urgency.

> **Not so good:** What you need to know about Denver real estate
>
> **Better:** What you need to know *now* about Denver real estate

> **Not so good:** Flower sale
>
> **Better:** Flower sale – early entry information

> **Not so good:** Seminar invitation
>
> **Better:** Last chance to register

> **Not so good:** Tips for remodeling your kitchen
>
> **Better:** Tomorrow's tips for remodeling your kitchen today

Including value words

Value words are words that your audience associates with information that is personally relevant to them. Value words tell your audience that your e-mail contains personalized information rather than general information. Here are some ideas for using value words in your Subject line:

✔ **Words that highlight a particular topic of interest in your e-mail:** For example, if your e-mail includes information about a new type of golf club, write a Subject line that includes the word *golf,* as in

```
Inside: new golf club info improves your game
   immediately
```

Baiting your audience with your Subject lines

I'm a lousy fisherman, but I like to go catch-and-release fishing now and then, so I decided to subscribe to a fishing tips e-mail newsletter written by the owner of a local fly fishing shop. One of the e-mail issues I received read, See huge trout caught in Colorado in the Subject line. I opened the e-mail. The picture of the trout was right at the top of the preview pane, but it was too small to see. The caption under the picture read, Click to see full picture, so I clicked and was immediately taken to the shop owner's fly fishing Web site where there was a larger picture of a father and his very happy son holding a huge trout. Right next to the picture was a picture of the fly that was used to catch the trout and the shop owner's offer to tie several of the flies and take eight lucky people on his next guided fishing trip to the exact same place where the father and son team had caught the huge fish. The main point of the shop owner's e-mail was communicated so well that by the time I called, the guided tour was already full. The rest of the e-mail newsletter contained the shop owner's valuable fishing tips and his guided trip schedule in order to deepen his relationship with anyone who wasn't ready or able to purchase a guided trip immediately.

✔ **Words that highlight the beliefs and attitudes of your audience:** For example, if you sell automobiles and your audience believes in driving fuel-efficient vehicles, you could write an e-mail newsletter with a Subject line that reads

```
3 ways to improve your fuel economy overnight
```

✔ **Words that motivate your audience:** For example, if your audience is motivated by saving money, include words that demonstrate the extent of the savings you're offering in your e-mail, as in

```
Over $50 in savings inside this e-mail
```

Working from a theme

Using a similar theme over the course of many e-mail campaigns can help you to come up with several good Subject lines in a row. For example, a printer might use *Colors that sell* as a theme and highlight a different color in every Subject line, as in

```
Why green increases your sales
```

or

```
Why blue puts your customers at ease
```

Avoiding Subject lines that look like spam

You might want to look at your junk folder occasionally to see what the spammers are up to so you don't inadvertently copy some of their Subject line techniques. Here are some Subject line mistakes to avoid:

- Excessive punctuation, such as lots of exclamation points or question marks

- Symbols, such as dollar signs and asterisks

- Words with all capital letters (usually perceived as yelling)

- Your recipient's first name in the Subject line

- Using RE: unless the e-mail is really a response to a previous e-mail Subject line

- A blank Subject line

- Vague Subject lines that attempt to trick the reader into opening your e-mail. For example

  - Hey you

  - Check this out

  - RE:

  - Personal information

  - Hi!

The current CAN-SPAM laws prohibit Subject lines that are "likely to mislead a recipient, acting reasonably under the circumstances, about a material fact regarding the contents or subject matter of the message," so make sure your Subject lines clearly and honestly represent the content in every e-mail. For more information about Subject line compliance, see Chapter 3.

Chapter 8

Including Text in Your E-Mails

*T*ext is mandatory in e-mail marketing messages. Plain, text-only e-mails significantly underperform compared with e-mails that include HTML design elements along with the text in the message, so applying design elements to your text is a balance. Too much plain text can make your e-mails appear unapproachable and difficult to read. Comparatively, too many design elements can cause distractions and make your messages more difficult to understand.

When used correctly, different fonts and text styles can create moods in your e-mails and change the tone of the words that you use:

- *Headlines* can help to entice your audience to read longer sections of text or take action on your e-mail content.

- *Paragraphs of text* can give your audience important information, help them form opinions, and give them compelling reasons to purchase your products or services.

- *Links* in your e-mails let your audience click keywords and phrases to take action on the content of your e-mails without having to use another medium.

In this chapter, I tell you how to choose fitting text elements for your e-mails to enrich your e-mail's meaning, and also how to use text to communicate the main idea of your e-mail quickly and effectively.

Choosing the Correct Font and Style

Fonts are graphical representations of letters in the alphabet. Fonts are useful for

- ✔ Making your words more legible
- ✔ Giving your words more emphasis
- ✔ Suggesting moods and emotions to reinforce your words
- ✔ Tying content to make your e-mails look more professional

In addition to applying different fonts to your text, you can also alter your fonts by applying different style elements to the font. This section includes tips for choosing fonts and applying stylistic changes to them so that the appearance of your text matches your e-mail's theme and message.

Picking a font

Because most e-mail programs use HTML to display e-mails to their users, you need to apply fonts and styles to your e-mail text by using the HTML code that tells the e-mail program which fonts and styles to apply when it displays your text to the user. Here's an example of a line of HTML code that defines various font elements for a headline:

```
<font color="#FFFFFF" face="Arial, Verdana, Helvetica,
        sans-serif" size="5" style="FONT-FAMILY: Arial,
        Verdana, Helvetica, sans-serif;FONT-SIZE:18pt;
        FONT-WEIGHT:bold; COLOR:#FFFFFF;">
        Headline Here</font>
```

To avoid the HTML hassle, most E-Mail Service Providers (ESPs) allow you to specify fonts and apply style elements to your fonts by using font tools in a special user interface. Figure 8-1 shows a font and style toolbar in an ESP interface.

Fonts specified in HTML tell the user's computer to display the applicable text, using the specified font. Any font specified in the HTML code has to be available on the user's computer to display properly.

Because most people don't go to the trouble of installing the latest fonts on their computers, formatting e-mail text by using fonts that are common to the majority of computers helps ensure that your text looks the same on your audience's computer as it does on yours. Figure 8-2 shows a list of fonts that are commonly available on default operating systems.

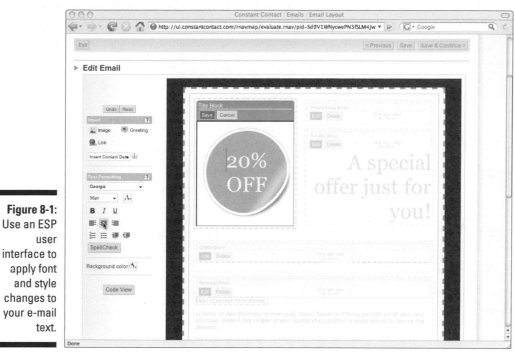

Figure 8-1: Use an ESP user interface to apply font and style changes to your e-mail text.

Courtesy of Constant Contact

Figure 8-2: Using commonly available fonts ensures that text displays properly on your audience's computer.

Arial	Lucida Console
Arial Narrow	System
Comic Sans MS	Tahoma
Courier New	Times New Roman
Garamond	Trebuchet MS
Georgia	Verdana
Impact	

If you want to use text in a font or style that's not commonly available or one that's not possible with HTML, you can use graphic design software to create an image of the text you want to use. Just remember that the text might not display if your recipient has image blocking enabled on his e-mail application or receives e-mail in a text-only format. See Chapter 9 for more information about inserting a stylized image in your e-mail.

Including too many different fonts in a single e-mail can make your text look disorderly and cluttered, so make sure you limit your e-mail's text to only two or three different fonts. Using one font for all headlines and another font for all body text is an acceptable standard.

Applying style elements

Style elements are alterations to the font that give emphasis to the text without changing the font. The following sections give you the most useful style elements and their most appropriate applications.

Bold

Bold text changes the weight of the text between the HTML tags <b> and </b> and creates a contrast that emphasizes or stresses certain words in bold. Most e-mail editors allow you to change text to bold without inserting the HTML tags. Reserve bold text for

- ✔ Headlines
- ✔ Short phrases (as shown in Figure 8-3)
- ✔ Entire sentences
- ✔ Captions
- ✔ Words or phrases that stand alone

Figure 8-3:
This e-mail bolds a portion of the text to emphasize the importance.

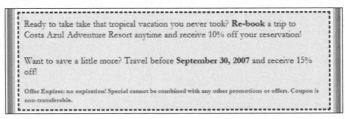

Ready to take take that tropical vacation you never took? **Re-book** a trip to Costa Azul Adventure Resort anytime and receive 10% off your reservation!

Want to save a little more? Travel before **September 30, 2007** and receive 15% off!

Offer Expires: no expiration! Special cannot be combined with any other promotions or offers. Coupon is non-transferable.

Courtesy of Costa Azul Adventure Resort. Photo by Preston Hall

Using bold text in the middle of a paragraph of text to give emphasis to single words usually takes too much attention away from the surrounding text, so avoid using bold text when you want to emphasize only one word in a paragraph.

Making your e-mails accessible

People with disabilities and physical challenges need to be able to read your e-mail content and respond accordingly. Some disabled and aging e-mail users are able to read and respond to your e-mails only if you design your e-mails with their challenges in mind, and some disabled people, such as those with visual impairments, have special tools that verbally read your e-mail or otherwise aid them in the comprehension of e-mail and other online content. Some e-mail designs make such tools cumbersome to use, so it's important to design your e-mails accordingly or provide two versions of your e-mail.

Visual impairments aren't the only disabilities that might make your e-mail difficult to understand. Here are some tips for making your e-mails accessible to many types of disabled and aging subscribers:

✔ Provide a link to a text-only version of your e-mail to allow text reading devices to easily read your content to people with visual impairments. Make sure your e-mail begins with the link and a summary of your e-mail content so visually impaired subscribers can tell whether your e-mail is worth listening to in its entirety. Also make sure your text version adequately describes any video, images, charts, and graphics in your e-mail.

✔ Use image descriptions (*alt text*) when including images in your e-mail. Reading devices read alt text so a visually impaired person knows what images are in the e-mail. This is especially important when you use images that contain text.

✔ Use fonts and point sizes that are easy to read so that people with low vision can interpret them. Make sure the text version of your e-mail avoids the use of absolute font sizes in your HTML so that your fonts can be enlarged.

✔ Use text and background colors with sufficient contrast so that words are easy to read.

✔ Provide a link to a text-only transcript of any audio used in your e-mail.

✔ Make sure any forms you ask your subscribers to fill in can be tabbed through in a logical order and design your forms to minimize the number of keystrokes necessary to complete the form.

✔ Keep your e-mail designs short, concise, and easy to scan. Avoid distracting design elements such as blinking text, flashing images, or audio and video streams that cannot be easily turned off.

If you use an E-Mail Service Provider to design your e-mails, ask about accessibility requirements. You can read more about making all your Internet marketing efforts accessible at `www.w3.org/WAI`.

Italic

Italic text is a slanted version of a font and provides subtle emphasis to your words. Italic text is a good choice for

✔ Emphasizing a single word or short phrase within a larger body of text

✔ Subheadings

  ✔ Calling attention to proper names

  ✔ Titles of books, movies, newspapers, and magazines

Italic text can be difficult to read on a computer screen, so limit the use of italics to single words and short phrases instead of using italics to emphasize large bodies of text. Figure 8-4 shows an e-mail with no italic (top figures) with the addition of italics to add emphasis (bottom figure).

Figure 8-4:
Italic text
gives subtle
emphasis to
words and
phrases.

Underline

<u>Underlined text</u> is another way to emphasize words and phrases. Underlined text is a best reserved for

  ✔ Text links

  ✔ Column headlines used to group bulleted lists

  ✔ Headlines, to visually divide the headline from the text appearing beneath the headline

Use underlining sparingly because people usually expect underlined text to represent a clickable link.

Point size

Changing text point size makes a font larger or smaller. If you decide to mix different point sizes, make sure that every type of textual content shares the same point size. For example, if you have multiple headlines in your e-mail, each type of headline should use the same point size (see Figure 8-5). Altering point size is useful for

- ✔ Making words easier to read on a computer screen
- ✔ Emphasizing headlines and links
- ✔ Deemphasizing large bodies of content
- ✔ Fitting text into a column or other confined space

Figure 8-5:
This e-mail uses consistent point sizes for main column headlines and side column headlines.

Courtesy of Yang's Fitness Center & Martial Arts

Font colors

Using different font colors can enhance the overall look and feel of your text and your entire e-mail. Using darker text and a lighter background usually produces more legible text onscreen. Altering text color is useful for

- ✔ Adding emphasis to headlines and subheadings
- ✔ Making links appear in a color that contrasts with other text

✔ Enhancing readability of words in front of various background colors

✔ Enhancing the overall look of your e-mails by matching text color to the colors used in the other design elements in your e-mail

Applying color to your text might make your words difficult to read. Make sure you have enough contrast between your font color and the background color of your text.

Including Headlines

Headlines are statements that summarize or announce larger bodies of text. Without a doubt, headlines are the most important text in your e-mails because headlines get noticed when your audience scans through your e-mail to determine whether your content is relevant and valuable enough to read.

Headlines are useful in many places within your e-mails. The following is a list of useful headlines and tips for including them in your e-mails:

✔ **Titles and main headlines:** *Titles* are headlines that summarize multiple groups of content with multiple themes. Titles should be used to describe the main idea of your entire e-mail and prompt your audience to read beyond your title. Whenever possible, use the text in titles and main headlines to communicate one or more of the following:

- The *immediate benefits* of reading your e-mail

- The *main reason* why you're sending the e-mail

- The *main action or response* you expect from your audience, even if that action is simply to read your e-mail

✔ **Paragraph headlines:** Because consumers tend to scan e-mail, looking for relevant content, paragraph headlines should summarize the text beneath your headlines in as much detail as possible (as shown in Figure 8-6). Paragraph headlines are easier for your audience to identify when you match each paragraph headline by using the same font and style.

Paragraph headlines should be short, but you should value clarity over length when you feel that you need a few extra words to make your point.

✔ **Paragraph subheadings:** *Subheadings* — lines of text that appear directly below headlines — are typically used to add important details to the main headline. The best way to use subheadings in your e-mails is to tell your audience which headlines are personally relevant. For example, a headline that reads `Local E-Mail Marketing Seminar` could be followed by a subheading that reads `Omni Hotel - June 22 at 7:00 p.m.` so that the additional article information can be easily skipped by people who aren't attending the seminar. Like all headlines, subheadings should match in font and style.

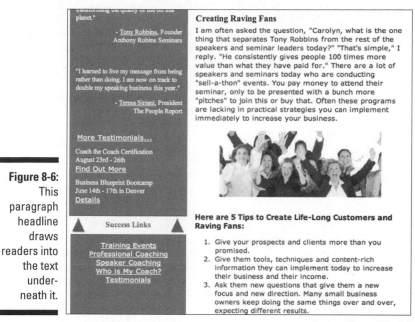

Courtesy of Personal Edge, Intl.

Figure 8-6: This paragraph headline draws readers into the text underneath it.

✔ **Captions:** Images sometimes need additional text — a *caption* — to reinforce the message related to the image or to describe the meaning of the image. Captions should almost always be placed under the image. Image captions can also be used as a link related to the image or to point out that the image itself is a link to additional information or more images. Image captions also help to identify images if they're blocked by e-mail programs. I cover image blocking in more detail in Chapter 6.

✔ **Navigation links:** Clicking a *navigation link* scrolls the user directly to a section of content within your e-mail. Navigation links can be used to help your audience skip over irrelevant content and find information quickly when the links are pointed directly to headlines and their related text. E-mail content links can be grouped as headlines in a table of contents (such as in Figure 8-7) or used as headlines at the conclusion of paragraphs to link interested readers to similar content. I show you how to make navigation links later in this chapter.

✔ **Calls to action:** Asking your audience to take action usually takes the form of a headline or a linked phrase. Headlines that call for action should stand alone, using fonts and styles that are different from the other headlines in your e-mail. Sometimes, using links that call for action within the body of a paragraph is appropriate. I cover calls to action in more detail in Chapter 10.

Figure 8-7:
Navigation
links help
readers
skip to the
sections
they want
to read.

Courtesy of Personal Edge, Intl.

Using Longer Sentences and Paragraphs

Communicating your entire message in the body of your e-mail can be tempting. If your message is concise and interesting to your readers, including your entire message in your e-mail might suit your objectives and your audience. E-mails are generally more effective, however, when sentences and paragraphs of text are used as summaries and teasers to entice readers to seek more information and take action outside the content of your e-mail.

If you have a lot of text to communicate or if you have several topics of unrelated content to deliver, I recommend that you post the bulk of your text content to your Web site and provide a link for interested readers to continue reading at the end of each summary.

The sentences and paragraphs in the body of your e-mail can include

- ✔ **Short articles and stories:** Stories and articles should generally be summarized and linked to the entire text on a Web site. Using an excerpt from a story or article is also an effective alternative to summaries when you want to highlight the main points of a story or article and generate interest in reading the entire body of text.

- ✔ **Salutations:** Greetings and closing bodies of text help personalize your e-mails and summarize the content for your audience. Greetings and closings paragraphs should be no more than two to three sentences.

  ESPs usually allow you to insert database fields so you can merge your audience's first name and other database information to personalize your salutations, as shown in Figure 8-8.

- ✔ **Product and service descriptions:** Product and service descriptions should concisely communicate the immediate benefits of making an immediate purchase decision or entice your audience to click and view additional information. Figure 8-9 shows an e-mail that includes products.

Figure 8-8:
This
message
begins with
a short
greeting
paragraph.

Courtesy of Centennial Leasing & Sales

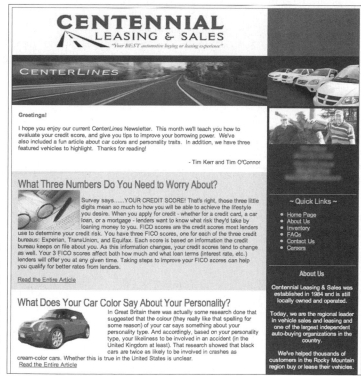

Figure 8-9:
Product
descriptions
prompt
readers to
consider a
purchase.

Courtesy of Centennial Leasing & Sales

- ✔ **Directions:** Most of the time, telling your audience exactly how to take action on the content your e-mail is necessary. For example, including your phone number in the body of your e-mail probably won't generate any calls unless you ask people to call you for a specific reason. When asking your audience to take action in multiple steps, use a headline followed by a bulleted or numbered list instead of a paragraph.

- ✔ **Testimonials and facts:** Customer testimonials and facts that support the main idea of your e-mail or the call to action should be stated in quotes and should include the source of the quote. If you have lots of testimonials, you can include one or two examples in your e-mail and provide a link so your audience can read more of them.

- ✔ **Lists:** Bulleted text makes longer sections of text and lists easier to scan and read. Bullets and lists should summarize the most important information within a particular section of your e-mail. Lists are also a good way to provide links that are related to your business but not necessarily related to the content of your e-mail.

Posting the bulk of your text content on your Web site and providing links has another advantage besides saving your readers from sorting through too much content. E-mail links are trackable, so you can tell when someone clicks to get more information about a topic you summarized in your e-mail. If you include all your content in the body of the e-mail, you won't know whether anyone read it or to whom it was interesting. I cover link tracking in Chapter 11.

Using Text Links

Text links are clickable words or phrases that result in certain actions when clicked. Links use HTML to tell the computer what to do when someone clicks the link, so your e-mail links need to contain HTML to work in e-mail programs.

If you're using raw HTML to create links for your e-mails, a simple link to a Web site looks like this:

```
<a href="http://www.yourwebsite.com">Link Text Here</a>
```

Most ESPs and e-mail applications allow you to add a link without typing in the HTML code by highlighting the text you want to turn into a link and typing the address of the Web page or file you want the text to link to. Figure 8-10 shows an ESP interface that allows you to create text links in your e-mails.

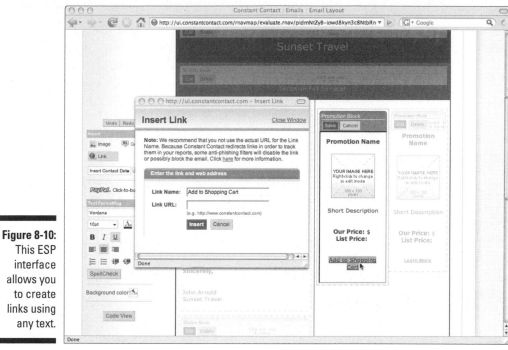

Courtesy of Constant Contact

Figure 8-10:
This ESP interface allows you to create links using any text.

Creating links

Most e-mail programs and ESPs allow you to enter a URL into a user interface, and the program then takes care of adding the HTML behind the scenes to turn your text into a link that points to the URL you entered. Follow these steps for finding a URL for the most common types of linked content.

To link to a landing page on your Web site (HTML Web sites only)

1. **Open your Web browser and navigate to the page where you want your link to point.**

2. **Highlight all the text in your browser's address bar (including the http part).**

3. **Copy the text:**

   • *Windows:* Right-click the selected text and choose Copy.

   • *Mac:* Control-click the selected text and choose Copy.

4. **Paste the URL into your e-mail program's link-creation user interface.**

   • *Windows:* Right-click and choose Paste.

   • *Mac:* Control-click and choose Paste.

To link to an e-mail address: Type **mailto:**, followed by the e-mail address you want to link to into your e-mail program's link creation user interface. For example

```
mailto:email.company@test-email.com
```

If you want an e-mail link to pre-fill the Subject line or From line, or if you want to use an e-mail link to include several e-mail addresses, you can find a free, e-mail link encoder that automatically generates the code you need at the following Web site:

```
http://email.about.com/library/misc/blmailto_encoder.htm
```

To allow someone to add an item to an online shopping cart (HTML links only)

1. **Open your Web browser and navigate to the item you want to feature in your e-mail.**

2. **Copy the link:**

   • *Windows:* Right-click the link that adds the item to your shopping cart and then choose Copy Shortcut.

   • *Mac:* Control-click the link that adds the item to your shopping cart and then choose Copy Link Location.

3. **Paste the shortcut into your e-mail program's link-creation user interface.**

E-Mail links tell the user's computer to open the default e-mail program on the user's computer. If the person clicking your link uses a Web-based e-mail program, such as AOL or Yahoo!, instead of a desktop e-mail program, such as Outlook or Outlook Express, the link won't allow them to use their Web-based application. To eliminate confusion for Web-based e-mail users, spell out the e-mail address in your link so that anyone can type it into their preferred e-mail program when necessary. (See Figure 8-11.)

Naming links

One of the most important things about text links is choosing the appropriate words to name the link. Although you can't employ every tip for every link you name, you can apply these tips to links throughout your e-mails as appropriate:

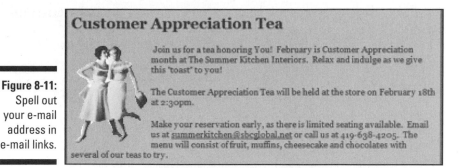

Figure 8-11:
Spell out
your e-mail
address in
e-mail links.

Courtesy of Summer Kitchen Interiors. Image of "the girls" courtesy of Fenderskirts Vintage

✔ **Name your links intuitively.**

A good rule for naming links is "what you click is what you get." In other words, name your links to tell your audience exactly what is going to happen when they click the link. Here are some examples:

- *If your link downloads a file:* Include the file type in parentheses. For example, a link that downloads a portable document format file could read

```
More Info On This Product(PDF)
```

- *If your link takes the reader to a Web site where he might have to search or scroll to view information:* Include the directions in your link. For example, if a link takes your audience to your blog, your link could read

```
Details on my blog (scroll to article 5)
```

- *If your link requires additional clicks or actions after the initial click:* Name your link describing the first step in the process. For example, a link that reads `Donate your car` isn't as clear as a link that reads

```
Read 3 steps to donating your car
```

- *If you're linking to an e-mail address:* Include the e-mail address in the link because e-mail links open the resident e-mail program on the user's computer, and users who use a Web-based e-mail program won't be able to use the link. For example, instead of using a link that reads `E-mail us`, your link should read

```
E-mail us at company@yourdomain.com
```

✔ **Name links using the text in your articles and headlines.**

Link names, such as `Click Here`, should be avoided because links attract attention and your audience won't be able to identify interesting text links if you give them generic names. Figure 8-12 shows an example of text links within the body of a paragraph.

Figure 8-12:
This e-mail
uses text
links in the
body text.

✓ **Name links to give you information about the clicker.**

Because e-mail links are trackable back to the clicker, naming your links in ways that give you insight into the motivations of the clicker makes your click reports more meaningful. For example, if your e-mail newsletter contains an article that includes three of the best places to golf with kids and you provide your readers with a link to view more information about family golf vacations, getting a group of people to click a `Read More` link isn't as valuable as getting a group of people to click a link that reads

```
Are your kids under 12? Read about best places to golf
            for younger kids.
```

✓ **Name links by describing the immediate benefits of clicking the link.**

You're likely to get more clicks when you give your audience good reasons to click. Instead of naming links by highlighting the mechanics of the click — as in, `Go to our Web site` — include the benefits in the link. For example, try

```
Shop on our website and receive an additional 10% off
            and free shipping.
```

Adding Navigation Links

Navigation links are HTML links that allow your audience to jump to visual anchors within the body of your e-mail. If your e-mails have one or more headlines or bodies of content that your audience has to scroll to for viewing, you can include navigation links in your e-mail to

✓ Highlight the content that your audience can't see immediately.

✓ Allow your audience to access the information by clicking a link instead of scrolling.

You can also include links to your Web site to allow your audience to jump from your e-mail to specific content on your Web site.

Navigation links are actually anchor links in HTML. *Anchor links* are HTML tags that reference a specific portion of content within an HTML document and automatically scroll the browser to the top of the referenced content when clicked. To create an anchor link, you have to create a name for the anchor using an anchor tag and place the anchor at the beginning of the content you want to link to:

1. **Use an anchor tag to name your anchor.**

   It's a good idea to use the first word of the headline or section of content for your name so you can remember how to name your anchor link later.

   - *To name text as an anchor,* include a name tag within your paragraph tags:

   ```
   <p><a name="anchorname">headline or title</p>
   ```

   - *To name an image as an anchor,* include the name tag within the image tag:

   ```
   <img name="anchorname" src="http://www.emailtrainer.com/
             sample/image_file/imagename.jpg">
   ```

2. **Create your anchor link by using a link tag with the anchor name and a # character.**

   - *To create a TOC link that scrolls to your anchor tag,* use the following:

   ```
   <a href="#anchorname">TOC link text</a>
   ```

   - *To create a navigation link that scrolls to an anchor link on your Web site,* use the following:

   ```
   <a href="http://www.yourwebsite.com/page.html#anchorname>
             navigation link text</a>
   ```

Most ESPs allow you to create navigation links in your e-mails, and many include navigation links in basic e-mail template designs. This section gives you tips for including navigation links in your e-mails that help your audience to easily find the information they are interested in.

Including a table of contents in your e-mails

An e-mail *table of contents* (TOC) lists headlines; each headline is linked to a different section of content within your e-mail. Figure 8-13 shows an e-mail that includes a TOC in the upper-left quadrant.

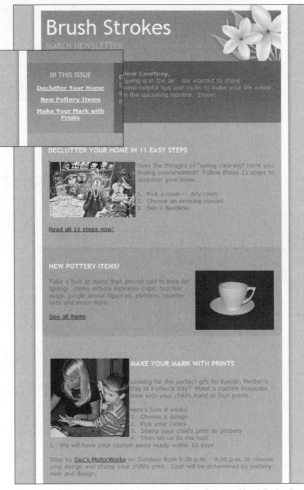

Figure 8-13:
This e-mail includes a TOC to help readers find information quickly.

Courtesy of Brush Strokes Pottery

TOCs are necessary only when your e-mail has lots of content that your audience has to scroll to view. If you decide you need a TOC in your e-mail because of the amount of content in your e-mail, take a moment to think about whether you're sending too much information in a single e-mail. Cutting down on your content and increasing your frequency might be a better solution to making your e-mails easier to scan.

If you can't cut down on your content, a TOC is a great way to summarize your content and allow your audience to find and access the content that interests them most. Here are some tips for including a TOC in your e-mails:

Text only, please

Text-only e-mails are a reality for people who check their e-mail on most portable devices. Some people also install e-mail filters and firewalls on their computers to convert HTML e-mails into text to protect their systems from malicious programs and files. When a device or filter converts an HTML e-mail into text, the results can be pretty scary. Some conversions result in displaying the entire HTML code, and others show the text along with long lines of code for links, images, and other design elements.

Because sending text-only e-mails to everyone eliminates links and tracking altogether, you might want to use an ESP that allows your e-mail list subscribers to choose a preformatted, text-only version of your HTML e-mails. That way, your e-mail is converted before it is sent and formatted to look good to the recipient. Some services even allow you to create and edit text-only versions of your HTML e-mails so you can control the content of the text version completely.

✔ **Include a heading above your table of contents.** Use wording, such as `Quick Links` or `Find It Fast`.

✔ **Keep your link headlines short.** You can use the first few words of the article headlines to which you're linking, or you can repeat short headlines as your main headlines and then use subheadings in your articles to expand on main headlines.

✔ **Make your link headlines clear.** Links should clearly communicate the content readers will see when they click. Clever links that intend to generate curiosity are generally harder to understand than clear link headlines and might cause disappointment if the linked message doesn't meet the clicker's expectations.

✔ **Keep your TOC above the scroll line.** The *scroll line* is the point at the bottom of your audience's screen where the e-mail content is no longer visible in the preview pane without scrolling. The whole point of a TOC is to keep people from scrolling. Thus, if your TOC is so long that it stretches beyond the preview pane, your e-mail probably has too much content.

Including Web site navigation links

If you intend your e-mail to drive traffic to your Web site, consider including some of your Web site's navigation links so people can easily find a link. Here are some ways you can include Web site links in your e-mails.

✔ **Across the top:** When the main goal of your e-mail is to increase Web site traffic, including Web site navigation links at the top of your e-mail is the most prominent way to position your links. Figure 8-14 shows an e-mail with navigation links across the top.

✔ **In a side column:** Including Web site navigation links in a side column is appropriate when you want to allow your audience to access your Web site without calling attention to Web site visits as your main call to action.

✔ **Across the bottom:** The bottom of your e-mail is a good place to put official Web site links related to your business operations. Examples include links to your Web site's privacy policy or job openings.

✔ **In the body of articles:** Any time you use text in an article or offer that references content on your Web site, you can make the text into a navigation link. For example, a music store could link every mention of a musical instrument to the product page for that instrument.

Figure 8-14: Using Web site navigation links across the top of the e-mail makes them easy to find.

Courtesy of Constant Contact

Linking to Files in Your E-Mails

E-mail can deliver attached files of all sorts, but attaching files should be reserved for sending personal e-mails to a small number of people at a time. Most e-mail programs and e-mail servers have security settings that send e-mails with attached files to a junk folder when the program suspects that the e-mail is commercial in nature.

Even though file attachments are e-mail delivery killers, you can still use files by linking to them within the content of your e-mails.

To link to a downloadable file (if your file is already accessible with a link on your Web site):

1. **Open your Web browser and navigate to the page that contains the link to your file.**

2. **Copy the link:**

   • *Windows:* Right-click and choose Copy Shortcut.

   • *Mac:* Control-click and choose Copy Link Location.

3. **Paste the shortcut into your e-mail program's link-creation user interface.**

   • *Windows:* Right-click and choose Paste.

   • *Mac:* Control-click and choose Paste.

If your file is not already on your Web site

1. **Upload the file to a public folder on your server.**

2. **Type the location of the file into your e-mail program's link creation user interface.**

   For example

   ```
   http://www.yourdomain.com/public/site/public_files/filename.pdf
   ```

The next sections describe some of the files that you might want to include in your e-mails along with tips on how to link to them.

Linking to video files

Video can be a powerful selling tool for some businesses, but deliverability is a challenge if you try to send an entire video file in an e-mail. Instead of delivering a video in its entirety — embedded in the content of an e-mail — insert a screen-shot image of your video and include a link to play the video on your Web site, as shown in Figure 8-15.

If your video has sound, warn people before they click in case they're reading your e-mail at the office or in a place where sound might cause a distraction.

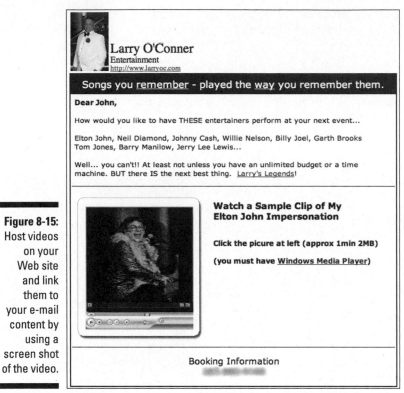

Figure 8-15:
Host videos
on your
Web site
and link
them to
your e-mail
content by
using a
screen shot
of the video.

Courtesy of Larry O'Connor Entertainment

Linking to sound files

Sound files can allow your audience to multitask by listening to information while they scan and click the links in your e-mail. Like other files, sound files should be hosted on your Web site and linked to text or images in your e-mail. Links to sound files that contain soothing music or other mood elements can distract your recipient from more important clicks, so make sure that sound helps to communicate your main message.

If the message itself is your sound file — say, you're announcing your latest podcast or an archived radio show appearance — link the user to your Web site to play the sound file so they can surf all your valuable information while they listen. Figure 8-16 shows an e-mail with a link to a sound file.

Figure 8-16:
This e-mail
uses an
image of
playback
controls to
link to an
audio file.

Courtesy of The Mark Crowley Radio Show

Linking to document files

Portable Document Format files (PDFs) are the most popular files for e-mail delivery. Like with other files, don't attach PDF files to your marketing e-mails. Instead, link to their location on your Web site. When linking to a file, make sure you tell your clickers that their click will result in a download.

For example, if a short, summarized article in your newsletter ends with a link to the entire article in PDF format, make sure the link includes (PDF) in the text of the link or use an icon to indicate that clicking will result in a document download. If the document is long and the information the clicker wants to obtain isn't on one page, make sure and tell the clicker where to find the information. For example, your link might read

```
Read entire article (PDF page 3)
```

Chapter 9

Including Images in Your E-Mails

*I*mages can enhance the look and feel of your e-mails and help to reinforce the messages contained in the body of your e-mails. Images are strong visual anchors that help to communicate your main message and divide your text into more-easily scanned sections.

Proper image positioning makes your e-mail appear inviting and easy to read. Arbitrarily positioned images are cumbersome to scan and can cause your e-mail to appear cluttered.

Placing images in your e-mails requires more than an eye for design, however, because images and e-mail browsers don't always play well together. Embedding images into the body of your e-mail can cause deliverability issues and make your e-mail slow to download, so you need to employ a few extra steps to ensure your images are ready to include.

This chapter covers what kinds of images you can include in your e-mails and how to effectively place them in your e-mails.

Choosing a File Format for Your Images

Images are graphic files that graphics programs can read and display on a computer screen. Whether you obtain your images with a digital camera or buy them online from a provider of royalty-free stock photography, make sure that your images are formatted for use in e-mail.

✔ **Use a file format that e-mail browsers can read.** An *image file format* is the type of compression used on an image in order to limit the amount of data required to store the image on a computer. *Compression* changes the amount of space the image takes up when stored on a computer, and image compression causes the graphics to display differently (especially when you reduce or enlarge the dimensions of the image). The three best file formats to use in e-mail browsers are

  • *JPG or JPEG (Joint Pictures Expert Group):* This format is a standard for Internet and e-mail images, and works well for most images.

  • *GIF (Graphic Interchange Format):* This format is best for images with only a few colors.

  • *PNG (Portable Network Graphics):* This format is similar to GIF compression but has the ability to display colors more effectively.

If your image isn't already in one of these three formats, use a graphic design application or image editor to save the image as a JPG file.

✔ **Check your file size.** The *file size* of your image refers to the amount of data your image contains measured in kilobytes (K). Images should be less than 50K to download quickly enough for most e-mail users. If an image you want to use in your e-mail is more than 50K, you can change the file size in a graphic design or image editing application.

  • *Reduce the dimensions of the image.* Smaller images contain less data.

  • *Reduce the image resolution to 72 dpi or less.* Image resolution, also known as dots per inch (dpi) or pixels per inch (ppi), refers to how many dots (or pixels) are in each inch of your image. The more dots per inch, the more detail your image is capable of displaying. More dots require more data, however, so images with higher resolutions download and display more slowly than images with lower resolutions.

Using 72 dpi provides enough resolution to appear properly on a computer screen, but images printed at 72 dpi are likely to appear fuzzy. If your audience is likely to print your e-mail and it's important that your images are printed with more definition, link your audience to a PDF version of your e-mail containing print-quality images 300 dpi or higher.

Don't Embed: Referencing Your Images

Never embed images in your e-mail as a file or attached to your e-mail because embedded and attached images usually cause a higher percentage of your e-mails to be filtered into junk folders.

Instead of embedding or attaching images, use image references that point to images stored in a public folder on your Web site server. An *image reference* is a line of HTML that tells your computer to display an image that's located in a folder on a remote server. Here's an example:

```
<img src="http://www.yourwebsite.com/public/imagefolder/imagename.jpg">
```

If you aren't comfortable using HTML to create image references in your e-mails, you can use an E-Mail Service Provider to help you reference images. If you can't store images on your Web site server or if you don't have a Web site, you can use an ESP with an image-hosting feature. That way, you can store your images on that server and automatically create image references to insert the images you upload to your e-mails. Figure 9-1 shows an ESP interface that allows you to reference images in a folder on your server or images that you upload to the ESP's server.

Figure 9-1:
Use an ESP
to insert
image tags
in HTML
to avoid
attaching
images to
your e-mail.

Courtesy of Constant Contact

Whether you code your own image references or use an ESP, you need to know the URL of the image you're referencing.

To find the URL of an image that's on your Web site, follow these steps:

1. **Open your Web browser.**

2. **Navigate to the page that contains the image you want to include in your e-mail.**

3. **View the image properties by right-clicking (Windows) or Control-clicking (Mac) and choosing Properties or open the image in a new browser window.**

Some browsers allow you to view the URL by selecting image properties, and other browsers require you to open the image in a new browser window to view the image URL.

If you're viewing the image properties, you can find the URL in the Address (URL) field of the Properties dialog box.

If your image isn't already on your Web site, follow these steps to find the location of your image file:

1. **Upload the image file to a public folder on your server.**

2. **Go to your Web site server's file manager and find the folder that contains your image.**

   The image URL is the folder location followed by the image filename. For example

   ```
   http://www.yourdomain.com/public/site/image_files/filename.jpg
   ```

When you reference image locations, you must have permission to use the images if you don't own them, even if they're publicly accessible on a Web site. Also keep in mind that you can't determine the location of background images and images that appear in Flash Web sites by clicking the image. You have to find the image location by using the folder address on your server or by finding the reference in your Web site's HTML.

Deciding Which Images to Use

Images should reinforce the text in your e-mails or tell the story of your e-mails all by themselves. You never know whether someone will decide to scan your e-mail just to look at the images.

Although using some kinds of images (such as photographs and clip art) works well when telling a story, other kinds of images (such as logos and stylized text) are more useful for branding your business or making your e-mails more attractive to the eye. The following sections explain how to use different kinds of images in the manner best suited to the image.

Photographs

Photographs are the most versatile images because they can communicate so much information. Examples of photos that you can use in your e-mails include

- ✔ Products and your services in action
- ✔ Key representatives in your business (see Figure 9-2)

✔ Your business or site (if your location is visually memorable; look ahead to Figure 9-3)

✔ Events and public appearances

✔ Customers who give you permission to share testimonials

Most photographs are copyrighted, so make sure you have permission to use someone else's photographs or your own photograph of a person. Of course, you can capture your own digital photographic images — or scan a photographic print to create a digital image — but you can also purchase royalty-free photographs online. You can find online photo library recommendations at www.emailtrainer.com.

Figure 9-2:
Photographs of key representatives help familiarize your audience with key people.

Courtesy of American Autowire, design by Jeff Moore

Created art

Created art consists of images made by utilizing a graphic design software. Created art can include manipulated photos, drawings and sketches converted to image files, abstract designs, and other creative uses of colors, lines, and shapes. The following sections explain several types of created art along with tips for making good choices when deciding to use them in your e-mails.

Logos

Placing a logo at the top of your e-mail is a good choice when you want to brand your e-mail without using a top-bar image (see Figure 9-3). Your logo is an important part of your brand and helps reinforce your identity. The best practice for logo inclusion is to use the same logo that's on your Web site so that people who click through to your Web site are reassured by the consistency in your brand identity.

Most people expect your logo to link to your Web site's home page, so including link functionality in every logo allows your audience to easily access your home page information. You can read more about making your images into links later in this chapter.

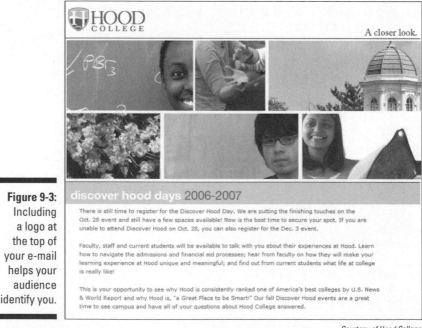

Figure 9-3: Including a logo at the top of your e-mail helps your audience identify you.

Courtesy of Hood College

Logos are most effective when you position them at the top left or top center of your e-mail. Like with any image included at the top of your e-mail, your logo should be small enough to allow your audience to view the content appearing in the upper left in the preview pane. Usually 150 pixels tall is a good maximum height. If your logo doesn't look good unless it's large, consider designing a top-bar image to brand your e-mails instead. You can read more about top-bar images later in this chapter.

Clip art

Clip art is an illustration created with a software application, or an illustration that is created by hand and converted to an image file. Clip art is useful when you don't have a photograph to precisely illustrate your message, or when you have created customized clip art to reinforce your brand identity. Figure 9-4 shows an example of an e-mail that uses clip art.

Examples of clip art that you can use in your e-mails include

- **Objects:** A clip art image of a tennis racket might be used by a tennis club to help reinforce the announcement of a new pro shop.
- **People:** A clip art image showing two people in a boat might be used by a fishing store to reinforce a boat sale.
- **Imaginative concepts:** A clip art cartoon of a bear wearing a napkin while holding a fork and a knife might be used by a zoo to reinforce a message telling people not to feed the animals.

Avoid using theme-less clip art images that don't add any meaning to your message. I also recommend choosing clip art images that contain colors that match the design of your e-mail.

Like photographs, clip art images are usually copyrighted so make sure you purchase your clip art images through a business that provides you with a license with royalty-free usage. You can find clip art library recommendations at www.emailtrainer.com.

Animated GIFs

Animated GIFs are image formats that display multiple images in a fixed rotation. Using these is a great way to include multiple images in your e-mails using the space for one image. Creating animated GIFs requires using image-design software with a GIF creation tool.

GIF animations that appear to blink quickly have a better chance of annoying your audience than reinforcing your message, so make sure your image rotation is set no faster than $^{200}/_{1000}$ second when you create your GIF animation.

When you use GIF animation to make objects appear to move within the GIF image, make sure you test the speed of your animation in several e-mail browsers to ensure your animation isn't distracting.

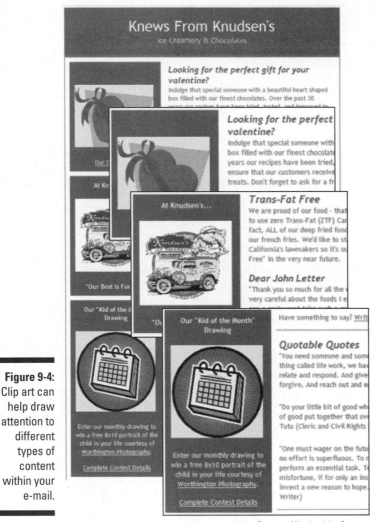

Courtesy of Knudson's Ice Creamery

Figure 9-4:
Clip art can help draw attention to different types of content within your e-mail.

Icons

Icons are small graphics that help to break up blocks of content, tie related content, or add to the look and feel of your text.

Icons are great for adding to the look and feel of your e-mails, but I recommend limiting your icon usage to a particular theme. For example, a seafood restaurant that decides to have icons next to each headline in a newsletter could use the same fish icon next to each headline or use different seafood icons that share a similar look and size. Other useful icons could include

✔ **Bullets:** Using icons as bullets next to lists of information is a good way to tie your list under a particular theme. For example, an association could use a Members Only icon as bullets in a list of Members Only events.

✔ **Buttons:** *Buttons* are clickable graphics. Icons that are used as buttons often incorporate text in the graphic to reinforce the fact that the button is clickable, but icons can also be designed as intuitive buttons to your audience. For example, an icon that looks like the Play button on an audio device could be used as a link to download an audio file.

✔ **Content dividers and borders:** Icons can be repeated to form rows and columns to divide sections of content. When using icons in this fashion, create one graphic with the row of icons or use your ESP or HTML to repeat a single icon as a border (see Figure 9-5). I also recommend limiting content divider icons to a few locations.

Figure 9-5:
Use small repeating icons to enhance your e-mail designs.

Courtesy of Great Harvest Bread Company

Mood icons or emoticons

Mood icons, or *emoticons*, are groups of keyboard characters that form representations of faces showing different kinds of expressions. Mood icons can help your audience interpret your tone in text-only e-mails so they don't get confused when you are being sarcastic, giving constructive criticism, or addressing a sensitive topic. The following table gives some examples.

Icon	*When to Use It*
:-) or :)	smiling or joking
;-)	winking, like when you don't really mean something
:-(	sad or not satisfied
:'(	crying
;-o or :o	surprised

Some e-mail applications replace commonly known emoticon keystrokes with actual graphics and others allow you to insert mood icon graphics into your e-mails by selecting them with your mouse. Figure 9-6 shows an example of a palate of mood icons.

Figure 9-6:
Mood icons.

Text images

When you need to display text in a style or font that's impossible with HTML, you can create images of your text to include in your e-mails. Text images are useful when your brand identity includes fonts and styles that are impossible to re-create in HTML.

Images are often blocked by e-mail applications until the recipient of your e-mail enables them to display, so make sure your stylized text isn't vital to your e-mail's main idea. You can read more about image blocking in Chapter 6.

Words and headlines

Creating words and headlines using a graphic design tool allows you to customize your text visually so you can

- ✔ Create unique moods.
- ✔ Draw extra attention to your words.
- ✔ Reinforce the main idea of your words.

Figure 9-7 shows an example of a stylized text image used as a visual anchor to draw attention and to reinforce the meaning of the words. Word images are also useful when your logo consists of text with unique styles and fonts that can't be displayed in HTML.

Signatures

Using a scanned image of your signature can give your e-mails a personal touch by making your e-mail appear as though it were as personally signed by you. Signature images are ideal for business letters, press releases, and event invitations (see Figure 9-8).

Figure 9-7:
Use stylized
text images
to draw
attention
to your
headlines
or reinforce
the main
idea.

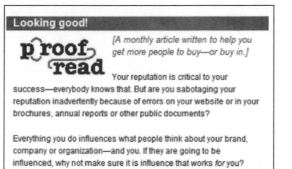

Looking good!

p roof read

[A monthly article written to help you get more people to buy—or buy in.]

Your reputation is critical to your success—everybody knows that. But are you sabotaging your reputation inadvertently because of errors on your website or in your brochures, annual reports or other public documents?

Everything you do influences what people think about your brand, company or organization—and you. If they are going to be influenced, why not make sure it is influence that works *for* you?

Courtesy of Adams Jette Marketing & Communications

Ask someone else to sign your name — or sign your name in a way that differentiates your e-mail signature from the signature you use for signing documents — so no one can copy your e-mail signature and use it for forgery.

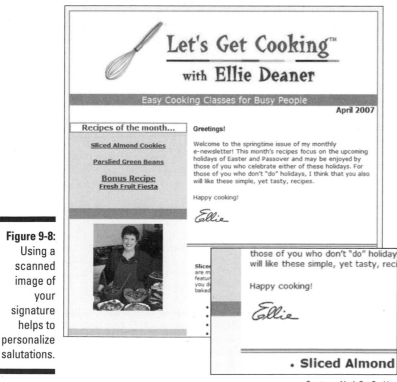

Figure 9-8:
Using a
scanned
image of
your
signature
helps to
personalize
salutations.

Courtesy of Let's Get Cooking

Image combinations

The following types of images can consist of photos, text images, or created art used separately or in combination for designing the look and feel of your e-mail.

Top-bar images

Top-bar images appear at very top of an e-mail and span its entire width. These images are a good choice when your Web site includes a top-bar image at the top of every page, and you want to match your e-mails to your Web site design. Figure 9-9 shows an example of an e-mail with a top-bar image that includes a photo, created art, and stylized text images.

Make sure that your top-bar images are thin enough to allow the content in the upper-left quadrant of your e-mail to display in the preview pane. Anything taller than 200 pixels is probably too tall. You can read more about utilizing the preview pane in Chapter 6.

Figure 9-9:
This top-bar image spans the entire width of the e-mail and includes a photo, created art, plain text, and a text image.

Courtesy of Safari Ventures

Background images

Background images are those that appear behind the text in your e-mails or in the background surrounding your e-mail (see Figure 9-10). Background images should be simple because busy background images with lots of designs make your text more difficult to read.

Background images outside the body of your e-mail often remain in the background when people reply to your e-mails, so choosing busy backgrounds can cause the text in your audience's replies to be unreadable. As of this writing, background images do not display in Microsoft Outlook 2007, so use background colors instead of images if your e-mail list consists of subscribers who are likely to use Outlook to read their e-mails, such as people who work for large companies.

Figure 9-10:
This e-mail uses a background image to create a shaded background behind the company logo and main headlines.

Courtesy of McDonald Garden Center

Placing Images Properly in Your E-Mails

When placed properly, images can help to break up the text in your e-mails and make your e-mail text easier to scan and read. Images can be positioned as visual anchors that attract attention and give your audience reasons to stop scanning and start reading your e-mails. Improperly placed images can distract your audience from the main idea of your message and cause clutter.

This section tells you where to place the images and how to arrange multiple images into eye-catching configurations that reinforce your message.

Positioning single images

You have three basic choices for single-image placement in the body of an e-mail. Images can be centered, or left- or right-justified.

Image justification is made possible by adding an align command followed by left, right, or center in your image reference in HTML. Here's an example.

```
<img align="left" src="http://www.yourwebsite.com/filename/imagename.jpg>
```

Most e-mail applications and ESPs allow you to justify images with a user interface so you don't have to know the code.

When you have one article and one image in your e-mail, these layouts work the best:

- ✔ **Centered:** Your image displays in the center of a column above your text. (No text is placed to the left or right of your image.) Centering is usually the best choice when an image is much wider than it is tall. (See Figure 9-11.)

- ✔ **Left justification:** Your image displays on the left side of a column with text placed to its right. (See Figure 9-12.) When you use left-justified images and text to the right, make sure that your text and image are the same height or that the paragraph text wraps underneath the image for at least two lines.

- ✔ **Right justification:** Your image displays on the right side of a column with text placed to its left. (See Figure 9-13.) When you use right-justified images and text to the left, make sure that your text and image are the same height or that the paragraph text wraps underneath the image for at least two lines.

Positioning multiple images

When you have multiple articles and images in a single column, arrange your articles and images in patterns. Five basic patterns are effective for organizing images into visually attractive anchors in the same column:

- ✔ **All images centered:** If you have multiple articles in a single column and the first article begins with a center-justified image, you should also center justify the images in the remaining articles for that column.

- ✔ **All images left-justified:** Left-justifying your images works best when you have one column and you want your images to be the main focus of your content. Your audience is likely to follow several images repeating down the page before scanning across the page to view the text.

- ✔ **All images right-justified:** Right-justify your images when your e-mail has a narrow left column that you want to draw attention to. Right justified images aren't as likely to be noticed right away.

- ✔ **Alternating justification left to right or right to left:** Alternating justification gives your audience reasons to scan across the e-mail page instead of just looking straight down the page at a number of repeating images. Figure 9-14 shows an e-mail that positions images in an alternating pattern.

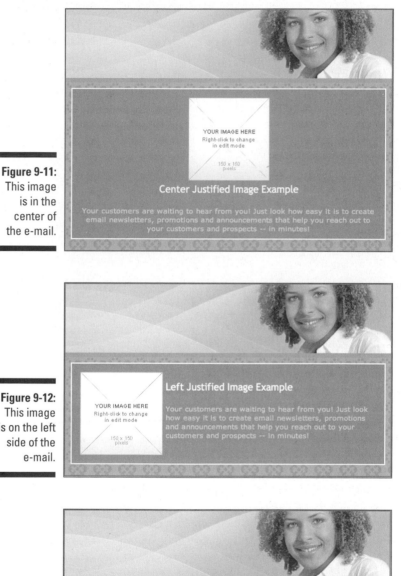

Figure 9-11:
This image is in the center of the e-mail.

Figure 9-12:
This image is on the left side of the e-mail.

Figure 9-13:
This image is on the right side of the e-mail.

Figure 9-14: Use images in an alternating pattern to draw attention across and down the page.

✔ **Bottom-justified images:** Including images at the bottom of a body of text can be effective in catching your reader's attention before he scrolls past the end of your article. Bottom-justified images can be positioned to the left, right, or center, depending on the image and the content that begins directly under the image. Here are some examples of bottom-justified images that are effective.

• *An image of your signature in a closing paragraph:* Draw attention to contact information or a call to action.

• *A small picture or icon pertaining to a call to action:* For example, an icon of a telephone might be used to draw attention to a phone number.

• *A symbol or logo that displays credibility:* For example, a logo displaying your certification as an authorized dealer might be used to draw attention to a link to view a list of testimonials.

Placing images in multiple columns

When your e-mail uses multiple columns, leave plenty of space between images in adjacent columns so that your images don't bunch up and cause your audience to scan away from the content related to each image. Here are some tips for arranging images in multiple columns:

- ✔ **A narrow left column with images:** Keep the images in your right column right-justified or centered, or include plenty of space between the columns. See Figure 9-15.

- ✔ **A narrow right column with images:** Keep the images in your left column left-justified or centered.

- ✔ **More than two columns:** Keep your image dimensions distinct and consistent for each column. You can use images with various dimensions, but all the images contained in each separate column should be the same size.

Figure 9-15: Use plenty of space between images.

Courtesy of Kansas Professional Photographers Association

Making Your Images into Links

Consumers like to click images, so making your images clickable gives your audience more opportunities to engage in your information. Image links are also trackable, so you can tell who your image clickers are. Making images into links requires using an image tag `<src>` combined with a URL link tag `<href>` in HTML. Here's an example:

```
<a href="http://www.yourwebsite.com">
    <img src="http://www.yourwebsite.com/filename/imagename.jpg/></a>
```

If you aren't familiar with coding your own image links, use an ESP with a user interface for creating image links. Figure 9-16 shows an ESP interface that allows you to insert a URL in order to add a link to an image.

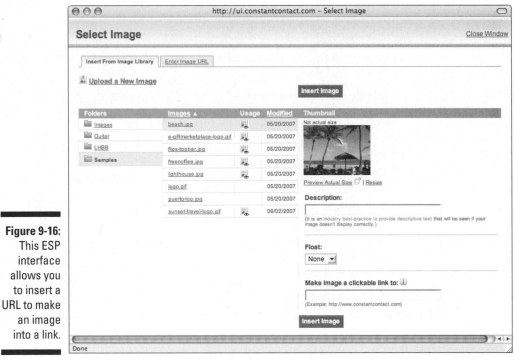

Figure 9-16:
This ESP interface allows you to insert a URL to make an image into a link.

Courtesy of Constant Contact

Here are some tips for making your image links more effective when you include them in your e-mails.

- ✔ **Make your image links intuitive.** If your image doesn't make the destination of your link clear to your audience, you're probably better off with a text link or using text to tell your audience what will happen when they click on the image.

- ✔ **Link logos to your Web site.** Most people expect your logo to link to your Web site's home page, so including link functionality in every logo allows your audience to easily access your home page information.

- ✔ **Link single images to more images or larger images**. When space allows for only one image or for smaller-size images, you can link your images to Web pages that contain more images and images with higher resolutions. Remember to make sure the content related to the image states or implies that the image links to more images.

Chapter 10

Making Your E-Mail Content Valuable

*W*hen people subscribe to your e-mail list, they share personal information with the expectation of receiving something valuable. Consumers aren't likely to value multiple e-mails that highlight only the distinguishing characteristics of your business. Repetitive e-mail content results in subscriber boredom. And boring your audience leads to low open rates, lost clicks, and unsubscribe requests.

Keeping your e-mail content valuable over time helps ensure that your list subscribers keep their attention and their subscription active while you attempt to capture purchases from them throughout the course of each buying cycle. The two basic types of value when it comes to e-mail content are

✔ An offer that is valuable when acted upon

✔ An *inherent* value: that is, content that is valuable in and of itself

Valuable content won't automatically make your audience rush to your business in order to part with their money. Your e-mail also needs to have a strong call to action to give your content a purpose and prompt your audience to help you meet your objectives.

This chapter covers some fundamental guidelines for including value in your e-mail strategy to deliver important information about your business while giving your audience continued reasons to open, read, and take action on your e-mails no matter which stage of the buying cycle they're in.

Making Sure Your Offers Are Valuable to Your Audience

Offers are conditional statements that give your audience one or more reasons to make an immediate decision instead of postponing a decision. Figure 10-1 shows an e-mail promotion that includes offers to make an immediate purchase decision.

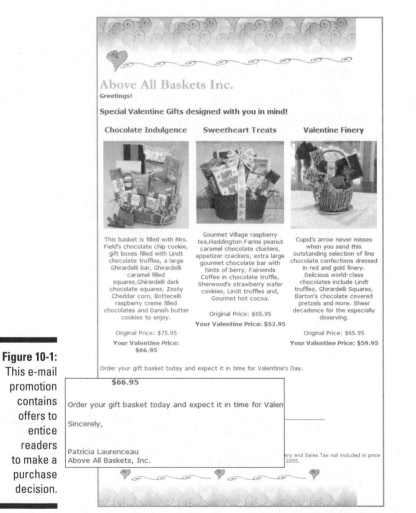

Above All Baskets Inc.

Greetings!

Special Valentine Gifts designed with you in mind!

Chocolate Indulgence   **Sweetheart Treats**   **Valentine Finery**

This basket is filled with Mrs. Field's chocolate chip cookie, gift boxes filled with Lindt chocolate truffles, a large Ghirardelli bar, Ghirardelli caramel filled squares, Ghirardelli dark chocolate squares, Zesty Cheddar corn, Bottecelli raspberry creme filled chocolates and Danish butter cookies to enjoy.

Gourmet Village raspberry tea, Haddington Farms peanut caramel chocolate clusters, appetizer crackers, extra large gourmet chocolate bar with hints of berry, Fairwinds Coffee in chocolate truffle, Sherwood's strawberry wafer cookies, Lindt truffles and, Gourmet hot cocoa.

Cupid's arrow never misses when you send this outstanding selection of fine chocolate confections dressed in red and gold finery. Delicious world-class chocolates include Lindt truffles, Ghirardelli Squares, Barton's chocolate covered pretzels and more. Sheer decadence for the especially deserving.

Original Price: $75.95

Your Valentine Price:
$66.95

Original Price: $65.95

Your Valentine Price: $52.95

Original Price: $65.95

Your Valentine Price: $59.95

Order your gift basket today and expect it in time for Valentine's Day.

$66.95

Order your gift basket today and expect it in time for Valen

Sincerely,

Patricia Laurenceau
Above All Baskets, Inc.

ery and Sales Tax not included in price
2005.

Figure 10-1: This e-mail promotion contains offers to entice readers to make a purchase decision.

Courtesy of Above All Baskets

Giving something away — whether of cash value or your knowledge — doesn't mean that your audience automatically understands nor appreciates the value in your offer. Offers become more valuable to your audience when

✔ Your audience gets closer to the decision stage of the buying cycle.

✔ The benefits of your offer outweigh postponing a decision.

Because the accessibility of the Internet allows your prospects and customers to easily compare competing offers, determining whether your e-mail offers are valuable depends on how your audience views your offer in light of the other choices available at the time of the offer. For example, sending an e-mail that features a new product available in your store could prompt your audience to compare prices online and purchase the product from a well-known competitor instead of from you if you aren't aware that your competitor has a better offer.

Taking the choices available to your audience into account helps ensure that your offers outweigh other easily accessible offers. Here are some of the things to consider when you decide which types of offers to include in your e-mails:

✔ **Research your competition.**

Information that's easily accessible to your audience is easily accessible to you as well. Determine where your audience is likely to search for more information and look at the offers that your competition uses. You can do research on the Internet, visit your competition, and sign up for your competition's e-mail list. If your main offer includes discounts or other price incentives, don't worry if you can't compete with your competition on price alone. Instead, use the opportunity to point out the reasons why your products or services are a better choice even though the discount isn't as significant.

✔ **Own your links.**

When your e-mails include links to additional information that supports your offer, post the information on your Web site, blog, and other online presences that you can control.

If you need to link to outside information, ask for permission from the outside source to include the information on your Web site to keep your clickers on your site. If you have to link to content on shared Web sites — such as public blogs, discussion boards, or other Web sites you don't own — make sure that you own the banner ads and other advertising space on those sites so that your message is reinforced when your audience clicks through and your competition can't take advantage of your e-mail list subscribers.

✔ **Know your audience.**

If your audience includes groups of people who are likely to respond to different offers, divide your audience into different lists based on the offers they tend to respond to and then adjust your offers accordingly. For example, a travel company might divide its customer list into segments based on recreational interests to send offers for golf vacations to golfers and family vacations to families. Here are some examples of other offer lists you can create:

- Customers who value the latest styles or highest quality and are willing to pay more for them

- Customers who value convenience and time and are more likely to purchase products or services when the purchase process is fast and easy

- Customers who value financial savings and are willing to take extra steps or settle for less to save money

Sending Valuable Offers

Offers don't necessarily have to require a purchase decision in order to have value. Sometimes offers are necessary just to motivate your audience to consider all the information related to making a purchase decision. Whether your offers ask for an immediate purchase or just a visit to your Web site, your offers have to be valuable, or your audience won't take action on them.

Because the value in postponing a decision almost always has to do with the fact that people prefer to hold on to their money, offers usually take the form of discounts and savings. However, some people value other types of offers. The following sections describe money-saving offers as well as other types of offers.

Creating content to promote something

When the main idea of your e-mail is to promote your products or services, your e-mails need to include descriptions and images that support your promotion. Here are some ideas and sources for creating promotional content to include in your e-mails:

✔ **Ask manufacturers for content.**

Companies that manufacture your products are great sources for product descriptions, images, and headlines.

✔ **Take digital photos.**

Use a digital camera to create product photos and show your services in action.

✔ **Ask your customers for descriptions.**

Sometimes your customers are able to describe your products or services in ways that speak to your audience better than you can.

✔ **Ask people to write testimonials.**

Asking people to tell you about their experiences can be interesting and relevant to your audience as well as powerful motivators. Testimonials don't have to come from your customers. Sometimes you can find examples of other people who have used products and services like yours and demonstrate how their testimonial applies to your business.

Make sure you have permission to use personal testimonials.

✔ **Check your e-mail.**

Keeping track of the types of e-mails your customers and prospects are sending to you can give you insight into the topics that interest your audience. When your customers and prospects ask questions and make inquiries about your business, use your answers to help you develop content that promotes the way your products or services help to solve their problems.

Cashing in on coupons

Coupons are traditionally printed on paper and redeemed in person, but e-mail coupons can take many forms, such as

✔ Printable HTML designs on a Web page or in an e-mail for use in a brick-and-mortar store

✔ Coupon codes that customers enter into a form field when making an online purchase

✔ Links that include special HTML code that applies a change to the price field of a product database when someone clicks to view the product or add it to an online shopping cart

Most ESPs allow you to create dotted-line borders to give your coupon content the appearance of being clipable.

If you format your coupons to have a traditional cut-out look on the screen, make sure that your coupons include redemption directions because consumers need to know how to redeem your coupon. For example, if you intend for your consumers to print the coupon, cut it out, and drive down to your store for redemption, include those instructions in your e-mail. Figure 10-2 shows an e-mail that includes more traditional-looking coupons as well as directions for using the coupons.

Figure 10-2:
Include
redemption
directions
with
coupons.

Coupons contained in the body of your e-mail can be forwarded to anyone, so make sure you're ready to honor the unlimited use of your coupon by individuals who aren't on your e-mail list. If you want to make sure your coupon is used only by a few selected individuals, you can ask your audience to request an official copy of the coupon or give every coupon a unique code and tell your audience that you will allow only one use per coupon code.

Some ESPs allow you to merge database fields into your e-mail so you can assign unique numbers to each customer's printable coupon. If your coupon is redeemable online, you can use the same code on every coupon and require your audience to create an account or log in before using the coupon code so you can keep track of unique redemptions.

You should also think through the financial implications that your coupon might create if someone tries to abuse your offer. Including an expiration date and limiting the number of redemptions per product or customer can help to limit any attempts to maliciously exploit your coupon's basic intentions.

Including incentives

Incentives are limited-time offers that reward a specific action. Incentives differ from coupons in that no physical redemption process is involved to take advantage of an incentive. Incentives are highly flexible; they can take the form of financial savings or special privileges. For example, a low financing rate might be the initial incentive to purchase a particular car, but membership to an exclusive automobile club is an additional incentive for purchasing the same car.

Incentives are particularly useful when you can identify your audience's specific interests and then match your audience's interests with your incentive. For example, if you know that your audience likes baseball, you might include two free tickets to a baseball game as an incentive for making an immediate purchase.

Using giveaways

Giveaways are complimentary products or services that are awarded to a single winner or a limited number of participants who take a specific action. Giveaways allow you to offer your audience a chance at a valuable prize or special privileges without having to worry about meeting the demand for a high number of requests for freebies. In addition to rewarding purchases, using giveaways can motivate your audience to

- ✔ Share more of their interests and contact information.
- ✔ Respond to surveys and polls.
- ✔ Forward your e-mails to friends and colleagues.

Figure 10-3 shows an e-mail that offers a giveaway to reward a visit to the store.

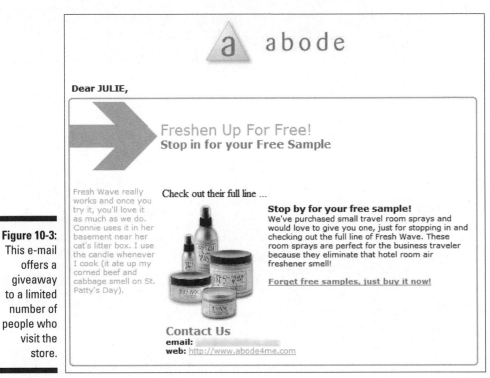

Figure 10-3:
This e-mail offers a giveaway to a limited number of people who visit the store.

Courtesy of Abode

When your giveaway involves a prize drawing or contest, make sure that your giveaway complies with all applicable laws in your area. You can usually find your local contest laws online at your state's Secretary of State Web site.

Making gains with loss leaders

A *loss leader* is an offer to purchase a product or service that results in a financial loss to your business to gain a new customer who represents more profitable revenue in the future. For example, a camera store might be willing to sell a specific type of camera for far less than all their competitors to obtain highly profitable printing and accessory sales from those customers.

Loss leaders are useful when some of the people on your e-mail list have to experience the quality of your products or services firsthand before they will understand the true value inherent in your regular prices. Loss leaders represent a customer acquisition cost and should therefore be reserved for obtaining customers who have never purchased from you before. You can read more about customer acquisition costs in Chapter 2.

Extending urgent offers

Sometimes, products or services are valuable enough to cause an immediate purchase decision all by themselves because they fulfill a need that your audience perceives as an emergency. For example, a landscaping company might offer to blow out sprinkler systems for their audience because a cold front is moving in that has the potential to freeze pipes and cause serious water damage.

E-mail offers that highlight urgent needs are most effective when used sparingly.

Writing an Effective Call to Action

Even when your content is valuable, most consumers simply scan and delete your e-mails unless you prompt them with alternatives. If increasing your deletion rate isn't one of your objectives, every e-mail you send needs to include a strong call to action. As I talk about elsewhere in the book, a *call to action* is a statement that prompts your audience to complete one or more specific tasks in favor of your objectives.

Calling your audience to action isn't as simple as including your phone number in the body of your e-mail or giving your audience lots of links to click. Consumers need directions and compelling reasons for taking specific actions, especially when their actions require spending time or money.

This section explains the basic principles of writing a strong call to action and includes examples of calls to action that are applicable to the most common types of valuable content.

Constructing a call to action

Anyone who reads e-mail is familiar with the stalwart phrase *Click Here,* but such generic phrases are not necessarily models for writing an effective call to action. An effective call to action acts like a little sign that allows your audience to visualize the steps involved to take advantage of your e-mail's content. Figure 10-4 shows an example of an e-mail offer that includes a call to action.

Figure 10-4:
This e-mail includes an offer and a call to action.

Courtesy of Impressions Marketing

Words are the building blocks of a strong call to action, and the quality and the number of words that you choose significantly affect the number of responses that your call to action receives. The most effective way to write a call to action is to begin with one or more *action* words: verbs that propose a specific task to your audience. Examples include

- ✔ Visit
- ✔ Call
- ✔ Download
- ✔ Read
- ✔ Print

Here's how you can use action words to create a strong call to action. You can see the progression of the call to action as you make it stronger and stronger:

1. **Combine your action word with the subject of the action word.**

   Order *this item*.

2. **Include the place where the action happens.**

   Order this item *online*.

3. **Add the urgency of the action.**

   Order this item online *before Friday*.

4. **Finish with an adjective to underscore the value inherent in the action.**

   Order this *hilarious* item online before Friday.

The combination of one or more action words along with your supplementary words makes a complete call to action. Writing an effective call to action can become more of an art than a science, but becoming a good call to action writer is just a matter of practice.

Turning your action words into links is a great way to prompt your audience to click to take action. When using one or more action words as a link, select words that allow your audience to visualize the steps involved in taking your proposed action after they click. (You can read about creating links in Chapter 8.)

Calling for specific actions

Calling your audience to action is useful only when you have meaningful actions for your audience to take. The following examples of different types of calls to action include ideas for calling your audience to specific actions, such as forwarding your e-mail or making a reservation to attend an event advertised in your e-mail.

Read your e-mail

When you send lengthy articles or when your main call to action appears after a long body of text, writing calls to action that prompt your audience to read a specific portion of your e-mail is useful. Calls to action prompting your audience to read your e-mail might take the form of

✔ **Stand-alone headlines and short phrases, such as Read On or See Below, as shown in Figure 10-5**

   Calling attention to content placed farther down in your e-mail helps ensure that your audience reads beyond the bottom of the screen.

Call to action prompts readers to scroll.

Courtesy of The Clutter Diet, www.clutterdiet.com

Figure 10-5: This call to action is placed toward the bottom.

- ✔ **A table of contents with links to various sections of content within your e-mail**
- ✔ **Action words used in your e-mail's Subject line**
- ✔ **Links to additional content outside the body of your e-mail**

Try these action words to entice your audience to read your e-mails:

- ✔ **Read:** For example, *Read below for this month's tech-tip.*
- ✔ **Look:** For example, *Look in the left column for a list of events.*
- ✔ **Consider:** For example, *Consider the following free options.*
- ✔ **Notice:** For example, *Notice the price under each image.*
- ✔ **Scroll:** For example, *Scroll to the bottom for our contact information.*

Save your e-mail

Most consumers don't think to save the e-mails they receive. When you want your audience to refer to your e-mail, you need to incorporate a call to action to keep folks from deleting your e-mail.

You can prompt your audience to easily save your e-mails in these three ways:

- ✔ Ask your readers to save the e-mail to any Inbox subfolder in their e-mail program.
- ✔ Archive your e-mail on a page within your Web site and ask your readers to bookmark the page in their Web browser.

✔ Provide a link to a Portable Document Format (PDF) version of your e-mail that your audience can save.

Make sure to include specific directions or a link to directions in your call to action.

To write a strong call to action when you want readers to save your e-mail, try these action words:

✔ **Save:** For example, *Save this e-mail now for future reference.*

✔ **Keep:** For example, *Keep this e-mail in your inbox until next Friday.*

✔ **Store:** For example, *Store the following linked files on your computer.*

✔ **File:** For example, *File this e-mail away to continue using the enclosed menu.*

✔ **Move:** For example, *Move this e-mail to a saved folder in your e-mail program.*

Print your e-mail

Printed e-mails are useful when your e-mail's ultimate objective requires your audience to produce a paper copy of your e-mail. Examples of e-mails that are valuable in printed form include e-mails that contain

✔ Coupons that must be printed to be redeemed. I cover the ins and outs of coupons earlier in this chapter.

✔ Maps or driving directions.

✔ Valuable information that your audience is willing to post for others, such as an advice column, a restaurant menu, or a list of available products that a specific group might be interested in.

Some e-mail programs need to be configured to print background colors and images, so your printed e-mail might not look the same as it does onscreen. Instead of giving your audience complicated instructions for enabling background printing, use simple designs for your print-worthy e-mails or provide a link to a printable version of your e-mail in PDF form.

When you're writing a call to action to get your readers to print your e-mail, start with these action words:

✔ **Print:** For example, *Print this e-mail before you delete it.*

✔ **Post:** For example, *Post this e-mail in your break room during your lunch break.*

✔ **Bring:** For example, *Bring this e-mail with you when you visit.*

✔ **Hang:** For example, *Hang this e-mail up today so others can read it.*

Forward your e-mail

When the goal of your e-mail is to deliver your content to people outside your e-mail list, prompting your audience to forward your e-mail to friends and colleagues is a great way to get beyond your own reach.

Your audience has two choices for forwarding your e-mails:

✔ **Click the Forward button in an e-mail program.**

An exact copy of your e-mail is forwarded to the e-mail address. Because the forward button sends an exact copy of your e-mail, the links in the e-mail — including the unsubscribe link — are attributed to the person who received the original e-mail. Turn to Chapter 13 to find out how to keep track of your e-mails.

When your audience forwards your e-mail by clicking the Forward button, your E-Mail Service Provider (ESP; if you use one) can't track your e-mail.

✔ **Click a forward link that your ESP provides.**

A completely new copy of your e-mail is forwarded to the e-mail address. Your forwarded e-mail can't log an unsubscribe request or track clicks in the name of your original recipient, and your ESP can track this forward progress. An ESP allows you to create and include trackable forward links in your e-mails (as shown in Figure 10-6).

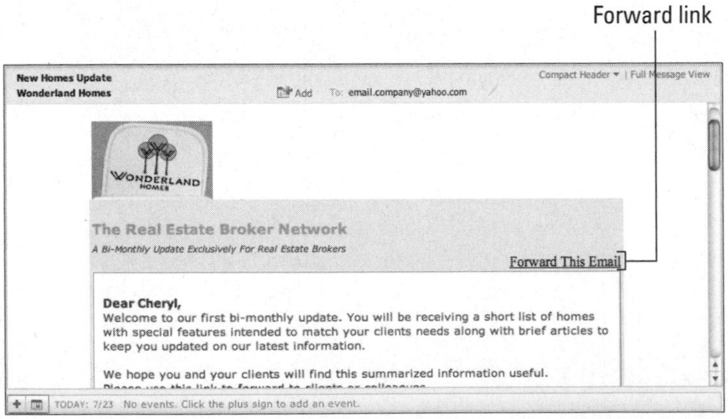

Forward link

Figure 10-6:
Include
a link to
forward
your e-mail.

Courtesy of Wonderland Homes

If you intend to prompt your audience to forward your e-mails, make sure that the Forward link in your e-mail's body draws attention away from the Forward button in your audience's e-mail program. Make your forward link into an eye-catching button or place a text link in a prominent position. You might also want to offer an incentive to encourage your audience to use the link in the body of your e-mail.

These action words are a good start to a call to action when you want your readers to forward your e-mail:

- ✔ **Share:** For example, *Share this informative e-mail with your boss before your next meeting.*

- ✔ **Forward:** For example, *Forward this funny story to a friend today.*

- ✔ **Send:** For example, *Send a copy to a friend by Friday for free admission.*

- ✔ **Refer:** For example, *Refer some friends before the event and enjoy it together.*

Make a purchase

E-mail purchases always involve more than one step because, well, an e-mail can't complete financial transactions all by itself. For example, someone who clicks a link that reads `Buy This Item Now` still has to go to a Web site shopping cart or visit your store to pick up the product. Make sure that every call to action that prompts your audience to make a purchase includes intuitive language or instructions for following through on the purchase process.

Here are some tips for prompting your audience to make a purchase:

- ✔ Help your audience visualize an online transaction by prompting your audience to `Add` *(the item)* `to the Online Shopping Cart` instead of prompting them to `Order` or `Buy` an item that must be purchased online.

- ✔ When your purchase process involves an online order form other than a shipping or billing form, include a call to action that allows your audience to view the order form before filling it out.

- ✔ If your purchasing process isn't online, give your audience directions in conjunction with action words, as in `Order by Phone at` *(number)*.

Use these action words to build a strong call to action:

- ✔ **Buy:** For example, *Buy this one-of-a-kind item online today.*

- ✔ **Add:** For example, *Add this quality item to your shopping cart now.*

- ✔ **Order:** For example, *Order your personalized (item) before we run out using this link to our order form.*

- ✔ **Phone:** For example, *Phone in your secure purchase between 9am and 5pm.*

- ✔ **Ship:** For example, *Ship your surprise present overnight when you call before 3pm.*

- ✔ **Own:** For example, *Own it today when you visit one of our convenient locations.*

Fill out a form

Online forms are useful for collecting information from your audience and for prompting your audience to contact you when you don't want to share an e-mail address that invites contacting you at will. Useful Web forms include

- ✔ Survey forms used to collect opinions and other information, as shown in Figure 10-7. (You can read more about surveys in Chapter 13.)
- ✔ Contact forms that send information to your e-mail address using form fields instead of an e-mail link.
- ✔ Forms that collect interest and contact information and place them in a database for use in future communications.
- ✔ Forms that submit order information.

Figure 10-7:
A link to call your audience to action when you want them to fill out a survey form leads to the survey itself.

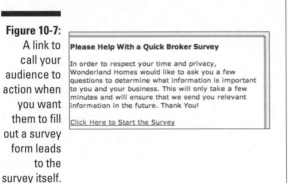

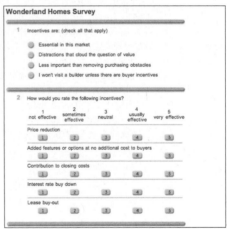

Courtesy of Wonderland Homes

When you want your readers to fill out a form, start a call to action with these action words:

- ✔ **Contact:** For example, *Contact us on our Web site.*
- ✔ **Respond:** For example, *Respond to our customer survey.*
- ✔ **Comment:** For example, *Comment on this article.*
- ✔ **Reply:** For example, *Reply with your preferences.*

Visit your Web site

Using a call to action to drive traffic to your Web site is useful when your main offer and call to action exist on your Web site. For example, your e-mail might contain a short summary of a larger body of text to entice your audience to read the entire article on your Web site. When your audience clicks through to read, your main offer and call to action appear next to the article on the Web site. You can read more about optimizing your Web site in Chapter 13.

To write a strong call to action when you want your readers to check out your Web site, try these action words:

- ✔ **Visit:** For example, *Visit our amazing online learning center.*
- ✔ **View:** For example, *View the entire article on our Web site.*
- ✔ **Go:** For example, *Go to our home page and click on Join Now.*
- ✔ **Navigate:** For example, *Navigate to the account login page to enroll.*

Visit a physical location

Driving traffic to your store or office is useful when you have a product or service that must be seen in person to appreciate. Here are some tips for prompting your audience to visit a physical location:

- ✔ Include important directions with your call to action, such as driving directions and parking information. You might also want to include a photograph of your storefront or a landmark if your building is difficult to see from the road, as shown in Figure 10-8.
- ✔ Ask your audience to bring a copy of the e-mail when they visit so you can track how many attendees came from your e-mails.
- ✔ Ask your audience to forward your e-mail to a friend or colleague if they are unable to visit in the near future.

Figure 10-8: Including directions along with visual aids helps your audience avoid confusion.

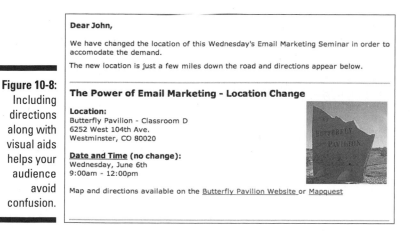

Dear John,

We have changed the location of this Wednesday's Email Marketing Seminar in order to accomodate the demand.

The new location is just a few miles down the road and directions appear below.

The Power of Email Marketing - Location Change

Location:
Butterfly Pavilion - Classroom D
6252 West 104th Ave.
Westminster, CO 80020

Date and Time (no change):
Wednesday, June 6th
9:00am - 12:00pm

Map and directions available on the Butterfly Pavilion Website or Mapquest

When you want your readers to come to you, try these action words to create a strong call to action:

- ✔ **Drive:** For example, *Drive down this weekend and see the clarity for yourself.*
- ✔ **Park:** For example, *Park for free behind the building when you visit during the week.*
- ✔ **Visit:** For example, *Visit with our friendly staff before the end of the month.*
- ✔ **Attend:** For example, *Attend Saturday's entertaining live event.*
- ✔ **Go:** For example, *Go tonight for free admission.*
- ✔ **Reserve:** For example, *Reserve your seat with our speedy online system.*

Request information

If your sales cycle involves multiple steps and lots of consideration on the part of your audience, calling your audience to request information helps you to deliver in-depth information to only the most interested prospects. Here are some tips for prompting your audience to request information:

- ✔ **If your in-depth information is available online:** Link your audience to the exact page where the information appears on your Web site instead of linking your audience to your home page, expecting them to click around.
- ✔ **If you don't have a Web site or you can't keep your Web site up to date with the information you want your audience to have:** Ask your audience to e-mail their request so you can reply with the information attached.
- ✔ **If your information must be delivered by postal mail:** Ask your audience to phone in their request or fill out a form with their mailing address and phone number so you can follow up personally and make sure they received the information.

You can write a strong call to action when you want your readers to request information with these words:

- ✔ **Download:** For example, *Download the facts in our PDF brochure.*
- ✔ **Request:** For example, *Request our free informative video.*
- ✔ **Learn:** For example, *Learn more at our next live seminar.*
- ✔ **E-Mail:** For example, *E-mail us with your questions.*

Register for an event

Calling your audience to register for an event (see Figure 10-9) is useful when you need to know how many people will attend an event or when you're selling tickets to an event.

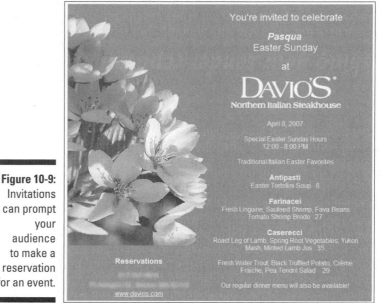

You're invited to celebrate

Pasqua
Easter Sunday

at

DAVIO'S
Northern Italian Steakhouse

April 8, 2007

Special Easter Sunday Hours
12:00 - 8:00 PM

Traditional Italian Easter Favorites

Antipasti
Easter Tortelini Soup 8

Farinacei
Fresh Linguine, Sautéed Shrimp, Fava Beans
Tomato Shrimp Brodo 27

Caserecci
Roast Leg of Lamb, Spring Root Vegetables, Yukon
Mash, Minted Lamb Jus 35

Fresh Water Trout, Black Truffled Potato, Crème
Fraiche, Pea Tendril Salad 29

Our regular dinner menu will also be available!

Reservations

www.davios.com

Figure 10-9:
Invitations
can prompt
your
audience
to make a
reservation
for an event.

Courtesy of Davio's Northern Italian Steakhouse

Here are some tips for prompting your audience to register for an event:

✔ **Give clear registration details.** Because event registration is often a multistep process, make sure that your calls to action clearly describe your registration process. Linking your audience to lengthy registration information instead of including all your registration information in the body of your e-mail is a good way to keep your event registration e-mails concise.

✔ **Confirm attendance.** If your event is free or if you can't charge your guests until they arrive at the event, make sure you follow up with your expected attendees before the event to make sure they still plan on attending.

When creating a call to action for readers to register for an event, try these action words:

✔ **Register:** For example, *Register online or by phone to ensure priority seating.*

✔ **Reserve:** For example, *Reserve your seats today and save 10%.*

✔ **Sign up:** For example, *Sign up at our tradeshow booth after the seminar.*

✔ **RSVP:** For example, *RSVP before Friday.*

Make an appointment

Appointments are useful when your services are rendered in person or when your sales require a sales presentation. Making appointments via e-mail can be frustrating because hashing out a meeting time by sending and replying to multiple e-mails can take a lot more time than a quick phone conversation.

If your e-mail prompts your audience to make an appointment, ask them to phone you to schedule a time or use a Web site form that synchronizes with your appointment calendar so your prospect can search for an opening without getting bogged down in a lengthy e-mail conversation.

To encourage readers to make an appointment, use one of these action words in your call to action:

- **Schedule:** For example, *Schedule a 15-minute appointment by phone.*
- **Arrange:** For example, *Arrange a quick personal consultation.*
- **Meet:** For example, *Meet with one of our professional team members.*
- **Set up:** For example, *Set up a convenient meeting time.*

Phone you

Your audience's computer is probably within reach of their phone, so phoning your business in response to your call to action is almost as easy as clicking a few links. In fact, if your e-mail finds its way to someone's mobile phone, phoning your business *is* as easy as clicking a link because most mobile phones allow the user to click a phone number on their device to automatically dial the number. Here are some tips for prompting your audience to phone you:

- **Tell your audience what to say when they call.**

  For example, if they need to speak to a specific person to place an order, tell them to ask for that person when they call.

- **Use bold text when you include your phone number.**

  Using bold helps your number stand out from the rest of your text.

- **Ask your audience to leave a message if they can't reach you the first time.**

  You can handle your calls in the order they are received.

- **Give your audience directions for side-stepping calling phone trees if your business uses one.**

  For example, your call to action might read, `Call 555-1234 and press 23 for a sales representative.`

These action words make a good call to action when you want your readers to phone you:

✔ **Call:** For example, *Call (number) after 3pm for the fastest response.*

✔ **Phone:** For example, *Phone us toll free now at (number).*

✔ **Dial:** For example, *Dial (number) to talk to our experts immediately.*

✔ **Ring:** For example, *Ring our informative helpdesk as soon as you can.*

Combining multiple calls to action

Your e-mail list probably consists of prospects and customers at different stages of the buying cycle with slightly different interests, so a portion of your audience will never be ready to immediately respond to every call to action. Even if everyone on your e-mail list is ready for action, your calls to action are sometimes made more visible by combining multiple calls to action.

Using multiple calls to action can give your audience more than one choice for responding to your e-mail content and gives more visibility to each of your calls to action. The following three call-to-action combinations allow you to capture responses from a larger percentage of your audience:

✔ **Options call:** An *options call* gives your audience three options for responding by choosing from a list of three consecutive options, each requiring less of a commitment than the previous option. For example, an offer to purchase a new mountain bike might include the following options call, as shown in Figure 10-10:

  • *Order this unique bike online today to ensure your color preference.*

  • *Read more about this unique bike on our Web site now.*

  • *Share your mailing address so we can mail you a brochure.*

Figure 10-10: The options call gives your audience more than one choice for taking action.

GIANT YUKON - $550

When you're ready to hit the trails, the Yukon's light ALUXX aluminum frame, RockShox suspension fork and Hayes mechanical disc brakes respond with confidence. The perfect hardtail for your next mountain bike adventure.

FRAME TECHNOLOGY
Giant's ALUXX aluminum-framed Yukon features disc-brake capability and geometry optimized for 100mm of front-end suspension travel to tame your first singletrack adventures.

FEATURES
• RockShox Dart 1, 100mm suspension fork
• Shimano Alivio trigger shifting, Shimano Deore rear derailleur
• Hayes MX-4 mechanical disc brakes
• WTB Dual Duty XC rim/Formula disc hub wheelset

- Order this unique bike online today to ensure your color preference
- Read More about this bike on our website
- Share your mailing address so we can send you a brochure

✔ **Echo call:** An *echo call* gives a single call to action more visibility by repeating the same call to action in three places in your e-mail. Repetition reinforces the call to action and helps your audience to commit the call to action to memory as they scan through your e-mail's content. For example, an offer to design a new Web site for someone might include the following echo call:

- The call to action at the end of the e-mail's opening paragraph reads, *Take the Web site quiz below and then call for a free Web site checkup.*

- The call to action immediately following the quiz reads, *Call now for a free Web site checkup.*

- The call to action at the end of the e-mail's closing paragraph reads, *Thanks for reading. Don't forget to call for your free website checkup.*

✔ **Variable call:** A *variable call* allows the same call to action to address multiple interests by rewriting the same call to action with three different interests in mind. For example, an e-mail featuring information about ski vacations could include

- An article about the benefits of ski rental with a call to action that reads, *Free ski rental when you book your vacation online before Friday.*

- An article about the current snow conditions to target with a call to action that reads, *Book your vacation online before Friday to take advantage of current snowfall conditions.*

- An article about worry-free ski vacations with a call to action that reads, *Book your vacation using our concierge service for a worry-free experience.*

If your call to action requires multiple steps, try one of these:

✔ *Reply now and request our quick step-by-step guide.*

✔ *Proceed to step one now using this link.*

✔ *Download our easy-to-use action guide in a flash.*

✔ *View our incredible online video instead of watching TV tonight.*

Giving Your E-Mail Content Inherent Value

E-mails containing valuable information based on your knowledge and experience are generally more effective over long periods of time than e-mails that repeatedly contain only offers. Even when your offers are compelling, people aren't always ready to take action right away.

The longer your sales cycle and average time between repeat purchases, the more you need to include inherently valuable content in your e-mails to keep your audience subscribed and interested. Figure 10-11 shows an e-mail that contains an offer with a quick tip section included as inherently valuable content to enhance the overall value of the e-mail.

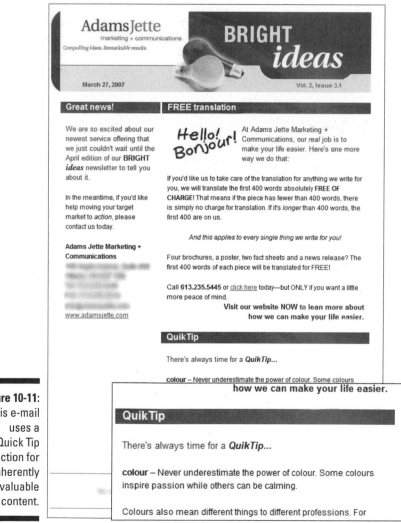

Figure 10-11: This e-mail uses a Quick Tip section for inherently valuable content.

Courtesy of Adams Jette Marketing & Communications

Inherently valuable content is most valuable when your content is relevant to your audience's stage in the buying cycle and targeted to your audience's interests. Survey your customers before you start creating inherently valuable content to make sure your content is appreciated. You can find out how to survey your customers in Chapter 13.

The following sections detail how you can create inherently valuable content or combine it with various related offers.

Creating content to inform your audience

When the main objective of your e-mail is to deliver information, you might find yourself looking for facts, data, and expert opinions to help you make your case and add an element of authority to your information. Here are some ideas and sources for creating informative content to include in your e-mails:

- **Be an aggregator.** Sometimes the best way to tell your story is to let someone else tell it. Information abounds on the Internet, and the chances that your audience is going to find exactly what you want them to read are relatively low. Aggregating information from the Internet is a great way to generate content and inform your audience with the information you want them to see.

  Make sure you have permission to include excerpts of other people's online information in your e-mails before you include them. Also, ask whether you can post the content on your Web site with a link to the outside source so that people who click links in your e-mail aren't sent to someone else's Web site.

- **Have an opinion.** If you don't have time to search for outside content and ask for permission in order to aggregate information, you can save yourself and your audience a lot of time by summarizing outside information for your audience. For example, a fashion designer who reads a lot of fashion magazines could create an e-mail that summarizes the two most stylish ways to tie a scarf so that the audience doesn't have to read all the scarf-tying articles in all the fashion magazines.

- **Be an expert interviewer.** If you find yourself running out of opinions, you can usually find someone with expert information and advice for your audience. Instead of borrowing content, ask someone whether you can interview him about their expertise and share it with your audience. Interviews can also be broken up into themes or individual questions and included in a series of e-mails.

- **Find a storyteller.** People love to tell stories, and some of them can help you to inform your audience. Start by asking your current customers to tell you stories about their experiences with your business and your products or services.

Adding tips and advice

If your products or services require special knowledge for customers to use them, or if your audience needs a trusted opinion to buy your products in the first place, including tips and advice in your e-mails can reinforce your expertise.

Here are some ideas for including tips and advice in your e-mails:

- **Start a tips and advice e-mail newsletter where the bulk of your content is informative.**

  For example, a gardening center might send an e-mail newsletter with tips for keeping gardens alive with less effort and advice on plants that thrive with little or no attention. The gardening newsletter could include related offers for plants mentioned in the newsletter, or separate offers could be sent after their audience has enough information to engage in the buying cycle.

- **Include one tip in each promotional e-mail you send with a link to additional tips on your Web site.**

  For example, a shoe store could include the location of a secret hiking trail in every e-mail with a link to an archive of hiking trails featured in the past. If you include single tips in your e-mails, make sure that your Web site's tips page includes related offers.

- **Share your opinion.**

  If you and your audience have the same beliefs, sharing your personal opinion can strengthen your customer relationships. For example, a store that sells recycled products might have a customer base that is more likely to be concerned about the environment. Such a customer base might be more loyal to a company that includes opinions concerning recycling issues along with offers to purchase recycled products.

- **Share another opinion.**

  If your audience doesn't perceive you as an expert in your field, find an expert who is willing to share an opinion. You can ask permission to include opinions in your e-mails or interview an opinionated expert and include the highlights of the interview in your e-mail.

- **Dedicate a section of your e-mail newsletter to answering customer questions.**

  For example, a Web site designer could answer a different customer question related to search engine optimization in every e-mail.

Providing instructions and directions

If your products or services require your customers to follow detailed instructions, include information that gives your audience timesaving shortcuts. For example, an e-mail promotion from an online auction might include steps for setting up account options. Here are some ways you can include instructions and directions in your e-mails:

✔ **Ask your customers to submit creative shortcuts.**

You can then feature the shortcuts in your e-mails.

✔ **If your directions involve several detailed steps, include one step with details in each e-mail.**

For example, a hobby store could include instructions for building a great model airplane beginning with choosing a model and ending with painting and displaying the model.

✔ **Include instructions that are valuable for reference and ask your audience to save them in their e-mail inbox.**

For example, a promotion for a product that includes a one-year warranty could include return and refund instructions along with instructions for saving the information in case there is a problem with a recent or future purchase.

Putting in entertaining content

Some audiences value e-mail content that gives them a good laugh or diverts their attention with an interesting story. If your products or services are related to entertaining content and your audience values diversion, the following examples of entertaining content might be appropriate:

✔ **Retell the stories you hear from your customers that relate to using your products and services.**

For example, a business that sells boats might include interesting stories about customers who live on the ocean or use boats to help people in the community.

If you include such stories, make sure you have permission from your customers before you send them to your list.

✔ **Include links to online videos that are related to your products or services.**

For example, a guitar store might include a link to a video showing a different guitar hero who plays the guitars that the store sells.

Like with any link to content you don't own, make sure you have permission to include the link, and also make sure that the content you're linking is legally obtained.

✔ **Write your own stories about your experiences or knowledge relating to your products or services.**

For example, the owner of a restaurant might include stories about her trips to the French vineyards that inspire the wines featured in the restaurant.

Including facts and research

If you sell products or services that are enhanced by helpful facts and research, you can include them in your e-mails in order to add value to related offers. Here are a few possibilities:

✔ **Conduct your own research and publish your findings in your e-mails.**

For example, a men's clothing store could conduct a poll and find out how many women think it's fashionable for men to wear pink shirts. The results of the poll could be included along with a pink shirt sale if the results support wearing pink shirts — or perhaps blue shirts if the results indicate that pink is out of favor.

✔ **Include facts and research though external sources.**

Facts and research abound on the Internet, and the people who publish them are usually willing to share their findings with proper attribution to the source. If you locate facts and research that interest your audience, ask the source whether you can include them in your e-mails.

Mixing and Matching Value and Relevance

After you determine which types of value make sense for your e-mail strategy, experiment with different combinations of valuable content to find the right match for your audience. Sometimes, mixing various percentages of each type of value in a single e-mail is appropriate, but sending valuable e-mail offers by themselves in rotation with inherently valuable content is sometimes more effective.

Keeping content relevant to your audience is also important when you mix different types of value. Sometimes, even valuable e-mails become irrelevant to the same audience because people become accustomed to your e-mails and begin to take your valuable content for granted.

Watching your open rates and click rates can help determine whether your content is relevant and valuable after you send each e-mail, but sending too many e-mails before you determine whether your e-mail content is valuable and relevant could cause you to lose subscribers before fine-tuning your strategy.

The following sections help you mix valuable content and keep your content relevant before you send your first e-mail and while you continue to experiment with mixing and matching value.

Combining different types of value

Here are the three basic ways to mix inherently valuable content with valuable offers:

- Create a valuable offer and include inherently valuable content in the same e-mail.
- Create inherently valuable content and include one or more valuable offers in the same e-mail.
- Create and send your inherently valuable content and valuable offers in separate e-mails in rotation with each other.

Deciding whether to mix different types of value in your e-mails or send them separately is a matter of determining

- **What your audience wants:** For example, a discount store that sends e-mail coupons along with lots of tips and advice might be better off sending the coupons by themselves if the audience is interested only in money-saving offers.

  Survey your audience members and ask them what they value. I cover surveys in more detail in Chapter 13.

- **What e-mail format you send:** For example, most people expect an e-mail newsletter to contain information that is inherently valuable instead of offers and incentives only. I cover e-mail formats in more detail in Chapter 6.

- **What you are asking your audience to do in response to your e-mail:** For example, if your audience generally needs to read a lot of information before making a purchase decision, you might want to send plenty of informative content that is inherently valuable before you send valuable offers.

- **How frequently you send e-mails in relation to your buying cycle:** For example, if you send monthly e-mails that contain an offer to buy a product most people buy only once per year, include inherently valuable content along with your offers to keep recent purchasers interested during the year-long buying cycle. I cover e-mail frequency in more detail in Chapter 3.

If you decide to include both types of value in a single e-mail, keep your e-mail focused on one main objective, or your audience might not clearly determine the purpose of your e-mail. Starting with an 80/20 rule is a good way to keep your content focused on your main objective until you determine the perfect amount of each type of value to include in each e-mail. If the main objective of your e-mail is to cause someone to

- ✔ **Take advantage of your offer:** Your offer should make up 80 percent or more of your content, and your inherently valuable content should make up the remaining 20 percent or less.

- ✔ **Internalize your message while still giving them an opportunity to take advantage of an offer:** Your e-mail's inherently valuable content should make up 80 percent or more of your content, and your offer should make up the remaining 20 percent or less, as shown in Figure 10-12.

If you decide to send valuable offers in rotation with inherently valuable content, you can use a similar 80/20 rule. If your audience

- ✔ **Needs a lot of information to make a buying decision or if you need to build a lot of trust before someone will buy from you:** Eighty percent or more of your e-mails should be inherently valuable, and 20% or less of your e-mails should contain only offers.

- ✔ **Responds to valuable offers without a lot of supporting information or if it's easy to build trust with your audience:** Eighty percent or more of your e-mails should contain offers only, and 20% or less of your e-mails should be inherently valuable.

Sending different percentages of valuable content in rotation can be done systematically in a number of ways. For example, a business that sends e-mail to only one list might send one valuable offer after every four inherently valuable e-mails. Another business might send 20 inherently valuable e-mails in a row to a list of prospects and then move those subscribers to a new list where they receive 5 valuable offers in a row.

Matching relevance to value

Adding a measure of relevance to your e-mail content helps ensure that your content is valuable every time your audience receives your e-mail. Here are some tips for adding relevance to value when you create your e-mail content:

- ✔ **Keep your e-mail content targeted to your audience's interests.**

    Because interests change, stay in tune with your audience and keep track of its interests. If you notice your e-mail open rates slipping, consider employing new topics or changing the theme of your e-mail value plan. You might also need to sort and organize your e-mail lists by interest periodically to continue refining and targeting your e-mail content.

✔ **Make sure your e-mails are on time.**

E-mails are more relevant when they refer to current events. Include content that relates to recent, impending, or timely events.

✔ **Give your e-mails multiple uses.**

Valuable content is more effective when you give your audience more than one way to use the content. For example, an interesting story with facts and research could be positioned as entertainment initially while also including a few tips for sharing the story to impress colleagues at work.

This offer takes up only
20% of the content.

Figure 10-12:
Balancing valuable content with offers helps keep your e-mail content focused on the main objective.

Courtesy of A to Z Sports and www.pitchsmarter.com

Finding Help with Content Creation

You can turn to many sources for help creating interesting and relevant content for your e-mails. Marketing companies and content providers can help you when

- ✔ You don't have time to create e-mail content.
- ✔ Your content isn't giving you the results you want.
- ✔ You don't like creating your own content for your e-mails.

Marketing companies and content providers often have services that range from small amounts of copywriting to fully outsourced, turnkey solutions. Most companies that provide content creation for e-mail marketing provide one or more of the following services:

- ✔ Copywriting, using themes and ideas you provide
- ✔ Formatting content that you provide into HTML for e-mail
- ✔ Custom e-mail template design
- ✔ Advice and consulting
- ✔ Image creation, design, and licensing
- ✔ Matching your Web site content to your e-mails
- ✔ Archiving e-mail campaigns to your Web site

For a list of marketing companies and content providers that can help you with e-mail content design and creation, go to

www.emailtrainer.com

Part IV

Delivering and Tracking Your E-Mails

The 5th Wave   By Rich Tennant

"They were selling contraband online. We broke through the door just as they were trying to flush the hard drive down the toilet."

In this part . . .

Making adjustments to improve your marketing strategy is easy with e-mail because you can track the interaction between your e-mail and the person you send your e-mail to. Finding out what happens after you send an e-mail and taking appropriate action can significantly improve your results and allow you to realize huge returns on investment (ROI).

Chapter 11 explains the trackable elements of an e-mail campaign and gives you insight into the meaning of e-mail statistics. The chapter also includes examples of many benchmark statistics against which you can measure your e-mail campaign results.

Chapter 12 tells you why e-mail bounces, how e-mail is filtered, and how e-mails get blocked. Here are tips for getting more e-mail delivered and nontechnical explanations of blocking and filtering technologies that aren't so easy to sidestep.

Chapter 13 gives you tips for using e-mail tracking and analysis to convert more of your e-mail list subscribers into customers. You find tips for improving your e-mail links and your Web site landing pages as well as tips for converting customers offline. I also offer tips for deepening your customer relationships and expanding your online presence with e-mail surveys and other marketing technology mediums.

Chapter 11

Tracking Your E-Mail Campaign Results

. . . .

In This Chapter

▶ Navigating e-mail tracking reports

▶ Understanding e-mail statistics

▶ Tracking other responses

. . . .

*O*ne of the most practical and valuable features of using e-mail to market your business is using e-mail tracking reports to find out what your audience is doing with your e-mails after you send them.

Most E-Mail Service Providers (ESPs) can track your e-mails and allow you to view the results in an e-mail tracking report. In this chapter, you find out how to make sense of the data in an e-mail tracking report as well as other creative ways to track responses not captured in a tracking report.

Understanding Basic E-Mail Tracking Data

You have to be an advanced HTML and database programmer to track e-mails on your own, so I recommend using an ESP to track your e-mails for you. ESPs automatically add special tracking code to the links you include in your e-mails. The tracking code is unique to each individual on your e-mail list and tied to each e-mail campaign. ESPs also have programs that automatically read the code from other e-mail servers when they return undeliverable e-mail so you don't have to do the hard work to determine why a particular e-mail wasn't delivered.

E-mail tracking reports are analytical summaries of the results of a given e-mail campaign that can tell you

- ✔ Which e-mails bounced
- ✔ Why they bounced
- ✔ Who opened your e-mails
- ✔ What links they clicked
- ✔ Who unsubscribed from your e-mails
- ✔ Who forwarded your e-mails

Figure 11-1 shows a summary e-mail tracking report, generated by an ESP, that allows access to the report details when the user clicks the summary statistics. Making sense of the data in an e-mail tracking report takes a little getting used to because the technology involved in the e-mail tracking process causes the data to take on a slightly different meaning than you might expect.

This section explains the origins of the data found in a typical e-mail tracking report so you can interpret the true meaning of each number being reported. This section also includes references to current industry statistics so you can decide whether your data warrants any action to refine your strategy.

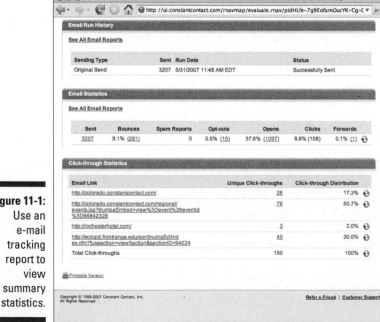

Figure 11-1:
Use an e-mail tracking report to view summary statistics.

Courtesy of Constant Contact

Calculating your bounce rate

Bounce rate is the number of e-mails that were returned as undeliverable expressed as a percentage of total e-mails sent. ESPs calculate bounce rate by taking the total number of bounced e-mails and dividing by the number of e-mails sent. You can calculate your own bounce rate as follows:

1. **Divide the total number of e-mails that bounced by the total number of e-mails sent to get the total number of bounces per e-mail.**

   For example, if you send 100 e-mails and 20 of them bounce, you bounced 0.2 e-mails for every e-mail sent.

2. **Take your bounces per e-mail and multiply by 100 to get your bounce rate as a percentage.**

   For example, the bounce rate for 0.2 bounces per e-mail is 20%.

According to a study conducted by ReturnPath (www.returnpath.com), the average bounce rate for commercial e-mails is 19.2%, as shown in Figure 11-2.

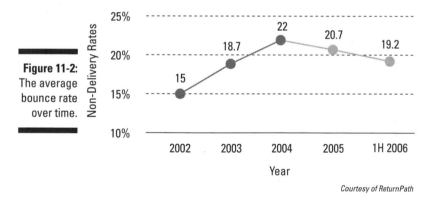

Figure 11-2: The average bounce rate over time.

Courtesy of ReturnPath

Calculating your non-bounce total

Non-bounce total is the number of e-mails that were not bounced and therefore assumed delivered. ESPs calculate non-bounce total by subtracting your total number of bounced e-mails from the total number of e-mails sent. You can calculate your own non-bounce total as follows.

Total e-mails sent
−Total bounced e-mails

Non-bounce total

For example, if you send 100 e-mails and 20 of them bounce, your non-bounce total is 80.

Non-bounce total is sometimes expressed as a percentage, but the non-bounce total is more useful as a real number because e-mail open rates are actually based on your non-bounce total instead of the total number of e-mails sent. (I explain open rate in more detail in the following section, "Calculating your open rate.")

Your non-bounce total isn't the same as the total number of e-mails delivered. Some e-mails aren't reported as bounced because software on the user's computer or a portable device bounced it — not an e-mail server — and some e-mail servers falsely deliver your e-mail to a junk folder that users can't access. (For more information about e-mail filters and other non-delivery issues, read Chapter 12.)

Even though you can't be sure whether your non-bounced e-mails are being delivered, you can assume that your non-bounced e-mails are reaching your audience until you have good reasons to believe otherwise. Because non-bounce total is basically the converse of the bounce rate, the average non-bounce rate is approximately 80.8%, according to ReturnPath.

Calculating your open rate

Open rate is the number of specific interactions with an e-mail server after the e-mail is sent expressed as a percentage of non-bounce total. Your e-mail isn't counted as an open until one of the following interactions occurs:

- ✔ The recipient enables the images in your e-mail to display either in the preview pane or in a full view of the e-mail.
- ✔ The recipient clicks a link in the e-mail.

ESPs calculate open rate by taking the number of tracked opens and dividing it by your non-bounce total. Here are the steps involved in calculating open rate:

1. **Take the total number of tracked opens and divide it by the non-bounce total to get opens per e-mail assumed delivered.**

   For example, if 80 of 100 e-mails you send don't bounce, and 20 of them are tracked as opened, you received 0.25 opens per e-mail.

2. **Multiply the number of opens per e-mail by 100 to get the open rate as a percentage.**

   For example, the open rate for 0.25 opens per e-mail is 25%.

You calculate your open rate by using your non-bounce rate instead of the total e-mails sent because your open rate indicates the strength of your e-mail's identity and content apart from the strength of your deliverability. Because e-mails that aren't delivered can't possibly be opened, they are excluded from your open rate calculation.

According to a 2007 study by Bronto Software (www.bronto.com), the average, tracked open rate for all industries is 23.6%, as shown in Figure 11-3. The average open rate depends highly on industry, as you can see in the figure.

Figure 11-3:
The average open rate depends on the industry.

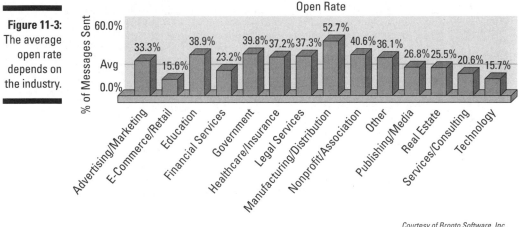

Courtesy of Bronto Software, Inc.

Because the default setting on an increasing number of e-mail programs is to block images until the user clicks to enable them, some people scan through e-mails without enabling images at all. In such cases, the true number of e-mails that your audience views is probably higher than your e-mail tracking report's open rate indicates.

Plain, text-only e-mails without any links or images are not trackable unless your audience replies to them directly. Make sure your ESP inserts a blank image in every e-mail to ensure that open tracking is possible.

Calculating your click-through rate

Your *click-through rate* is the number of unique individuals who click on one or more links in your e-mail expressed as a percentage of total tracked opens. ESPs calculate click-through rate by taking the total number of unique individuals who click a link in your e-mail and dividing by the total number of tracked opens. Here are the steps for calculating click-through rate:

1. **Take the total number of clicks on all links in the e-mail and subtract any multiple clicks attributed to a single subscriber to get total unique clicks.**

   For example, if your e-mail contains two links and ten people clicked both links or clicked the same link multiple times, subtract ten from the total number of clicks.

2. **Take the total number of tracked opens and divide by the total number of unique clicks to get clicks per open.**

   For example, if 30 of your e-mails track as opened and you receive 3 unique clicks, your e-mail received 0.1 clicks per open.

3. **Multiply clicks per open by 100 to get click-through rate.**

   For example, the click-through rate for 0.1 clicks per open is 10%.

Because clicking a link in your e-mail causes the e-mail to track as an open, your click-through rate never exceeds the number of tracked opens. Your e-mail might receive more total clicks than tracked opens, however, because some people click a single link multiple times or click more than one link in your e-mail.

Even if your audience clicks multiple times, your click-through rate represents only the number of unique individuals who click one or more links. Most e-mail tracking reports also allow you to view the total number of clicks attributed to each unique individual as well as showing you exactly which links are clicked.

Average click-through rates vary widely by industry. Figure 11-4 shows an ESP report that includes comparative tracking information along with e-mail tracking reports to compare results with ongoing averages.

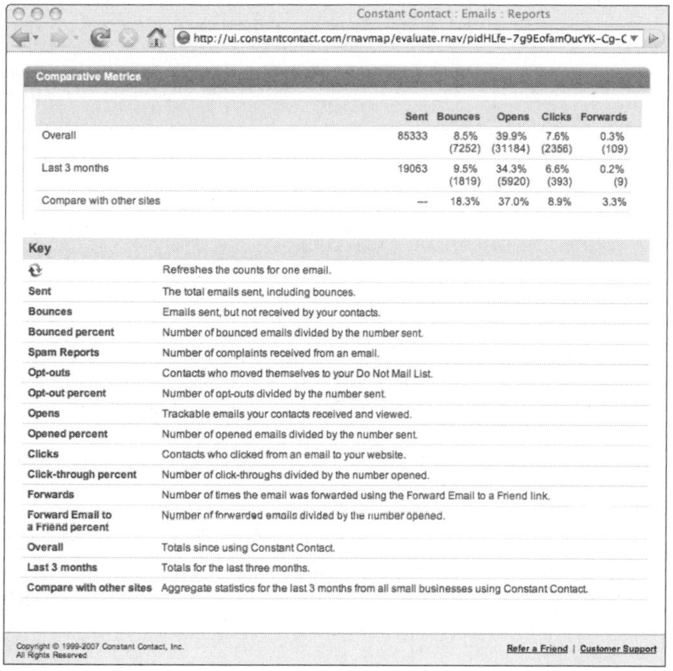

Figure 11-4: Compare click-through rates with larger groups to gauge your results.

Courtesy of Constant Contact

Tracking Non-Click Responses

Some e-mail marketing objectives can't be accomplished through a click. For example, if your goal is to increase the number of phone calls to your sales representatives to increase appointments — and, ultimately, closed sales — your e-mail requires an approach to tracking and evaluation apart from click-through reports and Web analytics.

This section explains how you can track non-click responses and calculate return on investment (ROI) so you can measure your effectiveness in converting customers outside the realm of your Web site. (You can read more about creating non-click offers in Chapter 12.)

Tracking in-store purchases

If the goal of your e-mail is to generate purchases in a brick-and-mortar store, you need to find a way to track the foot traffic that results from your e-mails and also compare any increase in foot traffic against any increase in sales.

Here are some ideas for tracking your in-store visitors and linking them to your e-mail marketing efforts:

- ✔ **Ask your e-mail audience to print the e-mail and bring it with them when they visit your store.**

  Count the number of e-mails you receive over a fair test of time such as one month or over the course of a series of e-mail campaigns.

- ✔ **Ask your e-mail audience to mention your e-mail when they visit your store.**

  Offer your audience a gift so they have an incentive to mention your e-mail — even if they don't walk up to the counter to buy something. Count the number of gifts you give away to determine how many visitors result from your e-mails.

- ✔ **Have your sales staff ask all store visitors whether they received your e-mail.**

  Count the number of visitors who say that they remember receiving it.

- ✔ **Promote a specific product or service and a specific offer in your e-mail.**

  Count everyone who visits the store in search of the offer. Figure 11-5 shows an offer that appears only in the e-mail so that all inquiries can be attributed to the e-mail.

Tracking phone calls

If the goal of your e-mail is to increase the number of inbound phone calls, your e-mail needs to include a method for tracking which phone calls result from your e-mail. Here are some ideas for tracking your phone calls and linking them to your e-mail marketing efforts:

- ✔ **Ask your e-mail audience to mention your e-mail when calling.**

  Count the number of callers who mention it.

- ✔ **Set up a special phone number to accept calls from your e-mails and publish that number in your e-mails.**

  Every time a call comes to that number, you can count the call as coming from one of your e-mails.

- ✔ **Promote a specific product or service in your e-mail.**

  Count each call related to that product or service.

Figure 11-5:
Mentioning a special in your e-mail (and nowhere else) allows you to track inquiries.

Courtesy of McDonald Garden Center

✔ **Ask your e-mail audience to request a specific person in your organization when they call, as shown in Figure 11-6.**

Count the increase in the number of calls that person receives.

✔ **Tell your sales staff to ask callers how they found your phone number.**

Count every caller who references your e-mail.

Tracking event attendance

If the goal of your e-mail is to increase event attendance, your e-mail needs to include a method for tracking how many event attendees resulted from sending your e-mail. Here are some ideas for tracking your event attendance and linking attendance to your e-mail marketing efforts:

✔ **Ask your e-mail audience to bring your e-mail to the event.**

Count the number of attendees who bring the e-mail.

✔ **Ask your e-mail audience to mention your e-mail or include a code in the e-mail that gets them into the event.**

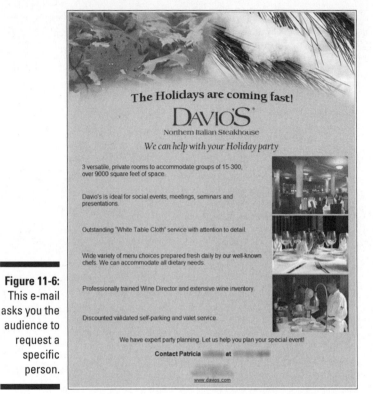

Figure 11-6:
This e-mail
asks you the
audience to
request a
specific
person.

Courtesy of Davio's Northern Italian Steakhouse

> Count the number of attendees who mention the e-mail or code.
>
> ✔ **Ask your e-mail audience to preregister by calling or replying to your e-mail.**
>
> Count the number of attendees who preregistered.

Tracking e-mail replies

Sometimes, asking people to reply to your e-mails is enough to meet your ultimate objectives. An ESP can't track a reply to your e-mail, but you receive an e-mail from your list subscriber with a Subject line that reveals the source of the reply. For example, say you send an e-mail with a Subject line that reads, `Last chance to register`. When someone replies to your e-mail, the Subject line reads, `RE: Last chance to register`.

Counting the number of replies you receive from your e-mails isn't particularly useful, but replies can be very useful when you track the qualitative information inherent in your replies. Here are two ideas for tracking replies and putting the information to good use:

✔ **Keep track of the nature of each reply.**

Record whether your reply contained a complaint, suggestion, or inquiry and then track the reply to its source. For example, if you receive enough replies from people who want to know your hours of operation, you might include a link to your normal business hours in your future e-mails or make the information easier to find on your Web site.

✔ **Keep track of your response to each reply and the result.**

For example, if your response to a complaint results in a resolution or an order fulfillment, make a note of the situation so you can address anyone with a similar complaint using your Web site, Help files, or blog. You can also share the information with everyone on your sales team so they can address future complaints successfully.

Simple event registration

Asking people to tell you in advance whether they're coming to your event is a great way to make room arrangements and prepare enough materials. However, asking people to fill out a long online registration form or take multiple steps to preregister before making a commitment might create a barrier to preregistration, especially if your event is free. Because you can track e-mail links to the clicker, you can create two links for each event and ask your audience to click one of them to indicate their intentions. For example, your two links might read, `I'd like to attend` and `No, thanks`.

After you create the links, you can point one link to a landing page that reads, `Thanks for` `confirming your attendance`, and you can point the other link to a landing page that reads, `Thanks for giving up your seat`.

Make sure that your landing page also has additional links, such as maps, directions, and other important event information. After you count the number of unique clicks on each link, you can plan for the appropriate number of visitors and send a follow up e-mail that delivers more event information and asks your preregistered guests to confirm their attendance or purchase their tickets.

Chapter 12

Maximizing E-Mail Deliverability

*T*hinking about the early days of postal mail delivery conjures up images of the Pony Express traveling long distances and risking their lives to get the mail delivered proudly in the name of the United States of America. While sticking a stamp on a letter or postcard and dropping it off at a U.S. Postal Service office doesn't necessarily ensure its delivery to someone's mailbox, mail carriers most often deliver your mail to a mailbox belonging to the addressee or return your mail to the mailbox specified in the return address with a clear reason for the failed delivery.

E-mail delivery isn't quite as trustworthy as the U.S. Postal Service because even e-mail sent to a correct e-mail address doesn't always reach the inbox, and returned e-mail doesn't always include unmistakable reasons for the failed delivery.

The good news is that the positives of e-mail marketing greatly outweigh the deliverability issues inherent to sending commercial e-mail. This chapter uncovers the various reasons why some e-mail fails to reach an inbox and then offers solutions for maximizing your e-mail delivery rates.

Managing Bounced and Blocked E-Mail

Sometimes, e-mail is simply returned to the sender either by the e-mail server or software application. You hear the terms *bounced* and *blocked* apply to returned e-mail somewhat interchangeably, but the two have some slight differences.

✔ **Bounced:** A *bounced e-mail* happens on a per e-mail basis when an e-mail is returned because of conditions that make a particular e-mail undeliverable.

✔ **Blocked:** A *blocked e-mail* happens on an all-inclusive basis when an e-mail is returned because of characteristics that make a particular type of e-mail unwanted.

E-mail is sometimes returned with code that indicates the reason for the block or bounce, and sometimes e-mail is returned with unintelligible code or no code at all. Figure 12-1 shows an example of an e-mail returned to the sender with bounce code.

If you use an E-Mail Service Provider (ESP), you don't have to read all the boring HTML. Most ESPs automatically file bounced and blocked e-mails into a bounce report. A *bounce report* shows the number of your e-mails that bounced and were blocked as well as the reason for the bounce or block response. Figure 12-2 shows a bounce report generated by an ESP. You can see the number of bounced e-mails by category as well as individual bounced e-mails and associated database records.

| Delete | Reply ▾ | Forward | ⬇ | ⬆ | Spam | Move ▾ | Print | More Actions ▾ | ⬜ |

failure notice   Compact Header ▾
"MAILER-DAEMON@n4.bullet.re4.yahoo.com" <MAILER-DAEMON@n4.I 📝 Add   To: email.company@yahoo.com

Sorry, we were unable to deliver your message to the following address.

<non.existentemailaddress@aol.com>:
Remote host said: 550 MAILBOX NOT FOUND [RCPT_TO]

— Below this line is a copy of the message.

Received: from [68.142.237.89] by n4.bullet.re4.yahoo.com with NNFMP; 06 Aug 2007 13:23:37 -0000
Received: from [66.196.101.133] by t5.bullet.re3.yahoo.com with NNFMP; 06 Aug 2007 13:23:37 -0000
Received: from [127.0.0.1] by rrr4.mail.re1.yahoo.com with NNFMP; 06 Aug 2007 13:23:37 -0000
X-Yahoo-Newman-Property: ymail-5
X-Yahoo-Newman-Id: 426070.74788.bm@rrr4.mail.re1.yahoo.com
Received: (qmail 59123 invoked by uid 60001); 6 Aug 2007 13:23:37 -0000
DomainKey-Signature: a=rsa-sha1; q=dns; c=nofws;
  s=s1024; d=yahoo.com;
  h=X-YMail-OSG:Received:X-Mailer:Date:From:Subject:To:MIME-Version:Content-Type:Message-ID;
  b=AEGQXhnXpgrUJHAFVhEciaaURB+fwYp/xnoiUvg15rOQhVDhxKxBMQHnKUH+1DC+fYJQ99aZRlhLEHHvHjWzCPmbqWQB6g17G/
X-YMail-OSG:
w.SLwY8VM1n8PljvJkLINg8aoKTxsR_BefGC5TOBSz6siV1McllFb1f8rJgQ0SAMcQHl4sxWwQ6s60ORafz3H93tvRQ9fN18eu5R
Received: from [71.229.220.106] by web57512.mail.re1.yahoo.com via HTTP; Mon, 06 Aug 2007 06:23:37 PDT
X-Mailer: YahooMailRC/651.41 YahooMailWebService/0.7.119
Date: Mon, 6 Aug 2007 06:23:37 -0700 (PDT)
From: John Arnold <email.company@yahoo.com>
Subject: is this your email address?
To: non.existentemailaddress@aol.com
MIME-Version: 1.0
Content-Type: multipart/alternative; boundary="0-189140787-1186406617=:58173"
Message-ID: <225327.58173.qm@web57512.mail.re1.yahoo.com>

--0-189140787-1186406617=:58173
Content-Type: text/plain; charset=us-ascii
Content-Transfer-Encoding: quoted-printable

Are you getting my emails?=0A=0A=0A=0A   =0A

◀ ▶

＋ 🗓 TODAY: 8/6   No events. Click the plus sign to add an event.

Figure 12-1:
Bounce
code can be
difficult to
interpret
without
the help
of an ESP.

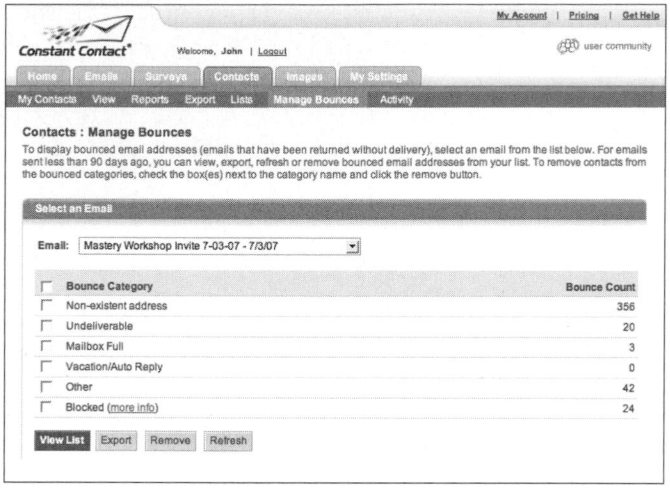

Figure 12-2: Use a summary bounce report to see the number of bounced e-mails by category.

Some bounced or blocked e-mail will never get delivered, but some bounced and blocked e-mail are temporary. This following sections explain how to take the appropriate action on each type of bounced and blocked e-mail in order to refine your e-mail list and get your e-mails delivered to more of your list subscribers.

Dealing with hard bounces

A _hard bounce_ is an e-mail that is returned because a permanent condition makes delivering the e-mail impossible. When your ESP's bounce report shows e-mails delivered to non-existent addresses, your e-mail can't be delivered to that address no matter what action you take. Non-existent e-mail addresses are either

✔ Misspelled (for example, _name@hotmai.1com_)

✔ Invalid (such as when your subscriber changes her e-mail address)

You can check your hard-bounce report for obviously misspelled e-mail addresses. However, most of the time, you can't tell whether an e-mail address is misspelled or invalid. In those cases, you need to obtain a new e-mail address. If your hard-bounce list is too large to contact each individual to obtain a new e-mail address, or if you don't have any alternative contact information for the subscribers, remove those e-mail addresses from your e-mail list.

Dealing with soft bounces

A *soft bounce* happens when the delivery of an e-mail is delayed temporarily. Soft bounces happen because of technical conditions inherent in the technology that makes e-mail delivery possible. Examples include

- ✔ A full mailbox
- ✔ A server that's temporarily down
- ✔ A software application that can't accept the e-mail

When an e-mail address bounces for a reason that is temporary in nature, try resending your e-mail later or simply wait until your next e-mail campaign to see whether the same address still bounces. If an e-mail address bounces repeatedly for temporary reasons, contact the subscriber for a more reliable e-mail address.

Keeping up with e-mail address changes

According to a study conducted by ReturnPath, more than 30 percent of your e-mail list addressees are likely to change their e-mail address each year. Because losing your entire e-mail list every three to four years isn't going to help improve your repeat business, you should periodically remind your list subscribers to update their e-mail addresses.

Because most people keep their old e-mail address active for a short period of time between changes, sending a subscription reminder every two to three months is a good way to ask your list subscribers to share their new e-mail address before their old e-mail address is completely deactivated. If you have a large e-mail list, make sure that your subscription reminder links your audience to a secure, online form where they can update their own information and save you from replacing your selling time with data entry. Here's an example of text you might use in your subscription reminder:

```
Subject Line: Subscription Reminder

Body: This e-mail is sent every other month to remind you that
you are subscribed to the ABC Company e-mail list. If your
contact information or interests should changed at any time,
please
select your interests (link to interests form) or update your
contact information (link to secure profile form) so we can
continue to send you valuable offers and information.
```

Reducing blocked e-mails

Blocked e-mails are sometimes temporary and sometimes permanent, depending on whether the server or software blocking the e-mail does so in response to the content of a single e-mail or the characteristics of a specific type of e-mail. The following sections show how you can keep from being blocked by someone on your e-mail list.

Responding to a challenge response system

A *challenge response system* is a software program that returns all unrecognized e-mail to the sender with instructions for getting the e-mail delivered that only a live person is capable of following, in order to verify that the sender is a real human being — not a computer generating e-mail addresses. Figure 12-3 shows an e-mail returned by a challenge response system.

Challenge responses are generated by third-party applications that integrate into e-mail applications. For example, someone who wants to eliminate computer-generated spam might purchase a challenge response application to verify all e-mails sent to his AOL e-mail address. If you send e-mail to someone with a challenge response system, the returned e-mail might ask you to click a link and enter specific characters in a form field or reply to the e-mail with a specific subject line. Following the instructions in the returned e-mail adds your server address or e-mail address to the subscriber's friends list or address book so that future e-mails are delivered without a challenge.

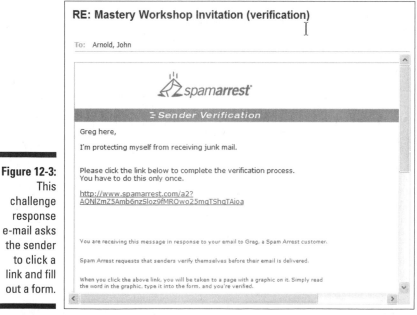

Figure 12-3: This challenge response e-mail asks the sender to click a link and fill out a form.

Courtesy of SpamArrest

Keeping your e-mail address or server off a block list

A *block list* (also known as a *blacklist*) is a database that contains the domain names and server addresses of suspected spammers. Block lists are maintained by Internet service providers (ISPs) and other companies that monitor spam complaints across the Internet. Server addresses and domain names are added to block lists based on the number of spam complaints logged by consumers.

If you send an e-mail that gets too many spam complaints, the server you use to send your e-mail might be added to one or more block lists. (You can read more about avoiding spam complaints in Chapter 3.)

Avoiding spam trap e-mail addresses

A *spam trap* is a false e-mail address that is placed on the Internet by a company with an interest in reducing spam. When spammers using Web crawlers to capture e-mail addresses to try to send an e-mail to the spam trap e-mail address, the sender's domain and server address are automatically added to the block list. (A *Web crawler* is a computer program that searches the Internet for specific types of content, such as lines of text that look like an e-mail address.) Many companies share their spam trap block lists. If you happen to send e-mail to a spam trap address, your deliverability could be doomed.

Here are some ways to avoid spam trap e-mail addresses:

✔ **Don't surf the Internet to obtain e-mail addresses.**

Besides risking your deliverability, this behavior is also illegal.

✔ **Don't send e-mail to a purchased list.**

Purchased lists are often collected without permission and can contain spam-trap addresses.

✔ **Send a welcome e-mail to every new list subscriber and immediately remove e-mail addresses that return your welcome e-mail.**

That way, you can weed out anyone who tries to maliciously join your e-mail list by using a known spam trap address.

Getting past e-mail firewalls

An *e-mail firewall* is a piece of hardware or a software application that's programmed to identify and block e-mails that appear untrustworthy. Firewalls can be customized and configured to block almost any e-mail element. For example, a system administrator at one company might configure a firewall to block e-mails with certain types of content, and another system administrator might configure a firewall to block e-mails from certain senders while ignoring the content altogether.

Because firewalls have so many variables, telling whether your e-mail is being blocked by a firewall is usually impossible. If you use an ESP that provides blocked e-mail addresses in its bounced report, however, you can at least find out which e-mail addresses are being blocked and then take action to try to get the e-mail delivered.

Changing your tactics to get e-mail delivered to a blocked address is difficult, but the following remedies might prove effective:

✔ **Ask your audience to add your e-mail address to their address book or contacts list when they sign up for your e-mail list.**

Some content-blocking systems allow e-mail to go through if the sender's e-mail address is in the recipient's address book.

In your welcome letter and subscription reminders, give your audience instructions for adding your e-mail address, as shown in Figure 12-4. This e-mail asks the reader to help ensure delivery by adding the sender's e-mail address to the reader's address book.

✔ **Obtain an alternative e-mail address from each of your blocked subscribers.**

Sometimes, half the battle with blocked e-mail is knowing that a particular e-mail address is being blocked. When your ESP's bounce report shows a particular blocked e-mail address, you can ask your subscriber to provide a different address.

✔ **If the blocked e-mail address is a work address, ask the IT expert at your subscriber's company to add your ESP's e-mail server address to the friends list on the company's e-mail server.**

A *friends list* (also known as a *white list*) is a database containing e-mail addresses from welcome senders. Some firewalls ignore their blocking instructions when the sender's e-mail address exists in the friends list.

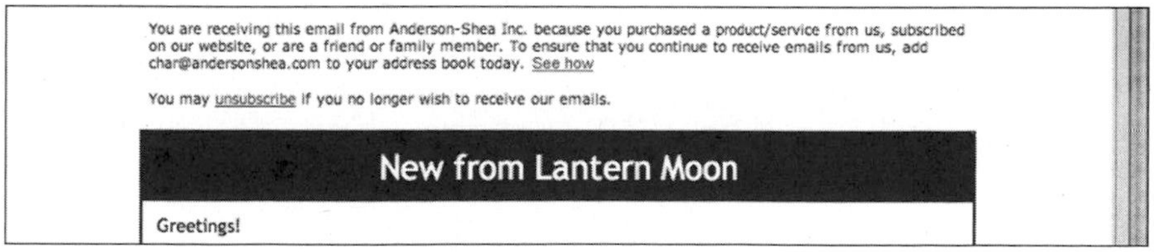

Figure 12-4:
Help ensure
delivery.

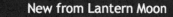

You are receiving this email from Anderson-Shea Inc. because you purchased a product/service from us, subscribed on our website, or are a friend or family member. To ensure that you continue to receive emails from us, add char@andersonshea.com to your address book today. See how

You may unsubscribe if you no longer wish to receive our emails.

New from Lantern Moon

Greetings!

Courtesy of Anderson-Shea, Inc.

Reducing Filtered E-Mail

An *e-mail filter* is a program that scans the content of your e-mail to identify whether your e-mail contains unwanted content. If your e-mail contains content that is identified as potentially unwanted, the program places the e-mail into a holding place (such as a junk folder) or tags the e-mail with a message to identify it as potentially unwanted.

Filters are different from programs that block and bounce e-mails because filters don't return the e-mail to the sender.

Sometimes an e-mail is filtered even though the recipient wants the e-mail. Desirable e-mail content that still gets filtered is a *false positive*. False positives are all too common because of the enormous amount of spam e-mail content that is similar in nature to legitimate e-mail content. Some e-mail filters result in more false positives than others because the people behind the filters get to decide what kinds of content are considered unwanted. For example, an e-mail that contains the word *drug* might be filtered by a systems administrator who believes that certain prescription drug advertisements are spam even if the word is being used by a bookstore to describe a book.

Unfortunately, you can't tell whether your e-mail is filtered unless the recipient notifies you that your e-mail landed in the junk folder or that your e-mail is being delivered with a filter tag. The following sections explain how you can get a higher percentage of your e-mail through the most common types of filters.

Establishing your sender reputation

Getting more e-mail delivered starts with sending your e-mail from a reputable e-mail server. According to a recent study conducted by ReturnPath (www.returnpath.com), 77 percent of e-mail delivery issues occur because of the sender's reputation, as shown in Figure 12-5. Most companies that provide e-mail delivery for their customers consider the reputation of the sender when filtering e-mail.

Figure 12-5:
Most companies consider the sender's reputation when filtering e-mail.

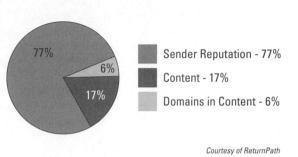

77%

6%

17%

■ Sender Reputation - 77%

■ Content - 17%

■ Domains in Content - 6%

Courtesy of ReturnPath

Because your own e-mail server isn't likely to have a reputation, delivering your mail through an ESP with a respectable and well-known reputation is one of the most important steps you can take to maximize your e-mail deliverability. Make sure you choose an ESP that can

- ✔ **Authenticate your e-mail:** *Authentication* allows e-mail servers to identify the sender of an e-mail. (I cover authentication later in this chapter.)

- ✔ **Eliminate customers with high spam complaints:** ESPs send e-mails from their own servers on behalf of their customers even though the e-mails appears to come from their customers. Because too many spam complaints might cause the ESP's servers to become block listed, I recommend associating with an ESP that takes action when one of its customers receives too many spam complaints. Reputable ESPs keep their overall complaint rates low — and your sender reputation as clean as possible.

- ✔ **Affirm the quality of their customer's e-mail lists:** Although ESPs can't guarantee or predetermine the quality of their customers' e-mail lists, reputable ESPs require customers to adhere to strict permission policies to caution their customers when attempting to use e-mail addresses that could generate a high number of complaints.

- ✔ **Confirm permission from their customer's list subscribers when necessary:** Some businesses, such as those in the financial industry, inherently receive a lot of spam complaints because their legitimate e-mail content looks similar to a lot of spam e-mails. Use an ESP that either has options for such businesses or has a policy to recommend such businesses to another service that specializes in working with e-mail senders that have the potential for generating a lot of spam complaints.

✔ **Keep customers from sending repeated e-mails to unknown users:** Spammers send billions of e-mails to every possible e-mail address hoping to uncover real addresses. Because ISPs (such as AOL, Yahoo!, and Hotmail) spend a lot of money bouncing e-mails sent by spammers, they aren't appreciative of e-mails sent to nonexistent addresses. Resultantly, your deliverability could suffer if your e-mail server is labeled as a nuisance. To help protect your sender reputation (as well as that of the ESP), most reputable ESPs stop sending your e-mail to nonexistent e-mail addresses after two or three attempts even if you don't remove the e-mail addresses yourself.

E-mail filters often rely on sender reputation before content filters, so make sure to put your ESP to the test. You can check your ESP's sender reputation against the competition by signing up for a free account at www. senderscore.org. Type the domain name of the company and then click each of their listed e-mail servers to see the sender score for each server used to send e-mail on behalf of the ESP's customers. A score of 0 on a particular e-mail server is the worst, and a score of 100 is the best. After you feel comfortable that you're sending e-mail via a reputable ESP, you can be sure that your efforts to optimize your e-mail content won't be wasted.

Understanding automatic content filtering

A small percentage of e-mail content filters are controlled completely by e-mail system administrators to keep their users from administering their own filter settings. The e-mail system administrator (usually IT personnel at a company, or an ISP) sets up the automatic filter with specific global parameters that apply to all e-mail users in the same way.

Because automatic e-mail filtering is generally controlled by technically knowledgeable people with all kinds of backgrounds, the types of e-mail content that get filtered through automatic filtering vary widely. For example, one system administrator might decide to filter HTML e-mails, but another might decide to filter e-mails with attachments. If someone on your e-mail list wants your e-mail and his or her system administrator has strict filter settings, your e-mail has a greater chance of false positive identification. (You can read about false positives earlier in this chapter.)

Automatic filtering effects a relatively small percentage of your e-mails. You can't do much about it unless you happen to know the system administrator and you can coax him or her into relaxing a particular company's filtering standards.

Understanding user-controlled content filtering

The majority of e-mail filters are included within e-mail programs and written with broad consumer preferences in mind to filter e-mail content that has spam-like characteristics. E-mail filters within e-mail programs almost always allow the user to access the default filter settings and alter them according to user preferences.

Filters often look for spam-like content, so avoid simulating spammer techniques. Recent examples include

- ✔ Generic Subject lines and anonymous From lines
- ✔ PDF attachments containing advertisements
- ✔ Images of entire advertisements without any plain text
- ✔ Excessive promotional phrases and words

Most consumers don't alter their default e-mail filter settings manually, so avoiding false positive filtering by the most common e-mail filters is partly a matter of building your e-mails to exclude the most commonly filtered content. Figure 12-6 shows a sample of the headers in a junk e-mail folder.

Read some of the e-mails in your own junk folder to see examples of what to avoid: namely, the most common types of content that spammers include in their e-mails.

		From	Subject	Received	Size	
		John Weber	Visit new internet shop of digital goods!	Fri 6/29/2007 7...	7 KB	
		Brianna Park	Re. Did you see this?	Fri 6/29/2007 3...	6 KB	
		Sharon Acker	{mactech2}	Thu 6/28/2007 ...	6 KB	
		Demetra Marshall	Saw them all	Thu 6/28/2007 ...	26 KB	
		Isabel Bingham	Best online pharmacy	Wed 6/27/2007...	6 KB	
		Essie Castle	Thanh - 100% results.	Wed 6/27/2007...	21 KB	
		Rex Dickinson	AutoCAD 2008 $129	Wed 6/27/2007...	19 KB	
		Wesley Gonzales	Best online pharmacy	Tue 6/26/2007 ...	7 KB	
		Pauline Pierson	Re. What	Tue 6/26/2007 ...	7 KB	
		isch LINTON	When overridden in a derived class, gets or sets the position within the...	Tue 6/26/2007 ...	14 KB	
		Jerold Funk	Re. Read This	Mon 6/25/2007 ...	6 KB	

Best online pharmacy
Isabel Bingham [katicika@mail.ru]

This message was converted to plain text.

To: Arnold, John

```
Replica Watch
Why spend thousands of dollars on the real deal when a replica watch looks so
much alike that only an expert could tell the difference...
And you only pay a fraction of the price.
```

Figure 12-6: Filters often look for spam-like content.

You can prevent your e-mails looking like spam if you do the following:

- ✔ **Don't include your subscriber's first name in the Subject line of your e-mails.**

  The practice is common among spammers because most consumers can't understand how a complete stranger could know their first name. (Spammers use Web-crawling programs to pull the information out of your e-mail headers.) After being tricked a few times, most consumers associate this technique with spam.

- ✔ **Always include a From line in your e-mail header.**

  Excluding the From line is an attempt by spammers to trick people into opening e-mails in the hope that the consumers are curious to find out who the e-mail is from. Most filters automatically identify e-mails with no From line as untrustworthy.

- ✔ **Avoid excessive punctuation such as strings of exclamation points or dollar signs.**

  Spammers often use strings of punctuation to make their offers more eye-catching, and the practice is just as attention-catching to e-mail filters.

- ✔ **Don't send marketing e-mails with attachments.**

  Consumers are understandably nervous about an e-mail with an unfamiliar attachments, and e-mails sent to more than a few people with attachments are usually filtered.

- ✔ **Don't write sentences in all capital letters.**

  Writing in all capital letters draws attention to e-mail headlines, and this tack is as annoying to consumers as it is noticeable by e-mail filters.

Building your e-mail content with the most common filter settings gets more of your e-mail delivered to the inbox, but several types of user-controlled filters aren't so simple to sidestep.

Individual filters

A small percentage of consumers do access their filter setting in order to make changes. Figure 12-7 shows some of the individual filter settings available in Yahoo! Mail.

If someone on your e-mail list accesses his personal filter settings to set up a filter, your e-mail content is obviously subject to being filtered based on the personal settings for that user. Because you can't know every personal setting in an individual filter, there is little you can do to get your e-mail through. Accessing filter settings allows the user to personally filter one or more of the following e-mails:

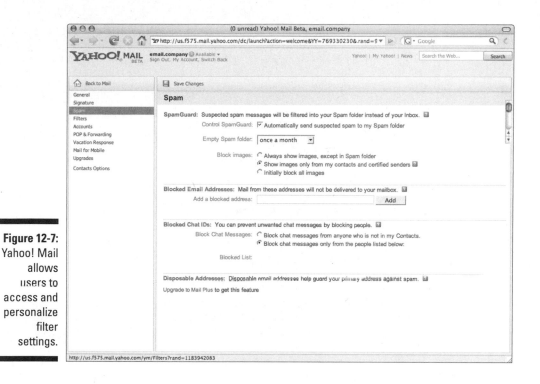

Figure 12-7:
Yahoo! Mail
allows
users to
access and
personalize
filter
settings.

✔ From specific senders

✔ Containing specific words or phrases

✔ With links or images (usually converted to plain text only)

✔ From senders not in the user's address book

✔ With certain domain extensions, such as `.biz` or `.info`

✔ With certain types of encoding, such as international languages

✔ With attachments

Trained content filters

Some filters begin with broad default settings and are automatically updated based on whether the user identifies certain e-mails as unwanted. The most common example is the Spam button. A *Spam button* (as you can read about in Chapter 3) is a clickable link in an e-mail program that reports the e-mail as spam to the e-mail system administrator. Clicking a Spam button not only reports an e-mail as unwanted but also scans the content to identify content that recurs frequently in the reported e-mails.

When a user clicks a Spam button, a filter scans the e-mail to look for words, phrases, and other types of content to determine whether there is a pattern to the types of content being reported as spam by the user. For example, if a user continues to click the Spam button on multiple e-mails containing the phrase *discount meds,* the filter begins to learn that phrase and automatically filters any e-mails containing that phrase to a junk folder.

Trained content filters work fairly well, but a filter can't distinguish between wanted words and unwanted words in an e-mail that is marked as spam. Because spam e-mails share many common characteristics with legitimate e-mails — such as the phrase Click Here — some legitimate e-mails are identified as false positives.

Keeping Up with Advancing Technology

Filtering and blocking technology are constantly improving. Although it might seem as if spammers are always one step ahead of the game, several promising technologies are emerging to help reduce spam.

Keeping up with emerging technology is important so that your e-mails are optimized for current deliverability standards as well as poised to comply with emerging technology that might cause your e-mails to go undelivered.

Spammers forge the e-mail addresses they send e-mails from by using technical tricks to replace the legitimate header information in an e-mail with false information. Several major ISPs have developed technology to validate the From information in an e-mail. The following is a list of the most popular sender authentication methods. The list also represents the most likely technology to emerge as standards for your own deliverability.

- ✔ **Sender ID:** A technology developed by Microsoft that uses an algorithm to select a header field containing the e-mail address responsible for sending the e-mail. The sending e-mail address is then checked against a list of authorized e-mail servers for that e-mail address.

- ✔ **DomainKeys:** A technology developed by Yahoo! that uses cryptography to generate a set of unique public and private encryption keys. All outgoing messages are digitally signed by the sender using the private key (known only to authorized senders), and the public key is published with the sender's Domain Name Service (DNS) so that recipients can use the public key to validate that the correct private key was used by the sender.

- ✔ **Sender Policy Framework (SPF):** SPF is similar to Sender ID in that the technology validates the sender's From information by allowing the owner of a specific domain to specify his or her e-mail sending policy or SPF. When someone receives an e-mail that appears to originate from the specified domain, the e-mail server receiving the message can check the SPF record to see whether the e-mail complies with that domain's specific policy.

Self-publishing your own authentication information is beyond the scope of this book, but you can easily employ authentication technology in your e-mails by using a reputable ESP that complies with current authentication standards to send your e-mail. You can find ESP recommendations at www.emailtrainer.com.

What's your spam score?

Instead of filtering specific types of content on an individual basis, some companies choose to score every e-mail by comparing the content in the e-mail with the content in known spam e-mails. These companies compare e-mails to lists of keywords, HTML structure, attachments, published block-lists, and domain names to determine how closely the e-mail resembles a typical spam e-mail. The more each e-mail's content resembles the content in spam, the higher the e-mail's spam score. The company sets a limit for the spam score and then tags, filters, or returns those e-mails that exceed the score. Some ESPs help you score your own e-mails before you send them as shown in the following figure. If you use such a service, make sure that your spam score is 0 before you send.

Chapter 13

Capitalizing on Clicks and Other Responses

● ●

In This Chapter

▶ Using e-mail click-through data

▶ Analyzing Web site visitors

▶ Creating e-mail surveys

▶ Extending your e-mail marketing

● ●

*Y*our e-mail marketing strategy is only as valuable as your ability to continuously convert your e-mail list subscribers into customers who support you and your business financially. Maximizing customer conversions with e-mail marketing is a matter of

✔ Driving interested prospects to a place where conversion is likely to happen, such as a Web site with compelling content or a store with good products, values, and salespeople

✔ Tracking and analyzing your results to determine which tactics positively or negatively affect customer conversions

✔ Repeating and cultivating tactics that increase customer conversions while correcting or eliminating tactics that hinder customer conversions

This chapter explains how to collect and analyze the information you need to identify the strengths and weaknesses of your e-mail marketing strategy and make adjustments to your tactics accordingly.

This chapter also explains how you can extend your e-mail marketing strategy beyond the basics to deepen your relationships and enhance other Internet marketing mediums such as search engine optimization (SEO), really simple syndication (RSS), blogs, and portable e-mail–receiving devices.

Evaluating E-Mail Click-Through Data

Every time someone clicks a link in your e-mail, you have the opportunity to track the click back to the individual and use the information to accomplish more meaningful objectives and increase the value of your e-mail list.

You have to be an advanced HTML and database programmer to write your own link-tracking code, so I recommend that you use an E-Mail Service Provider (ESP) that can generate link-tracking code automatically for you. An ESP also provides a click-through report for each e-mail campaign. Figure 13-1 shows a detailed click-through report, generated by an ESP, that shows each link in the tracked e-mail and allows the user to view the individuals behind each click.

The next sections include tips and techniques for extracting practical meaning from your click-through data and for acting on your click-through data to make your e-mail marketing efforts more effective over time.

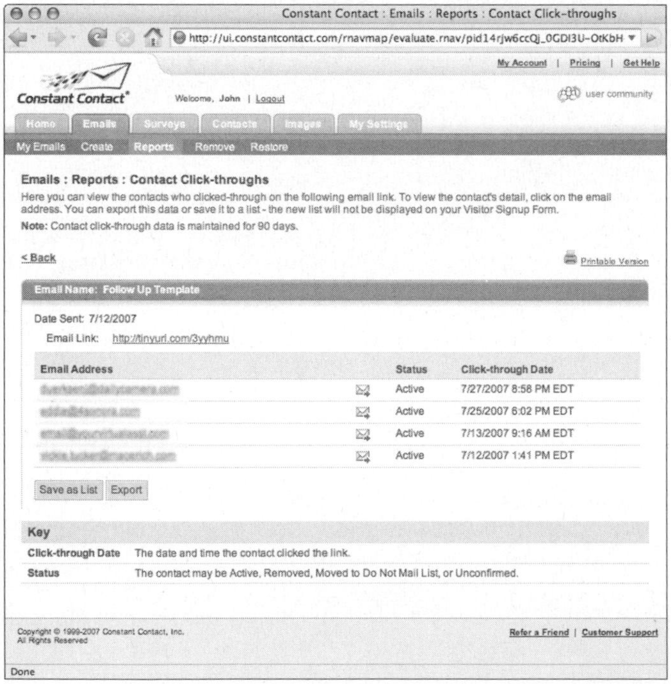

Figure 13-1:
Click-through reports show links in tracked e-mails.

Courtesy of Constant Contact

Using click-through data to target your e-mail offers

Someone clicking an e-mail link in response to an article or offer allows you to make assumptions about your clicker's interests. For example, a bookstore that receives 100 link clicks leading to information about a guitar book can assume that those 100 subscribers are interested in guitars.

Placing your clickers into different e-mail lists based on their interests allows you to send future e-mails with more-targeted offers. For example, if a bookstore compiles its 100 guitar book clickers in a guitar-interest list, the bookstore could include offers and information related to guitars in every e-mail sent to that specific list. Figure 13-2 shows an ESP interface that allows you to save clickers to a list.

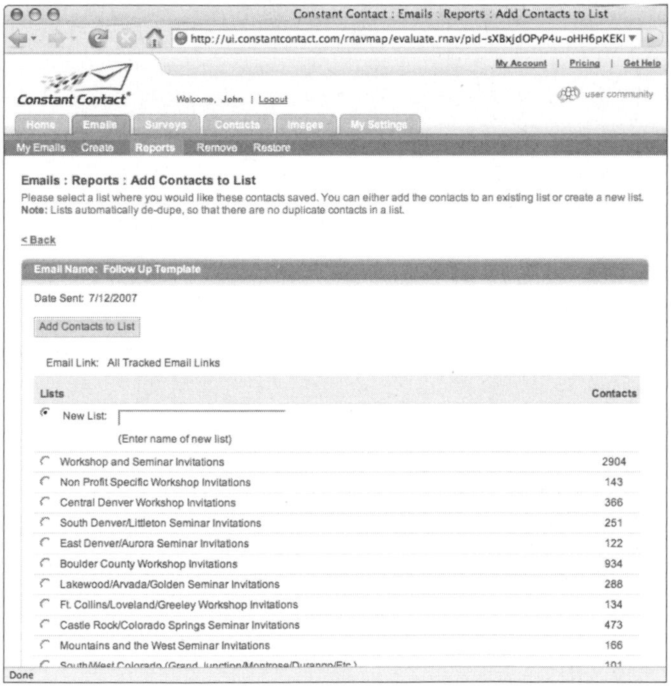

Figure 13-2: Save your clickers as a list to target future e-mails by interest.

Courtesy of Constant Contact

Here are some tips to help you determine your audience's interests and for dividing your e-mail list by using click-through interests:

✔ **Turn your links into data mines.** Clicks are much more meaningful when you write them in ways that affirm the clicker's personal information. For example, if a golf store sells kids' golf equipment as well as adult golf equipment, the store might include a link that points to kids' golfing tips:

```
Do you have kids under 12 who golf? Read our latest
        kids golfing tips.
```

The golf store can save the names of those who click the kids' tips link as a list and then target their kids equipment offers to those clickers because they are more likely to value them.

✔ **Rearrange your e-mails by interest.** You don't need to send a completely different e-mail to each subscriber with a different interest. Instead, you can make small changes to your e-mail content based on the interest list you're targeting. For example, you can send the same e-mail newsletter to all your lists while changing the Subject line or rearranging the order of your articles to highlight the most interesting content for each of your interest lists.

✔ **Change your offers by interest.** People often respond to calls to action in your e-mails based on the strength of your offers. When you send offers to different interest lists, keep your call to action the same but change your offer according to each interest. For example, if your e-mail contains a call to action asking your audience to take a survey, you might offer one interest list a discount for taking the survey while offering another interest list special privileges. (You can read more about creating valuable offers in Chapter 10.)

Using click-through data for intelligent follow up

When someone clicks an e-mail link but doesn't follow through with a purchase or other commitment, you can use your click-through report to follow up with your clicker and find out what might have caused him or her to abandon the conversion process.

Following up with e-mail can be effective, but it's also a good idea to collect phone numbers and mailing addresses from your subscribers in case you need to follow up outside the inbox. For example, a consultant who sends an event invitation with a registration link could compare the list of subscribers who click the registration link with the number of completed registrations and then call each person who clicked *without* registering. Such follow-up can help you determine what might have prevented the registration from going through. The phone calls might reveal that those who didn't register had questions that your Web site didn't answer or felt uncomfortable typing a credit card number into the registration form.

Here are some tips for following up on the data in your click-through reports using e-mail as well as other forms of communication:

- ✔ **Send a second-chance offer** to those clickers who did not follow through by making a purchase or other commitment. You can use another e-mail or a postcard highlighting a more compelling second-chance offer.

- ✔ **Send a postcard thanking your clickers** for considering your offer and asking them to consider an alternative product or service.

- ✔ **Call your clickers** and ask them whether they have any questions.

- ✔ **Send a survey to your clickers** asking them about any interests that the link seems to have uncovered. (You can read more about e-mail surveys later in this chapter.)

- ✔ **Thank your subscribers** who forward your e-mails.

- ✔ **Send a postcard to clickers who unsubscribe** from your e-mail list telling them that they are still valued and thanking them for considering your products and services.

Using click-through data for testing your offers and calls to action

A spike or a decline in your click-through rate usually means that your offers or calls to action aren't compelling. Sending your offers and calls to action to a small and random portion of your e-mail list and tracking your click-through rate allows you to test your offers and calls to action before sending them to your entire e-mail list. Here's how you can create and execute your own click-through test:

1. Randomly select ten percent of your e-mail list subscribers from your database and copy them to a new database or category in your database.

2. Create two versions of your e-mail and send each one to half of your test list.

3. Wait 48 hours and compare each e-mail's click-through report to see which links received the most clicks.

4. Create a final version of your e-mail using the elements that produced the most clicks and send it to your entire e-mail list.

If your sample click-through rates are lower than you expect in both versions of your e-mail, you can adjust your offers or calls to action accordingly and test again using a different test list. You can improve a low click-through rate with these simple techniques:

- ✔ Rewriting your headlines to attract more attention to your offer
- ✔ Adjusting your offer to deliver more value
- ✔ Moving your call to action to a more visible location
- ✔ Rearranging your layout to make your offer easier to scan

Tracking and Analyzing Web Site Visitors

E-mail applications can't track what happens after someone clicks an e-mail link, so your Web site needs to be ready to take the handoff from your e-mail links and track each click-through visitor. Tracking Web site visitors allows you to determine whether the people clicking your e-mail links follow through on their clicks in ways that help you to achieve your objectives.

Keeping track of Web site visitor behavior and analyzing the data is *Web (site) analytics*, and executing a Web analytics strategy involves using a software application that collects and organizes important visitor information every time someone visits your Web site, as shown in Figure 13-3.

Web analytics applications can collect mind-boggling amounts of information, but not all information is useful for e-mail marketing purposes.

This sections explains the Web analytics that are essential to maximizing your e-mail marketing results and tells you how to use the data to improve customer conversions. (You can find Web analytics software application recommendations at www.emailtrainer.com. Another great resource is *Web Analytics For Dummies,* by Pedro Sostre and Jennifer LeClaire, Wiley.)

Looking at your landing page

A *landing page* is the page on your Web site that your audience sees immediately following a click within your e-mail. A landing page might be one of the regular pages in your Web site or a special page that you create to host the content specifically related to your e-mail link. The content on a landing page might include

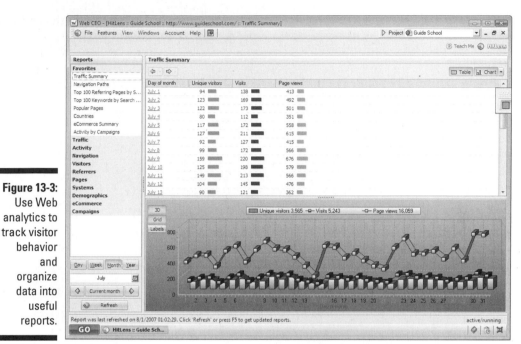

Figure 13-3:
Use Web analytics to track visitor behavior and organize data into useful reports.

✔ Expanded information on a product or service highlighted in your e-mail

✔ The remainder of an article or story that begins in your e-mail

✔ A shopping cart (if someone clicks a link in your e-mail that adds a product directly)

✔ A form that collects information, such as an order form, a survey form, or a request for more information

✔ A form that displays personal information, such as account status or an event calendar

✔ Instructions for taking action outside of your e-mail, such as driving directions or steps for making an in-store purchase

✔ An article in a blog or on a discussion board

✔ A list of archived files or other navigation links

✔ A coupon or other printable information

Linking to a landing page

Linking directly to a landing page involves determining the exact location of the landing page on your Web site and using the address of that page as your link address. Here are three steps to finding your landing page address so you can link directly to the page from your e-mail.

1. **Go to your Web site and navigate to your landing page.**

   If your landing page isn't accessible from your main Web site, load the landing page into a Web browser by using your Web site file manager.

2. **Use your mouse to highlight the address of the page located in the address bar at the top of your browser window.**

3. **Copy the text in the address bar and use it as the address for your link.**

If you use an ESP to create your links, you can paste the landing page address directly into your link creation interface. If you code your own links with HTML, you can use the following line of code to create your landing page link:

```
<a href="http://www.landingpageaddress.com/filename">
Name of Link Here</a>
```

For example, if you want to create a link that reads, `Register Now!`, your link code might look like this:

```
<a href="http://www.helpwithemailmarketing.com/events/
registration_page?event=3&id=3">Register Now!</a>
```

Checking your landing page bounce rate

Your *landing page bounce rate* is the number of landing page visitors who abandon your Web site after viewing only the landing page, expressed as a percentage of total landing page visitors. Web analytics applications report a landing page bounce rate for each page in your Web site.

A high landing page bounce rate is usually an indication that your visitors are interested when they click within your e-mail but become uninterested in visiting other pages in your Web site when they reach your landing page. Determining whether your landing page bounce rate is too high is a matter of figuring out how many landing page visitors need to see additional Web pages when they visit a specific landing page.

If your landing page asks visitors to make a purchase, you probably need a high number of visitors to move from your landing page to a series of other pages, such as a shopping cart and a confirmation page. If your landing page asks visitors to print the landing page because it contains a coupon, your landing page bounce rate might not be as important as the number of people who print your landing page and walk in to your store with a coupon.

Possible reasons for a high landing page bounce rate include

- ✔ **Your landing page doesn't match the design of your e-mail,** causing your visitors to lose confidence in your identity.

- ✔ **The offer in your e-mail doesn't match the offer on your landing page,** causing your visitors to question the original offer.

✔ **Your landing page content isn't what your visitors expect,** causing your visitors to feel led in the wrong direction.

✔ **Your Web site visitors can't find the information they expect** after clicking through, even though the information is on the landing page, causing your visitors to give up.

✔ **Your visitors are interested in your offer but aren't ready to buy,** causing your visitors to put off any further investigation.

✔ **Your landing page doesn't make the next step obvious enough,** causing your audience to wonder how to proceed.

Following your Web site visitor's click path

The *click path* lists every Web page that's viewed by a visitor in sequence, beginning with your e-mail link and ending when the visitor abandons your Web site. Figure 13-4 shows an example of a click path report generated by a Web analytics application.

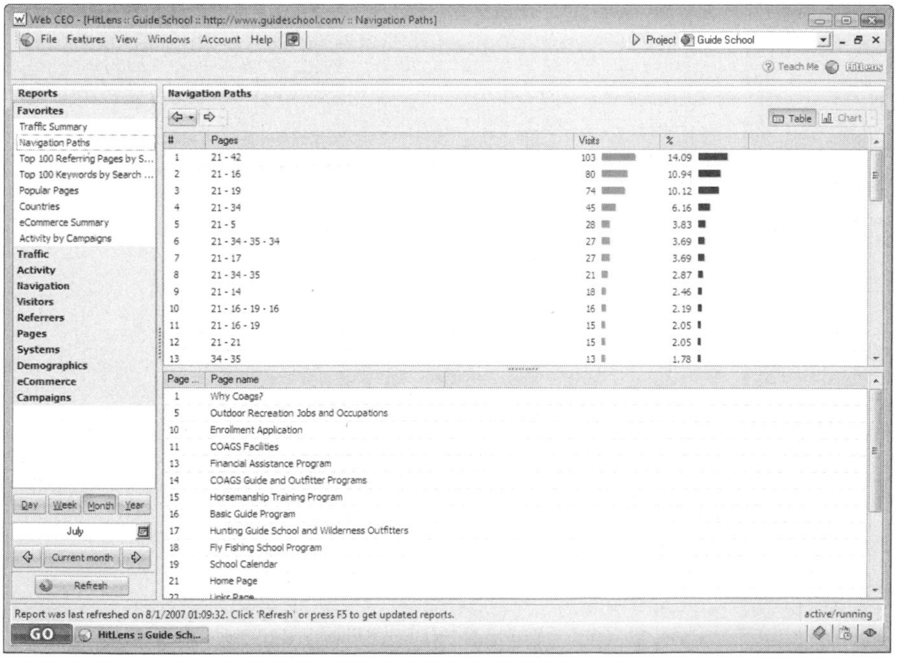

Figure 13-4: Track your visitors by a click path report.

Courtesy of Colorado Outdoor Adventure Guide School and SQV Technologies

Tracking the click path allows you to determine whether your Web site pages drive visitors toward or away from conversion. For example, if your Web analytics software tells you that 50 percent of your landing page visitors click to add an item to their shopping cart but later abandon the purchasing process on the shipping form, your shipping form probably represents a barrier to conversion — as well as an opportunity to improve your results by correcting the information on the Web page containing your shipping form.

Here are some tips for using the information in your click path report to increase your customer conversions:

- ✔ **Look for trends in how visitors move toward a specific page**, such as a shopping cart or registration page, to see whether you can create shortcuts for your visitors.

- ✔ **Look for trends in how visitors move away from a specific page**, such as a landing page or your home page, to see whether you can drive your visitors more effectively to the places on your Web site that produce the most revenue.

- ✔ **Keep track of the last page in the click pat**h to see whether any one of your Web site pages causes an above-average number of visitors to exit your Web site. Use the information to improve any pages that cause visitors to exit when they aren't supposed to.

- ✔ **Use your click path reports to identify your visitor's interests** so you can target future e-mails and link your visitors to landing pages that highlight their interests and then lead them down an interest-specific click path ending with conversion.

Measuring your conversion percentage

The main reason to track your Web site visitors is to ensure that your Web site is effectively converting the visitors referred by your e-mails into customers. A *conversion* happens when someone clicks through to your Web site and completes a transaction that helps you to achieve one or more of your ultimate objectives.

The Flash Web site click path dilemma

Designing a Web site with Flash instead of HTML doesn't allow you to link to a specific page within your Web site or track the movement between pages. Pages in Flash Web sites don't have unique URL addresses. If you have a Flash Web site, I recommend creating HTML landing pages so your audience doesn't have to begin at your home page and navigate through any additional links in your Web site to find the information you refer to in your e-mail links.

Usually, conversion rates are assigned to sales and other financial transactions, but your e-mail marketing strategy might include other objectives that qualify as conversions. Examples of clicks resulting in conversions include

✔ Adding an item to a shopping cart by using an e-mail link and following through by purchasing the item

✔ Clicking-through from your e-mail link to a survey form and following through by filling out and submitting the form

✔ Clicking an e-mail link to read an article and following through by purchasing a subscription to the publication that is the source of the article

✔ Clicking an e-mail link to view directions to your store and following through by visiting the store and making a purchase

✔ Downloading event information by using a document file link in your e-mail and following through by purchasing tickets to the event

Your conversion percentage is calculated by dividing the total number of conversion transactions resulting from your e-mail campaign by the total number of visitors referred by your e-mail. Web analytics applications are great for calculating online conversion percentages because they can easily count your online transactions and divide it by the number of visitors, as shown in Figure 13-5.

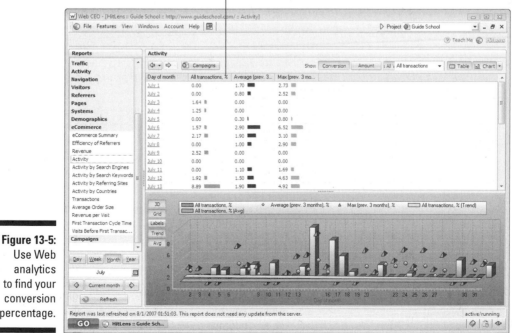

Figure 13-5: Use Web analytics to find your conversion percentage.

Courtesy of Colorado Outdoor Adventure Guide School and SQV Technologies

Comparing your conversion percentage and your click-through rate allows you to determine whether your e-mails and Web site work well together:

- **High click-through rate and a low conversion percentage:** This indicates that your e-mails drive interested visitors to your Web site, but your Web site content isn't effective for closing sales.

- **Low click-through rate and a high conversion percentage:** This indicates that your Web site is effective for closing sales, but your e-mail content isn't effective for driving visitors.

Keeping track of your overall conversion percentage is important, but keeping track of your conversion percentages by individual campaigns is also important so you can compare different e-mail offers and landing pages side-by-side to determine which tactics outperform others. Analyzing the e-mail campaigns and landing pages that give you the best results allows you to repeat effective tactics in future campaigns and eliminate tactics that aren't as effective.

Measuring your return on investment

Measuring and analyzing your return on investment (ROI) for each e-mail campaign and for your overall strategy is important so you can determine whether your e-mail marketing efforts are worth your time, money, energy, and effort. ROI is calculated by assigning a value to each conversion and then dividing the total value of all conversions by the total cost attributed to your e-mail campaign.

For your Web analytics application to calculate an accurate ROI, you need to assign monetary values to your conversions and marketing expenses, as follows:

- **Assign a value to each conversion.** For example, if someone makes a $200 purchase that results in $100 of profit before marketing costs, you can assign $100 to each purchase conversion. You can also assign a value to non-monetary conversions, such as completed survey forms or new e-mail list subscribers, by estimating the value of each completed task. For example, if you send an e-mail campaign that results in 100 of your e-mails getting forwarded to your subscribers' friends and colleagues, and you know that one of every ten forwards results in a sale that earns you $100, you can assign a value of $10 to each forward.

- **Assign a cost to your e-mail campaign.** For example, if you spend two hours building an e-mail and $100 for outside design and copywriting services, you might assign a value of $200 to your e-mail campaign.

After you enter your costs and expenses into your ROI calculator, the resulting calculation is expressed as a percentage and represents the amount of money your business receives in exchange for your marketing expenses. A ROI percentage lower than 100 percent indicates a financial loss; conversely, a ROI percentage higher than 100 percent represents a financial gain.

Going Deeper with E-Mail Surveys

Click-through data and Web analytics often reveal areas of concern or opportunities for improvement without revealing which actions are best for addressing the issue or how your audience is likely to respond when you make changes to your strategy. In such cases, e-mail surveys are a great way to determine the best course for corrective action or enhancements to your strategy.

This section explains some simple approaches to using e-mail for surveying your audience to overcome challenges, deepen your relationships, and improve your overall e-mail marketing strategy.

Planning your survey

Surveys can help your business to understand your customers and solve problems, but surveys that are conducted without sound marketing principles are likely to annoy your audience or encourage useless feedback.

Five steps are involved in surveying your audience:

1. Determine the issue you want to address.
2. Determine what type of survey addresses the issue best.
3. Write your survey questions.
4. Collect your data.
5. Implement your changes.

The following sections explain these steps in detail and also include tips for making sure your survey strategy unfolds with a sense of direction and purpose.

Step 1: Determine the issue you want to address

Sending an e-mail survey to your audience hoping to uncover potential issues before identifying the issue that needs improvement is a common marketing research mistake that usually results in suggestions for making improvements to problems that your audience wasn't even aware of before the survey. For example, a survey question that asks, "In what ways do you think our Web site could be improved?" is likely to generate lots of ideas for how you can improve your Web site — regardless of whether your Web site actually needs improvement.

Because people who respond to survey questions might be inclined to place undue importance on issues that you ask them directly about, a more reliable approach for uncovering areas for improvement is to use your click-through and Web analytics data to define potential issues and use your survey questions and responses to guide your decisions when executing improvements. The following is a list of issues that your data might expose:

- ✔ Click-through rate is low or declining.
- ✔ Conversion rate is low or declining.
- ✔ Conversion rate varies among different audiences.
- ✔ Unsubscribe rate is high or increasing.
- ✔ Forward rate is low or decreasing.
- ✔ Repeat customer counts are too low or declining.
- ✔ New customer counts are too low or declining.

Step 2: Determine what type of survey addresses the issue best

Most e-mail marketing issues can be attributed to the fact that your e-mails don't properly address the needs of your audience or that your audience is dissatisfied with your products or services. Two common types of surveys are useful for discovering the needs and attitudes in your audience:

- ✔ **Marketing research:** Asking your audience about their needs, preferences, and behavioral patterns is a part of marketing research. Marketing research surveys use questions about the marketplace and your industry in general rather than focusing on your business specifically.

- ✔ **Satisfaction:** Asking your audience about their attitudes toward your products, services, or business practices is a satisfaction survey. Satisfaction surveys help to determine whether your audience is dissatisfied with one or more aspects of your business and usually occur after your audience has a specific experience, such as a visit to your Web site or a purchase at your store.

Step 3: Write your survey questions

Whether you decide to take a marketing research or a customer satisfaction approach to your survey, the questions you use can make a significant impact on your results. When writing questions, you need to quantify the answers to your questions so your answers don't leave you with too many variables. Here are the four basic types of questions that result in quantifiable data:

- ✔ **Closed-ended:** *Closed-ended questions* have a limited number of answers — for example, asking a Yes or No question, or asking whether your respondent is male or female. Closed-ended questions are good for dividing your audience into segments so you can either ask them additional targeted questions or base your decisions on the majority of responses.

- ✔ **Open-ended:** *Open-ended questions* have an unlimited number of answers and allow your audience to freely address the question. Open-ended questions are quantifiable only when you can read all the responses and track similarities between the answers. These types of questions are best for getting an overall sense of your audience's opinions and attitudes.

- ✔ **Multiple choice:** *Multiple-choice questions* allow your audience to choose from a list of two or more answers. Multiple-choice questions can ask your audience to select only one answer from among the group, or you can allow your audience to choose more than one answer. They allow you to quantify answers to simple questions when you are aware of the possible answers yet still unsure which answer your audience agrees with.

- ✔ **Ranking and rating:** *Ranking questions* allow your audience to prioritize a list of possible answers in order of preference or importance. These questions allow you to create a scale and ask your audience to mark their answer according to the scale, as shown in Figure 13-6.

Ranking and rating questions are more effective than multiple choice questions when you need to address several issues at once and when you want to get a feel for which group of issues needs attention first.

Figure 13-6:
Use rating questions to focus on several issues, using a specified scale.

2. **When do you check email on the following devices?**

	Don't Use	Multiple times per day	Once daily	Once a week	Less than weekly
Work computer	○	○	○	○	○
Home computer	○	○	○	○	○
Mobile device	○	○	○	○	○

Comment:

150 character(s) left.

Courtesy of Constant Contact Survey

Step 4: Collect your data

Collecting survey data is a matter of creating online forms that capture responses and placing the responses into a database that can be queried for results. Writing your own survey collection forms and databases isn't practical, so I recommend using an online survey service to collect your data and summarize the information in easy-to-use reports. Figure 13-7 shows a survey report generated by a survey service. Survey reports summarize your survey responses so you can visualize the implications of your results. (I explain more about survey services in the upcoming section on creating an e-mail survey.)

Step 5: Implement your changes

Even when your survey data is compelling, test each of your proposed improvements with a small group before you make sweeping changes.

If the changes you make successfully address your issues in a small group, you can make the changes effective for your entire audience. If your changes don't work or have a negative effect, you might have to go back to your survey and determine whether your survey approach or your judgments were incorrect.

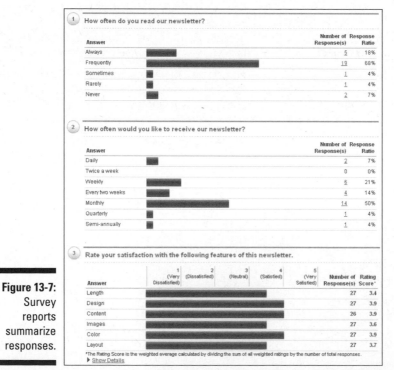

Figure 13-7:
Survey
reports
summarize
responses.

Courtesy of Constant Contact Survey

Creating an e-mail survey

E-mail is a great way to deliver a survey because you can link your audience directly to your survey form where they can answer the questions online. Because most e-mail is opened and read within the first 48 hours after delivery, e-mail surveys also allow you to gather information quickly.

Creating an e-mail survey is easy when you use a survey service to help you. Most survey services have survey templates designed to address common issues so you can use the surveys as-is or alter the questions to suit your individual objectives. Some survey services also allow you to integrate your survey links and response data into your e-mail marketing strategy. Figure 13-8 shows an e-mail survey generated by a survey service.

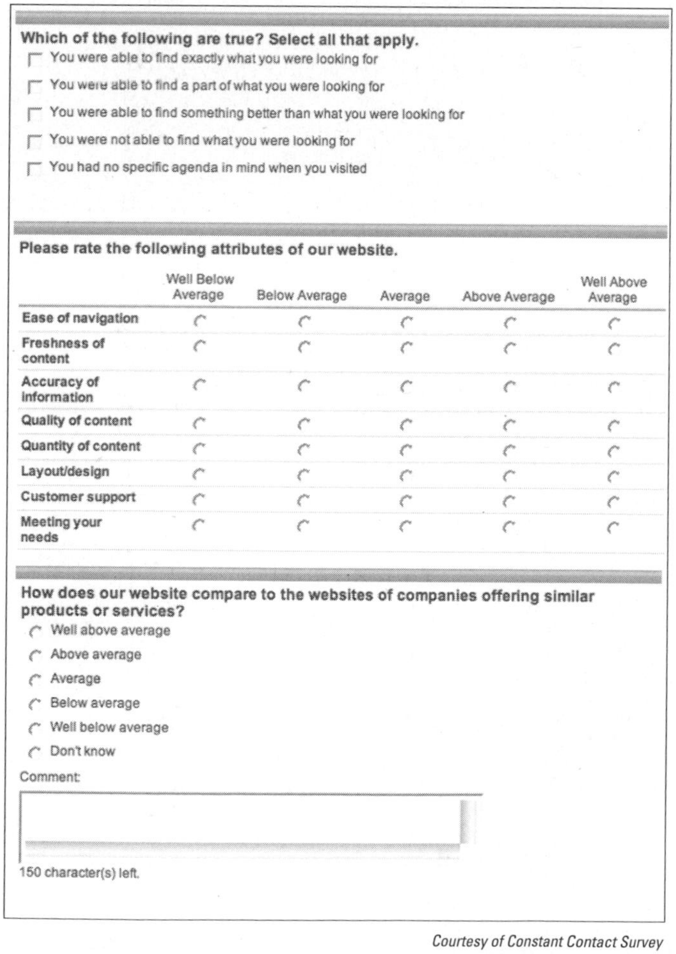

Which of the following are true? Select all that apply.

☐ You were able to find exactly what you were looking for

☐ You were able to find a part of what you were looking for

☐ You were able to find something better than what you were looking for

☐ You were not able to find what you were looking for

☐ You had no specific agenda in mind when you visited

Please rate the following attributes of our website.

	Well Below Average	Below Average	Average	Above Average	Well Above Average
Ease of navigation	○	○	○	○	○
Freshness of content	○	○	○	○	○
Accuracy of information	○	○	○	○	○
Quality of content	○	○	○	○	○
Quantity of content	○	○	○	○	○
Layout/design	○	○	○	○	○
Customer support	○	○	○	○	○
Meeting your needs	○	○	○	○	○

How does our website compare to the websites of companies offering similar products or services?

○ Well above average

○ Above average

○ Average

○ Below average

○ Well below average

○ Don't know

Comment:

150 character(s) left.

Figure 13-8:
This survey was generated by a survey service.

Courtesy of Constant Contact Survey

Here are some tips for creating an e-mail survey with a survey service. (You can find survey service recommendations at www.emailtrainer.com.)

✔ **Put a time limit on your survey.** Deciding when to analyze and implement the data your survey collects is a matter of determining whether you want your survey to be available only once or on an ongoing basis.

- *One-time surveys* are useful for addressing a specific issue quickly using a specific list, such as prospects or customers. A good time limit for using a one-time survey is anywhere from three to ten days.

- *Ongoing surveys* are useful for evaluating trends using your present and future audiences. For example, you might ask everyone who makes a purchase in your store to go to your Web site and take a survey so you can keep track of any perceived changes to your customer service.

✔ **Invite your survey participants.** You have to make people aware of your survey and tell them why it's important that they complete the survey if you want to attract a high number of survey participants. Here are a variety of ways you can make people aware of your survey and invite participants to complete the questions:

- *Send a special survey invitation e-mail with a link to your survey questions.* Special invitations should concisely explain the reason for your survey and the benefits of your audience's participation. You should also tell your audience how many questions your survey contains and approximately how long the survey should take. Survey invitation e-mails are good for sending a one-time survey to a large group or for prompting individuals to complete an ongoing survey after an experience with your business. Figure 13-9 shows an example of a survey invitation e-mail.

Figure 13-9:
This survey invitation e-mail prompts people to take the survey online.

Courtesy of Constant Contact Survey

- *Place a survey link in one of your regular e-mail formats.* When your survey is available for participants to take for a longer period of time, you can use your survey link as a call to action in your e-mail. For example, an e-mail newsletter that contains an article about cell phone technology overseas might contain a link to a marketing research survey related to cell phone usage overseas.

- *Place a link to your survey on your Web site.* If one of the goals of your e-mails is to drive traffic to your Web site, you can include survey links on your Web site so that your visitors have a chance to give you information. You can make your Web site surveys anonymous so that people who aren't willing to join your e-mail list and share their e-mail address have an opportunity to leave you feedback before leaving your Web site.

✔ **Keep your survey short.** Time is so important to consumers that your surveys need to be short and to the point to attract participants. Here are some tips for minimizing the time required to complete your survey:

- *Divide and conquer.* If your surveys require more than five questions and answers, break your survey into two parts and survey half your audience with each part.

- *Round-robin your questions.* Break your survey into individual questions and rotate them in your regular e-mail campaigns so that each member of your audience has to complete only one question at a time.

- *Keep it simple.* Use link tracking for closed-ended questions so your audience has to make only one click. For example, if you want to find out whether your audience likes chocolate or vanilla, your e-mail newsletter could ask your audience to click the link that reads, `I like chocolate` or `I like vanilla`. You can point each link to a page on your Web site that reads, `Thanks for your reply` and use your e-mail tracking report to count how many unique clicks you receive on each link.

✔ **Don't use your survey to sell.** Ending your survey with a sales pitch or a landing page that contains a lot of promotional information makes your audience feel used. Instead of using surveys to sell your products or services, use the responses and clicks in your survey to follow up with targeted e-mails that address the interests your survey responses suggest.

✔ **Publish your results.** If you're going to put your audience through all the trouble of completing surveys, make sure you tell them what you plan to do with their information so they feel like their efforts were valuable to your business and beneficial to their continued relationship with you. Post a summary of your results to your Web site or send an e-mail telling your audience about the positive changes you'll be making as a result of the survey. You don't have to get specific about the data — just summarize the results in a way that illustrates the benefits of your surveys.

Using E-Mail to Extend Your Online Presence

Combining e-mail marketing with other online marketing mediums, such as SEO, RSS, blogs, and mobile devices gives your audience multiple chances to run across your messages and makes your messages more memorable because of the added repetition.

This section explains how you can modify your e-mail marketing tactics to enhance other Internet and technology marketing mediums to extend your e-mail marketing strategy beyond the standard e-mail inbox in order to multiply your efforts and give your e-mail marketing messages more chances to get noticed.

Using e-mail to enhance search engine optimization

Making sure that your Web site is visible to search engines is becoming more and more important as the number of Web sites that compete for online revenue continues to grow. Whether you employ organic search tactics, paid search, or a combination of strategies to move one or more pages of your Web site closer to the top of a search engine list, including the following tactics in your plan increases your potential ROI and gives your search engine marketing tactics more ways to capture business over time:

✔ **Make sure every landing page that appears as a link on a search engine ranking includes your e-mail list sign-up link.** First-time visitors to your Web site are not likely to become instant customers, but if they show enough interest to click-through to your Web site after searching, they might be willing to respond to an offer to receive periodic information from you in the form of e-mails. Capturing contact information from as many of your search engine visitors as possible gives your search engine marketing efforts more than one chance to acquire a new customer and a more targeted way to follow up in hopes of a conversion.

✔ **Include your keywords in your e-mails and post your e-mails on your Web site as new content.** *Keywords* are words your customers and prospects are likely to type in a search engine when they are looking for the types of products or services you offer. Search engines pick up on the keywords in your Web site and display links to the pages that contain them when a consumer searches using your keywords. Because keyword pages are ranked and displayed by search engines based on how prominent your keywords are, using keywords in your e-mails and posting your e-mails to an archive page on your Web site allows search engines to find more of your keywords and improves your overall search engine rank-ing. If you're not sure what keywords to use in your e-mails, your Web analytics application can tell you which keywords people are using to find your Web site.

✔ **Exchange sign-up links with noncompeting businesses that share your customer interests.** Placing your sign-up link on other Web sites is a great way to improve your ranking, and it also allows you to capture contact information from people who are searching and landing on your col-leagues' Web sites.

✔ **Optimize your e-mail list sign-up page.** Make sure your e-mail list sign-up page is visible to search engines and use content that is attractive enough to invite visitors. For example, an e-mail list sign-up page with a headline that reads, `Free E-Mail Marketing Tips` has a better chance of being found by people who are interested in e-mail marketing than a sign-up page with a headline that reads, `Thanks for Your Interest in Our E-Mail List`.

Combining e-mail and RSS marketing

Really simple syndication (RSS; also known as *rich site summary*) allows you to announce changes to your Web site content so anyone with an RSS reader can receive and view all or part of the updated content. RSS is gaining popu-larity among consumers because it allows them to keep up with changes to their favorite Web sites without sharing their personal contact information and because the consumer has complete control over the information they receive and the terms of each subscription. Some of the other advantages include the following:

✔ RSS feeds aren't blocked or bounced (although RSS subscribers can filter their feeds by denying content containing certain keywords).

✔ RSS feeds can enhance your Web site's search engine ranking because the content is published across the Internet as well as on your Web site.

✔ RSS feeds are very reliable for delivering audio and video content.

Using RSS feeds for marketing purposes is gaining popularity among business owners. As of this writing, I recommend that you explore the possibilities. Having said that, though, here are some limitations to RSS marketing that you should be aware of:

✔ RSS feeds aren't delivered, per se, to an inbox folder, so they disappear as soon as you post a new feed. The old ones can't be saved by sub-scribers for future reference.

✔ RSS feeds can't be easily forwarded to your subscribers' friends and colleagues.

✔ Your prospects and customers have to subscribe to your RSS feeds online, which makes it difficult to collect subscriber information in person.

✔ RSS feeds don't allow your subscribers to reply directly to your feeds to help initiate a conversation.

Here are some tips for using RSS and e-mail marketing together while keeping the limitations and advantages of each medium in mind:

✔ Include links to your RSS subscription information in your e-mails so that your e-mail list subscribers have a chance to receive both forms of notification.

✔ Include e-mail list sign-up links in your RSS feeds so that you have an opportunity to collect an e-mail address and initiate one-to-one conversations with your subscribers as needed.

✔ Don't allow your RSS subscribers to join your feeds anonymously unless you can be sure that they're going to receive different information via your e-mail list.

✔ Ask the e-mail list subscribers who show up on your bounce report whether they would like to receive your RSS feed instead of your e-mail.

Using e-mail to enhance your blog

A *blog* is a Web site that hosts journal-style information sorted by date and topic. Most blogs are informative in nature, rather than promotional, but blogs are often used in subtle ways for marketing purposes. If your business benefits from blogging, you can use the following tips for combining e-mail marketing and blogging to increase your results from both mediums:

✔ Include e-mail list sign-up links on your blog pages so interested visitors can sign up to receive related information and promotions via e-mail.

✔ Use your e-mails to drive traffic to your blog by linking to new articles when they appear.

✔ Use your blog to support your e-mail offers by offering links to unsolicited positive comments left by your blog community.

✔ Enhance the value of your e-mail newsletter by highlighting comments and other feedback from your blog.

✔ Use your blog as a source of content for your e-mail newsletter and for pointing your readers to past content as an archive.

E-mailing to mobile devices

Mobile devices allow consumers to read e-mail on the go, and recent studies show that consumers who use mobile devices check their e-mail around the clock. Sending e-mail marketing messages to mobile devices hasn't been widely tested as of this writing. Because few e-mail formatting standards exist among mobile devices, I recommend doing a bit of your own testing before charging ahead with a mobile e-mail strategy. Here are some tips to get your testing started:

- **Ask people for mobile preference when they sign up for your e-mail list.**

  You can create specially designed mobile e-mails for specific subscribers.

- **Design your mobile e-mails with a width of 120 pixels or fewer.**

  If your e-mail links to a landing page, use the same dimensions for your landing page. (For a great example of a mobile landing page, go to `http://mobile.starbucks.com`.)

- **Use phone numbers to call for action in mobile e-mails rather than Web site links.**

  Phone numbers are clickable and automatically dial the phone number. Make sure that the phone number you use can receive a text message.

- **Use single column e-mail layouts.**

  Most mobile devices won't display multiple columns. Multiple column displays are more difficult to read on a small screen.

- **Limit your mobile e-mails to one small image and use a center-justified layout.**

  Your text should appear above or below the image.

- **Keep your mobile e-mails to one topic with a single headline and a short summary of your message.**

  Mobile audiences aren't likely to read a long message with multiple topics.

Part V
The Part of Tens

The 5th Wave   By Rich Tennant

In this part . . .

Marketing strategies need to be flexible enough to change with the times and stable enough to avoid reinventing the wheel every time a new trend or medium emerges. Chapter 14 keeps you from rediscovering ten e-mail marketing mistakes that others have already learned to avoid. Chapter 15 lists ten e-mail marketing resources to keep at your fingertips so your strategy can flex as new information and tools become available.

Appendix A contains an HTML primer to aid you when your e-mail requires a bit of customization. Appendix B contains an example of one small business' entire e-mail marketing portfolio as a guideline for creating your own.

Chapter 14

Top Ten Worst E-Mail Content Blunders

With e-mail, you can deliver lots of different kinds of content, but just because you can send something with e-mail doesn't necessarily mean that you should. Make sure your e-mails avoid the following content blunders that make your e-mails intrusive, unreadable, or difficult to take action on. You can read more about content creation in Chapter 8 and e-mail design in Chapter 6.

EX¢E$$1VE PUNCTU☺T1ON!!!!!!!

Your audience could misinterpret the emotion behind your text if you overemphasize headlines, subject lines, and other text elements in your e-mails. E-mails with excessive punctuation are also more likely to be marked as spam because spammers often use more "cutesy" punctuation in their e-mails. Be sure to avoid, minimize, or replace the following punctuation with more tactful font and style alterations:

- ✔ All capital letters
- ✔ Repetitive symbols, such as strings of dollar signs
- ✔ Strings of asterisks before and after headlines
- ✔ Multiple exclamation points or question marks

Long articles that seem to never end and keep on going while saying basically the same thing over and over again

Consumers don't want e-mails hanging around in their inbox the same way magazines and newspapers hang around next to the bed or on the coffee table. Your audience is more likely to immediately open and read a short and concise e-mail because it takes less time to decide whether to delete, save, or respond to the e-mail.

The longer your e-mail, the more likely your audience will decide to read it later. When your audience puts your e-mail on hold, your message is at risk of being discarded before being read because it is perceived as old information after a few days.

Instead of including all your content in the body of an e-mail, use short, summary paragraphs of text to highlight the benefits of accessing your content on your Web site. That way, your audience won't mind taking a few moments to read your e-mail immediately to get the gist of your message.

Unfamiliar From address

Most consumers look at the From line in your e-mail to decide whether to open your e-mail. If your From line or e-mail address is unfamiliar, your e-mail is more likely to go unopened or to be reported as spam. You can make your e-mails more familiar by

✔ Clearly identifying yourself and your business in your From line in a way that is familiar to your audience

✔ Sending your e-mails from an e-mail address that your audience recognizes

Click Here links

Links are one of the elements in e-mail that draw attention while your audience scans your e-mail. Links can be important headlines that should help tell the story of your e-mail in case your audience reads only the headlines and links.

Instead of naming every link Click Here, craft your links into phrases and headlines that call for action. For example, a dog trainer might write a link that reads View 3 Additional Dog-Training Tips.

Distracting images

Some people look only at the images in your e-mail, so make sure that your images help to tell the story of your e-mail and don't distract your audience from your main message. Images can enhance your e-mail's message when you

- ✓ **Avoid busy background images that make your text hard to read.**
- ✓ **Use small images and link them to larger versions on your Web site so interested people can view your images in more detail.**
- ✓ **Avoid clip art that distracts people from your e-mail's main theme.**
- ✓ **Make sure your images support the text in your e-mail instead of including generic images.**

- ✓ **Limit your image use to one image per article or offer.**

  If you need additional images, link readers to your Web site to view more images.

Boring subject lines

Subject lines should prompt your audience to open your e-mail instead of simply giving your e-mail a name. For example, an e-mail with a Subject line that reads, June Newsletter isn't likely to generate too much excitement. Try the following ideas to keep you subject lines from boring your audience:

- ✓ Include the immediate benefits of opening your e-mail in the Subject line.
- ✓ Use your Subject line to highlight one of the articles in your e-mail.
- ✓ Repeat your e-mail's main call to action in your Subject line.
- ✓ Repeat one of your e-mail's main headlines in your Subject line.

Keeping your Subject line interesting helps to improve your open rates over time, but remember to be honest and truthful in your Subject lines because consumers won't appreciate being tricked into opening your e-mails.

Links that surprise the reader

Your links should give your audience exactly what they expect when they click. For example, if your e-mail includes a link that reads More Information but it actually downloads a video with sound, make sure you include those details in your link's text or add supporting text before or after the link that tells your audience exactly what is going to happen when they click. Here's a video link that is more informative: Watch Our Informative Video (.mpg 4 minutes).

Unfamiliar advertising

If your e-mails mention sponsors or advertise other companies, keep the following best practices in mind:

- ✔ Make sure your sponsorships are related to your audience and your business.
- ✔ Keep your advertising space to a maximum of 20 percent of your overall content.
- ✔ Make sure the ads are not too large or positioned in a way that makes them seem like they are the main focus of your e-mail.

Including too many advertisements could make your e-mail unrecognizable to your audience.

Repetitive messages

Repetition helps your audience to remember your e-mails, but consumers stop opening e-mails that repeatedly convey the same basic facts about your business such as your location and contact information. If your audience won't take action unless they see the same information over and over again, include new and interesting content along with your repeat messages so your e-mails remain valuable and relevant to your audience over time.

Cluttered layout

Your e-mail's layout helps to break up your content so that your e-mail is easy for your audience to scan. When your put together your e-mail, do the following:

✔ **Organize your content into symmetrical groups.** For example, two articles could be displayed side-by-side or one after another down the page in the same column.

✔ **Use white space and images.** These design elements can break up multiple articles or offers.

✔ **Use columns to group related content together.** Separate less important content from your main message.

An E-Mail Service Provider (ESP) can provide you with e-mail templates to guide your content insertion. Chapter 6 covers the many kinds of templates an ESP provides.

Chapter 15

Ten E-Mail Marketing Resources

Keeping up with the latest e-mail markcting tools and trends is important because e-mail marketing is growing and changing so rapidly. Whether you need industry statistics to give you guidance or tools to optimize or simplify your e-mail strategy, the following list of ten e-mail marketing resources is a reference for finding the help you need.

EmailTrainer.com

    www.emailtrainer.com

This Web site is a companion to *E-Mail Marketing For Dummies,* featuring links to resources and tools for expanding your e-mail marketing knowledge and improving your results. You can sign up to receive a free e-mail newsletter containing the latest tips and ideas for improving your e-mail marketing strategy. The Web site also includes a calendar of live workshops and training events for anyone seeking more personal e-mail marketing instruction.

EmailStatCenter.com

    www.emailstatcenter.com

This site is a collection of e-mail marketing statistics pulled from hundreds of sources, organized into dozens of categories. The categories include technical industry facts (such as deliverability rates and response metrics) as well as statistics related to budgeting, copy, creative, and other less-technical marketing concepts. The Web site also has an e-mail list with a sign-up link so you can receive periodic e-mails containing the latest e-mail marketing facts and statistics.

Email Sender and Provider Coalition

`www.espcoalition.org`

This organization was formed to help reduce spam while protecting the deliverability of legitimate e-mail. Members of the coalition are committed to a set of consumer-friendly professional standards that all commercial e-mailers are wise to embrace.

The coalition's Web site contains useful links to pending legislation and press releases as well as position papers on industry best practices.

FTC spam site

`www.ftc.gov/spam`

The Federal Trade Commission (FTC) monitors commercial e-mail practices and pursues legal action in response to unsolicited commercial e-mail complaints. The FTC is also charged with proposing legislation and rules that govern commercial e-mail.

The FTC spam Web site contains links to current rules as well as information for consumers and business owners who use e-mail. The information for business owners contains details on spam laws and tips for securing your e-mail server. The information for consumers includes helpful steps for safeguarding your e-mail inbox.

Email Experience Council

`www.emailexperience.org`

This council is a membership organization that advocates e-mail for all types of business communications. The council has several chapters worldwide, and its members share ideas and resources in order to take positions on important e-mail trends and to suggest best practices for many e-mail marketing tactics.

The council also hosts and sponsors several industry events, and the Web site contains helpful industry resources and links.

Email-Marketing-Reports blog

www.email-marketing-reports.com/iland

This blog highlights the latest e-mail marketing trends through analysis and reasoned insights. The blog often contains links to comments and articles from reliable industry sources to support the topic. The topics are posted daily on the Web site or as a really simply syndication (RSS) feed, and you can subscribe to the information in the form of biweekly e-mail newsletter.

Eyetools

www.eyetools.com

This company can test your e-mail designs and layouts to determine how consumers are likely to view the content in your e-mail. The tests are conducted by showing your e-mail to sample consumers through an apparatus that tracks eye movement. The result of the test tells you how to improve your e-mail design to get the most important content noticed — before you send your e-mails.

Eyetools also tests Web site landing pages to make sure that anyone clicking through to your site doesn't get distracted from your main offer.

Spam Arrest

www.spamarrest.com

This software program eliminates e-mails sent by spammers who use automated e-mail delivery programs. Subscribers to the Spam Arrest service receive a special e-mail address that can be used separately or in conjunction with any other e-mail address. The special e-mail address replies to unknown e-mails with a challenge response requiring senders to verify that they are real — live human beings. After the sender verifies his or her identity, the sender is added to a *friends list* so that future e-mails are delivered unchallenged.

The software also allows the user to set up individual filters to reject any e-mails that become unwanted after a successful challenge.

Community home page, ConstantContact.com

http://community.constantcontact.com

This online community allows registered users to post questions, answers, and ideas to an e-mail marketing discussion forum. The forum is intended for postings by actual small business owners in the trenches rather than industry professionals or technical gurus, so the postings tend to reflect the concerns of small business owners.

You have to be a Constant Contact customer to post something to the discussion forum, but anyone can read the postings and ponder their e-mail marketing implications.

Stockxpert.com

www.stockxpert.com

This online stock photography community provides quality royalty-free images for use in e-mail campaigns and Web sites. Royalty-free images are licensed for certain kinds of unlimited use after paying a single fee as opposed to images that require payment every time the image is used. The stock photography is licensed by the photographers and artists who produce them and is brokered by Sockxpert.com at extremely low prices.

The Web site sells *download credits* in blocks so you can search for images and download them as needed without having to go through a checkout and payment process each time you want to download a new image for use in an e-mail or Web site page.

Appendix A

HTML Primer

When you want more control over your e-mail designs (whether you're starting from scratch or tweaking an ESP template), you have to break into the complex world of HTML. This Appendix gives you an overview of HTML.

To find out more about HTML, pick up a copy of *HTML 4 For Dummies,* 5th Edition, by Ed Tittel and Mary Burmeister (Wiley).

Headings

HTML includes six elements to help you define six different heading levels in your documents:

- ✔ <h1> is the most prominent heading (Heading 1). First-level headings are the largest (usually two or three font sizes larger than the default text size for paragraphs).
- ✔ <h6> is the least prominent heading (Heading 6). Sixth-level headings are the smallest and may be two or three font sizes smaller than the default paragraph text.

To create a heading, follow these steps:

1. **Add** <h*n*> **in the body of your document.**

   Note: *n* is a placeholder for the Heading Level number you desire.

2. **Type the content for the heading.**

3. **Add** </h*n*>.

The following excerpt of HTML markup shows all six headings at work:

```
<body>
   <h1>First level heading</h1>
   <h2>Second-level heading</h2>
   <h3>Third-level heading</h3>
   <h4>Fourth-level heading</h4>
   <h5>Fifth-level heading</h5>
   <h6>Sixth-level heading</h6>
</body>
```

Paragraphs

The paragraph element, p (which includes the `<p>` and `</p>` tags), breaks text into paragraphs. You can also

- Force line breaks by using the break element `<br />`.
- Create horizontal rules (lines) by using the `<hr />` element.

HTML doesn't recognize the hard returns that you enter when you create your page. You must use a `<p>` element to separate the contained block of text as a paragraph.

To create a paragraph, follow these steps:

1. **Add `<p>` in the body of the document.**

2. **Type the content of the paragraph.**

3. **Add `</p>` to close that paragraph.**

Here's what it looks like:

```
<body>
   <p>This is a paragraph. It's a very simple structure that you will use
      time and again in your Web pages.</p>
   <p>This is another paragraph. What could be simpler to create?</p>
</body>
```

Text Treatment

HTML allows you to decorate your text by using boldface, italics, and underline.

Bold

Using a boldface font is one of the more common text embellishments a designer uses. To apply boldface in HTML, use the <b> tag.

```
<b>The Daily Brainy</b>
```

Italic

Italics are commonly used to set off quotations or to emphasize text. To apply italics in HTML, use the <i> tag.

```
<i>Wednesday, September 26, 2007</i>
```

Underline

To apply underline in HTML, use the <u> tag.

```
<p>Your Source for <u>Everything</u> Cerebral</p>
```

Underline is not a common embellishment a designer uses because it is often perceived as a link.

Horizontal rules

The horizontal rule element (<hr />) helps you include solid straight lines *(rules)* on your page. A horizontal rule is a good option to

✔ Break your page into logical sections.

✔ Separate your headers and footers from the rest of the page.

When you include an <hr /> element on your page, like the following HTML, the browser replaces it with a line.

```
<body>
   <p>This is a paragraph followed by a horizontal rule.</p>
   <hr />
   </p>This is a paragraph preceded by a horizontal rule.</p>
</body>
```

Numbered lists

A *numbered list* consists of at least two items, each prefaced by a number. You use two kinds of elements for a numbered list:

✔ The ordered list element (`<ol>`) specifies that this is a numbered list.

✔ List item elements (`<li>`) mark each item in the list.

A numbered list with three items requires elements and content in the following order:

<ol>

<li>

Content for the first list item

</li>

<li>

Content for the second list item

</li>

<li>

Content for the third list item

</li>

</ol>

The following markup defines a three-item numbered list:

```
<body>
  <h1>Things to do today</h1>
  <ol>
    <li>Feed cat</li>
    <li>Wash car</li>
    <li>Grocery shopping</li>
  </ol>
</body>
```

Bulleted lists

A *bulleted list* consists of one or more items each prefaced by a *bullet* (often a big dot). A bulleted list requires the following:

✔ The unordered list element (<ul>) specifies that you're creating a bulleted list.

✔ A list item element (<li>) marks each item in the list.

✔ The closing tag for the unordered list element (</ul>) indicates that the list has come to its end.

An unordered list with three items requires elements and content in the following order:

<ul>

<li>

Content for the first list item

</li>

<li>

Content for the second list item

</li>

<li>

Content for the third list item

</li>

</ul>

The following markup formats a three-item list as a bulleted list:

```
<body>
  <h1>Things to do today</h1>
  <ul>
    <li>Feed cat</li>
    <li>Wash car</li>
    <li>Grocery shopping</li>
  </ul>
</body>
```

Fonts

You can define individual font properties for different HTML elements with

✔ Individual CSS properties, such as font-family, line-height, and font-size

✔ A group of font properties in the catchall shorthand font property

Font family

To define the font face by using the font family, do the following:

1. **Identify the selector for the style declaration.**

   For example, making the p the selector defines a font family for all <p> tags.

2. **Add the property name** font-family.

3. **Define a** value **for the property (the name of the font family).**

   Use single or double quotation marks around any font family names that include spaces.

To format all first-level headings to use the Verdana font, use a style declaration like this:

```
h1 {font-family: Verdana, Helvetica, sans-serif;}
```

In the preceding declaration, two more font families are identified in case a browser doesn't support the Verdana font family.

These font families are good to include in your style declarations:

- At least one of these *common* font families:

  - Arial

  - Helvetica

  - Times New Roman

  - Verdana

- At least one of these *generic* font families:

  - serif

  - sans serif

  - cursive

  - fantasy

  - monospace

Different elements may be formatted using different font families. These rules define a different font family for hyperlinks:

```
body {color: #808000; font-family: Verdana, sans-serif; font-size: 85%;}
hr {text-align: center;}
a {font-family: Courier, "Courier New", monospace;}
```

Font size

The style declaration to specify the size of text is

```
selector {font-size: value;}
```

The `value` of the declaration can be

- ✔ One of the standard font property measurement values
- ✔ One of these user-defined keywords:

  xx-small, x-small, small, medium, large, x-large, or xx-large

The value of each keyword is determined by the browser and not the style rule.

The following rules define

- ✔ A relative font value for all text
- ✔ An absolute value for the font size for all first-level headings

```
body {color: #808000; font-family: Verdana, sans-serif; font-size: 85%;}
h1 {color: #808000; font-family: Arial, Helvetica, sans-serif;
    font-weight: 800; font-size: 24pt;}
```

Color Values

HTML defines color values in two ways:

- ✔ **Name:** You choose from a limited list.
- ✔ **Number:** This is harder to remember, but you have many more options.

Color names

The HTML specification includes 16 color names that you can use to define colors in your pages.

Name	*Hexcode*
aqua	#00FFFF
black	#000000
blue	#0000FF
fuchsia	#FF00FF
gray	#808080
green	#008000
lime	#00FF00
maroon	#800000
navy	#000080
olive	#808000
purple	#800080
red	#FF0000
silver	#C0C0C0
teal	#008080
white	#FFFFFF
yellow	#FFFF00

This CSS style declaration says all text within <p> tags should be blue:

```
p {color: blue;}
```

Color numbers

Color numbers allow you to use any color (even salmon) on your Web page.

Hexadecimal notation uses six characters — a combination of numbers and letters — to define any color. When you use hexadecimal code to define a color, you should always precede it with a pound sign (#).

This CSS style declaration makes all text contained by <p> tags blue:

```
p {color: #0000FF;}
```

Some good online sources for hexadecimal color charts are

```
www.hypersolutions.org/pages/rgbhex.html
www.colorschemer.com/online.html
```

Color Definitions

CSS uses the following properties to define color:

- ✔ color defines the font color and is also used to define colors for links in their various states (active, visited).

- ✔ background or background-color defines the background color for the entire page or defines the background for a particular element (for example, a background color for all first-level headings, similar to the idea of highlighting something in a Word document).

Text

To change the color of text on your page

1. **Determine the selector.**

   For example, will the color apply to all first-level headings, to all paragraphs, or to a specific paragraph?

2. **Use the** color **property.**

3. **Identify the color name or hexadecimal value.**

The basic syntax for the style declaration is

```
selector {color: value;}
```

Here is a collection of style declarations that use the color property:

```
body {color: olive; font-family: Verdana, sans-serif;
      background-color: #FFFFFF; font-size: 85%;}
hr {text-align: center;}
.navbar {font-size: 75%; text-align: center;}
h1 {color: #808000;}
p.chapternav {text-align: center;}
.footer {font-size: 80%;}
```

In the preceding CSS rules, the color for all text on the page is defined by using the body selector. The color is applied to all text in the body of the document unless otherwise defined. For example, the first-level heading is defined as forest green by using hexadecimal notation.

Background color

To change the background color for your page, or a section of that page, follow these steps:

1. **Determine the selector.**

   For example, will the color apply to the entire background, or will it apply only to a specific section?

2. **Use the** `background-color` **or** `background` **property.**

3. **Identify the color name or hexadecimal value.**

The basic syntax for the style declaration is

```
selector {background-color: value;}
```

In the following collection of style declarations, the first style declaration uses the `background-color` property and sets it to light green by using hexadecimal notation:

```
body {color: #808000; font-family: Verdana, sans-serif;
    background-color: #EAF3DA; font-size: 85%;}
```

You can apply a background color to a block of text — for example, a paragraph — much like you define the background color for the entire page.

You use `background` as a shorthand property for all individual background properties or `background-color` to set just the color.

```
selector {background: value value value}
```

Basic Links

Hyperlinks, or simply *links,* connect HTML pages to other resources.

Web addresses

To create a link to a Web site, you need

✔ **The Web address** (called a *Uniform Resource Locator*, or URL) of the Web site or file you want to link. This usually starts with http://.

✔ **Some text** in your page to label or describe the link.

✔ **An anchor element** (<a>) with the href attribute.

For example, if you have a page that refers Web surfers to the World Wide Web Consortium (W3C), a basic link to the W3C's Web site, www.w3.org, looks like this:

```
<p>The <a href="http://www.w3.org">World Wide Web Consortium</a> is the
    standards body that oversees the ongoing development of the XHTML
    specification.</p>
```

You specify the link URL (http://www.w3.org) in the anchor element's href attribute. The text (World Wide Web Consortium) between the anchor element's open and close tags (<a> and </a>) describes the link.

Images

To create an image that triggers a link, you substitute an <img /> element in place of the text you would anchor your link to. This markup links text:

```
<p><a href="http://www.w3.org">Visit the W3C</a></p>
```

This markup replaces the text Visit the W3C with an appropriate icon:

```
<p><a href="http://www.w3.org"><img src="w3.jpg"
    alt="Visit the W3C Web Site" height="48" width="315" border="0" /></a>

</p>
```

The preceding markup creates a linked image to http://www.w3.org. When a user moves the mouse pointer over the image, the cursor changes from an arrow into a pointing hand (or any icon the browser uses for a link).

E-mail addresses

An e-mail link uses the standard anchor element and href attribute. The value of the href attribute is the receiving e-mail address prefaced with mailto:.

```
<p>Send us your
  <a href="mailto:comments@mysite.com">comments</a>.</p>
```

Locations within pages

Intradocument hyperlinks are such familiar features as

- Back to Top links
- Tables of contents

To identify and create a location within a page for direct access from other links, first place an empty anchor element with the name attribute, like this:

```
<a name="top"></a>
```

The anchor element that marks the spot doesn't affect the appearance. You can mark spots wherever you need them without worrying about how your pages look (or change) as a result.

An intradocument hyperlink uses a URL like this:

```
<a href="#top">Back to top</a>
```

The pound sign (#) indicates that you're pointing to a spot on the same page, not on another page.

This listing shows how two anchor elements work together to link to a spot on the same page.

```
   <title>Intradocument hyperlinks at work</title>
 </head>
 <body>
  <h1><a name="top"></a>Web-Based Training</h1>
  <p>Given the importance of the Web to businesses and
     other organizations, individuals who seek to improve
     job skills, or fulfill essential job functions, are
     turning to HTML and XML for training. We believe
     this provides an outstanding opportunity for
     participation in an active and lucrative adult and
     continuing education market.</p>
  <p><a href="#top">Back to top</a></p>
```

If the user clicks the Back to Top link, the browser jumps back to the top spot — marked by <a name="top"></a>.

Non-HTML resources

Links can connect to virtually any kind of files, such as

- ✔ Word-processing documents
- ✔ Spreadsheets
- ✔ PDFs
- ✔ Compressed files
- ✔ Multimedia

A great use for non-HTML links is on software and PDF download pages.

Non-Web files have unique URLs just like HTML pages. Any file on a Web server (regardless of its type) can be linked with its URL.

For instance, if users need to download a PDF file named `doc.pdf` and a `.zip` archive called `software.zip` from a Web page, you use this HTML:

```
<h1>Download the new version of our software</h1>
<p><a href="software.zip">Software</a></p>
<p><a href="doc.pdf">Documentation</a></p>
```

Basic Tables

The building blocks for your table's framework are the three basic components of any table:

- ✔ **Table:** `<table>`
- ✔ **Table row:** `<tr>`

  `<tr>` is always enclosed within `<table>`.

- ✔ **Table (data) cell:** `<td>`

  `<td>` is always enclosed within `<tr>`.

The `<table>`, `<tr>`, and `<td>` *opening* and *closing* tags are required. If you forget to include any, your table won't display correctly in most browsers.

Creating a simple table

The `<table>` tag and its markup typically appear between the `<body>` tags in your document. The following markup creates a simple table with two rows and two columns (four data cells) — replace cell 1, cell 2, and so on with your text.

```
<!DOCTYPE html PUBLIC "-//W3C//DTD XHTML 1.0 Transitional//EN"
    "http://www.w3.org/TR/xhtml1/DTD/xhtml1-transitional.dtd">
<html xmlns="http://www.w3.org/1999/xhtml">
<head>
    <title>Tables</title>
</head>
<body>
 <table>
  <tr>
    <td> cell 1 </td>
    <td> cell 2 </td>
  </tr>
  <tr>
    <td> cell 3 </td>
    <td> cell 4 </td>
  </tr>
 </table>
</body>
</html>
```

Creating a table-based page

To create the shell of your table-based page, follow these steps:

1. **Start with the** `<table>` **element:**

   ```
   <table>
      ...
   </table>
   ```

   The `<table>` element can have a number of optional attributes (for example, `border="1"` or `bgcolor="black"`) — for now, however, keep it simple.

2. **Decide how many rows you want the table to have:**

   The following markup creates a table with two rows:

   ```
   <table>
      <tr>...</tr>
      <tr>...</tr>
   </table>
   ```

Other table elements

- **`<th>`**: The table header element displays text in boldface with a default center alignment.

  You can use the `<th>` element within any row of a table, but you most often find and use it in the first row at the top — or head — of a table. Except for their position and egotism, they act just like table data (`<td>`) tags and should be treated as such.

- **`<tbody>`**: You can group table rows into a table body section with the table body (`<tbody>`) element.

  A recent addition to the HTML 4 specification, these elements allow table bodies to scroll independently of the table head (`<thead>`) and table foot (`<tfoot>`). The table body should contain rows of table data. The `<tbody>` element must contain at least one table row (`<tr>`).

- **`<thead>`**: You can group table rows into a table head section by using the table head (`<thead>`) element. The table head contains information about the table's columns.

  The `<thead>` element must contain at least one table row.

- **`<tfoot>`**: Much like the `<thead>` element, you can group table rows into a table footer section by using the table footer (`<tfoot>`) element. The table footer contains information about the table's columns and must contain at least one table row.

  Include your footer information before the first instance of the `<tbody>` element so that the browser renders that information before taking a stab at all the content data cells.

- **`<colgroup>`**: This element creates an explicit column group. You specify the number of columns by using the `span` attribute or by using the `<col>` element.

  You use the `span` attribute to specify a uniform width for a group of columns.

- **`<col>`**: The `<col>` element is an empty element. You use the `<col>` element to further define column structure. The `<col>` element shouldn't be used to group columns — that's the `<colgroup>` element's job. You use the `<col>` element after you define a column group and set a uniform width to specify a uniform width for a subset of columns.

3. **Create cells in each row with the table data cell (`<td>`) element.**

   Each `<td>` element creates a cell, so the number of `<td>` elements in a row is the number of columns.

   Here's a two-column table with three cells: the first row contains one cell, and the second row contains two cells. The markup for this arrangement looks like this:

```
<!DOCTYPE html PUBLIC "-//W3C//DTD XHTML 1.0 Transitional//EN"
    "http://www.w3.org/TR/xhtml1/DTD/xhtml1-transitional.dtd">
<html xmlns="http://www.w3.org/1999/xhtml">
<head>
    <title>Tables</title>
</head>
<body>
<table>
  <tr>
    <td> contents </td>
  </tr>
  <tr>
    <td> contents </td>
    <td> contents </td>
  </tr>
</table>
</body>
</html>
```

HTML Entities

To enhance your Web pages with symbols and characters that aren't available as keyboard commands, you can use HTML entities. The following table lists some of the more common entities and their character and numeric codes.

Character	Description	Character Code	Numeric Code
©	Copyright	©	&#169
™	Trademark	&trade	&#8482
®	Registered Trademark	&reg	&#174
•	Bullet	&bull	&#8226
<	Less Than	&lt	&#60
>	Greater Than	&gt	&#62
¢	Cent	&cent	&#162

You can find an expanded list of HTML entity codes at

```
http://www.w3schools.com/tags/ref_entities.asp
```

HTML Elements

Element	Common Name	Empty	Category	Description
a	Anchor	No	Link element	Creates document links
b	Bold text	No	Presentation	Sets enclosed text in boldface
big	Big text	No	Presentation	Bumps font size one level above default or basefont size
blockquote	Block-quote	No	Text element	Sets off long quotations from body text
body	Document body	No	Doc structure	Identifies (X)HTML document body
br	Line break	Yes	Text element	Forces line break in document text
caption	Table caption	No	Table element	Enclosed text defines a table caption
col	Table column	Yes	Table element	Defines a group of table column attributes
colgroup	Table column group	No	Table element	Groups a specified set of columns together
em	Emphasis	No	Text element	Provides typographic emphasis, usually rendered in italics

(continued)

(continued)

Element	Common Name	Empty	Category	Description
h1, h2, ..., h6	Header levels 1 through 6	No	Doc structure	Identifies heading level hierarchy six levels deep
head	Document head	No	Doc structure	Contains markup for (X)HTML document head
hr	Horizontal rule	Yes	Presentation	Inserts horizontal rule between lines of document content
i	Italic	No	Presentation	Sets enclosed text in italic
img	Image	Yes	Inclusion element	References an external image file in GIF, PNG, or JPEG format
li	List item	No	List element	Identifies item inside an (X)HTML list type: dir, menu, ol, ul
link	Link	Yes	Link element	Links current doc to other docs or resources, legal only inside head
ol	Ordered list	No	List element	List style that numbers included elements in order of appearance

Element	Name	Common Empty	Category	Description
p	Paragraph	No	Text element	Forms enclosed text into individual paragraphs
q	Quotation	No	Text element	Used to highlight short quotations from other sources
small	Small text	No	Presentation	Makes text one size smaller than the default or basefont size
strong	Strong emphasis	No	Text element	Strong visual emphasis for key words/ phrases within normal doc text
sub	Subscript	No	Text element	Render enclosed text as a subscript, lower than surrounding text
sup	Super-script	No	Text element	Render enclosed text as a super-script, higher than surround-ing text
table	Table	No	Table element	Container element for a table in an (X)HTML doc
tbody	Table body	No	Table element	Defines data portion of a table, known as the table body

(continued)

(continued)

Element	Common Name	Empty	Category	Description
td	Table data (cell)	No	Table element	Create a cell in a table
tfoot	Table footer	No	Table element	Defines rows that belong to the footer area in an (X)HTML table
th	Table heading	No	Table element	Creates a row or column heading in an (X)HTML table
thead	Table header	No	Table element	Defines the rows that belong to the header area in an (X)HTML table
tr	Table row	No	Table element	Creates a row in an (X)HTML table
ul	Unordered list	No	List element	List items enclosed show up in a bulleted list in order of appearance

HTML Attributes

Name	Function/ Value Equals	Value Types	Related Element(s)
bgcolor	Background color for element	Color	body, table, td, th, tr
cellpadding	Defines interstitial space between table cells	Length (p/%)	table

Name	Function/ Value Equals	Value Types	Related Element(s)
colspan	Number of table columns that single cell spans	Number	td, th
height	Image or object height in pixels	Length (p)	img, object
href	URI to a linked resource	URI	a, area, link
rowspan	Identifies number of rows that a single cell spans	Number	td, th
span.1	Number of table columns to which col attributes apply	Number	col
span.2	Default number of columns in a column group	Number	colgroup
type.1	Identifies list item style to use	{"circle"|"disc"|"square"} or {"1"|"a"|"A"|"i"|"I"}	li, ol, ul
valign	Defines vertical alignment for table cells	{"baseline"|"bottom"|"middle"|"top"}	col, colgroup, tbody, td, tfoot, th, thead, tr
width.1	Specifies column or column group width	CS Length (p/%)	col, colgroup

Appendix B

A Sample E-Mail Portfolio

A typical small business needs to deliver a variety of information to keep prospects and customers engaged in buying cycles. Branding your e-mail communications to establish a unique and recognizable identity is important so that your prospects and customers can distinguish your business from your competition, but distinguishing your own e-mail communications from one another is also important so that your audience can easily identify the type of message you're sending.

Someone who attended one of my seminars told me that she was very upset when her business flooded because of a broken pipe in her neighbor's store. And, she was even more upset that no one responded to her e-mail inviting customers and prospects to a flood sale that would have saved her from throwing away much of her perishable inventory during the period when the impending construction closed her store to the public.

After further investigation, I discovered that she had announced the flood sale by using her e-mail newsletter template, and the people on her e-mail list thought it was just a standard newsletter. Her customers and prospects simply weren't used to urgent announcements in an e-mail newsletter, so they didn't bother reading the e-mail right away — and they missed the sale.

Creating an entire portfolio of templates with consistent but distinguishing designs for each type of message ensures that your audience can mentally rank each message they receive according to priority. Then they can respond accordingly.

This Appendix shows an example of an entire e-mail marketing portfolio for LIGHTGROUP, which is a small business specializing in video and Internet media production. Use the portfolio as a guide for building your own branded e-mail marketing portfolio. To protect the privacy of this business, the footer has been removed from each e-mail. However, make sure that your e-mails contain a footer with your physical address, an unsubscribe link, and additional privacy information for subscribers.

New Subscriber Templates

Use new subscriber templates when you're obtaining new e-mail list subscribers. The process begins when someone visits a Web site and sees an offer to subscribe, and ends when someone receives an e-mail confirming a new subscription.

Sign-up link

A sign-up link (see Figure B-1) placed on a Web site helps to enlist new subscribers.

Figure B-1:
Sign-up link.

Sign-up form

A sign-up link takes interested subscribers to a sign-up form (see Figure B-2) where they can share contact information and join various lists specific to their interests.

Welcome letter

Send a welcome letter (see Figure B-3) when someone fills out and submits the information in the sign-up form.

LIGHTGROUP
CREATIVE MEDIA SOLUTIONS

Free Monthly Media Marketing Tips Delivered Via Email

A good creative strategy ensures the best return on your investment, and a good email strategy ensures that we deliver information according to your interests. Please select your areas of interest below and fill in the contact information you are comfortable sharing. We promise never to share your email address with anyone outside LIGHTGROUP without your permission.

Your Email Address   john@thelightgroup.com
Re-type Your Email Address:

Please Select Your Interests Here

Remember, you can always change this information later if your interests change.

☑ **Subscribe to All Lists**
   Tips, invitations, incentives, and press releases

☐ **Media Minutes**
   Short weekly tips to help strengthen your media strategy.

☐ **Project Promos**
   Periodic incentives based on our production schedule.

☐ **Event Invitations**
   Periodic workshops, seminars, screenings, and social events.

☐ **Press Releases**
   Newsworthy stories about LIGHTGROUP delivered as information develops.

Please Share Your Contact Information

Please share only what you are comfortable sharing at this stage in your search. Items marked with "*" require a response so we can send you relevant information.

*First Name:
*Zip/Postal Code:
Last Name:
Company Name:
Work Phone:

I would like to receive text-only emails ☐

Cancel   Submit   Unsubscribe All

Figure B-2:
Sign-up
form.

LIGHTGROUP
CREATIVE MEDIA SOLUTIONS

Welcome to the Email Community

About Your Subscription

Dear John,

Welcome to the LIGHTGROUP email community. Please add emails@thelightgroup.com to your email program's address book to help ensure delivery.

Privacy is important to us; therefore, we will not sell, rent, or give your name or address to anyone. At any point, you can select the Update Profile link at the bottom of every email to unsubscribe, or to receive less or more information.

Thanks again for joining the email community. If you have any questions or comments, feel free to contact us.

Sincerely,
John
LIGHTGROUP

Figure B-3:
Welcome
letter.

Subscriber Maintenance Templates

Every e-mail you send should contain a link in the e-mail's footer that allows subscribers to update their contact information and interests. That way, your subscribers can save you time by maintaining your contact database for you.

Change of profile request

When subscribers click the link to change their profile, the subscribers receive an e-mail with a secure link that takes them to the original sign-up form so they can sign up for new lists, unsubscribe to unwanted lists, and update their contact information. (See Figure B-4.)

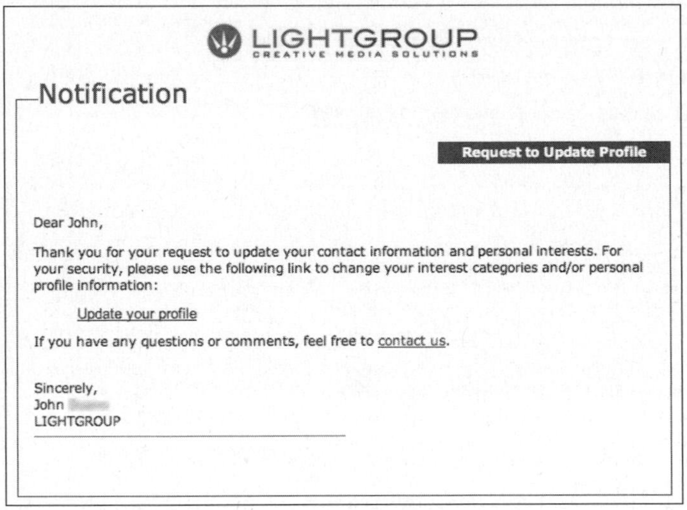

Figure B-4: Change of profile request.

Change of profile confirmation

When subscribers change their interests and contact information using the sign-up form, send a change of profile confirmation e-mail (see Figure B-5) to notify the subscribers of the changes they made.

LIGHTGROUP
CREATIVE MEDIA SOLUTIONS

Notification

Changes to Your Profile

Dear John,

We have recorded your changes in our database. Please review your changes below:

1. Changed email address.

If these changes are not correct, please select the link at the bottom of this email to return to our Subscription Center and make the appropriate adjustments. In the future, the emails we send to you will reflect these changes.

Thank you for your continued interest in LIGHTGROUP. If you have any questions or comments, feel free to contact us.

Thank you,
John
LIGHTGROUP

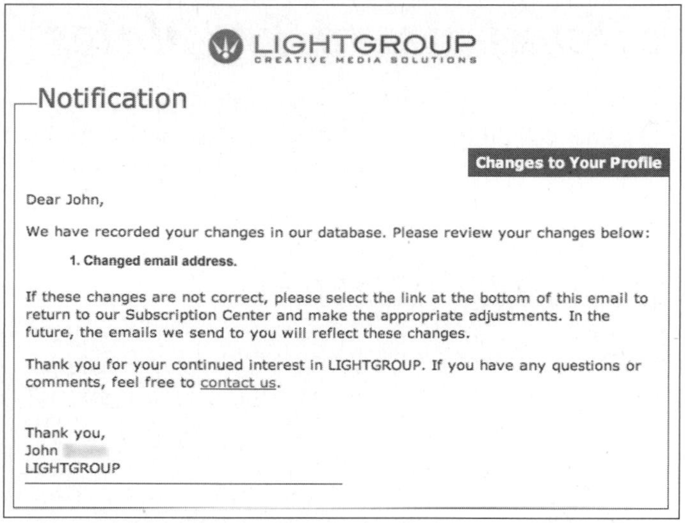

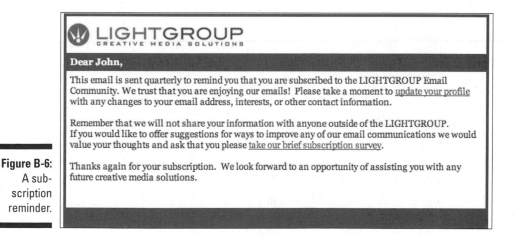

Figure B-5: Change of profile confirmation.

Subscription reminder

Send a subscription reminder e-mail (see Figure B-6) once per quarter to remind customers and prospects to keep their contact information current.

LIGHTGROUP
CREATIVE MEDIA SOLUTIONS

Dear John,

This email is sent quarterly to remind you that you are subscribed to the LIGHTGROUP Email Community. We trust that you are enjoying our emails! Please take a moment to update your profile with any changes to your email address, interests, or other contact information.

Remember that we will not share your information with anyone outside of the LIGHTGROUP. If you would like to offer suggestions for ways to improve any of our email communications we would value your thoughts and ask that you please take our brief subscription survey.

Thanks again for your subscription. We look forward to an opportunity of assisting you with any future creative media solutions.

Figure B-6: A subscription reminder.

Newsletter Template

Send a monthly e-mail newsletter (see Figure B-7) when you have informative content with links to additional content and offers hosted on the Web site. LIGHTGROUP's e-mail newsletter is called *Media Minute*.

Promotional Templates

Promotions usually contain offers to take specific actions, such as immediate purchases and commitments to attend an event or make an appointment.

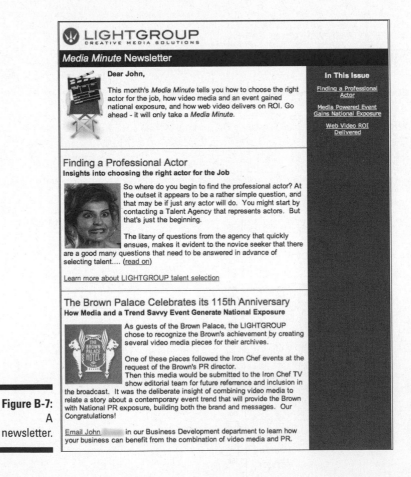

Figure B-7:
A
newsletter.

Promotional offer template

Send promotional offers periodically to help prospective customers engage in the buying cycle. LIGHTGROUP's promotional e-mail (see Figure B-8) is called *Project Promos*.

Event invitation template

Send event invitations for special occasions. Inviting people to an event is considered a promotion because there is usually a specific call to action asking your audience to make a decision. (See Figure B-9.)

Announcement Templates

Announcement e-mails don't require any specific action or response on the part of your audience. Using one template for all your announcements gives your audience a hint that the message doesn't need a response. You can also use a different template for each type of announcement.

Press release template

Most press releases are usually sent to a private media-only e-mail list, but some press releases are intended to impress customers and prospects. LIGHTGROUP allows anyone to subscribe to the press release e-mail list, but they don't send every press release to everyone on the list. (See Figure B-10.)

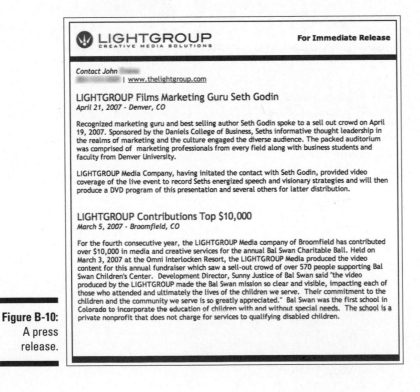

Figure B-10: A press release.

Announcement template

Send announcements (see Figure B-11) when short bits of information are important or urgent.

Figure B-11:
An announce-ment.

Holiday greeting template

Send holiday greetings (see Figure B-12) to remind customers that their business is appreciated. When possible, keep people who celebrate different holidays on separate private e-mail lists so that you can customize the greetings to reflect the beliefs surrounding particular holidays.

Figure B-12:
A holiday greeting.

Procedural e-mail

Procedural e-mails (see Figure B-13) deliver instructions or communicate official policies and guidelines as needed.

Figure B-13:
A
procedural
e-mail.

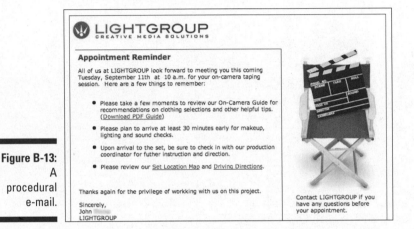

Survey Invitation Template

Survey invitations (see Figure B-14) are distinguished from event invitations because they require a different type of response.

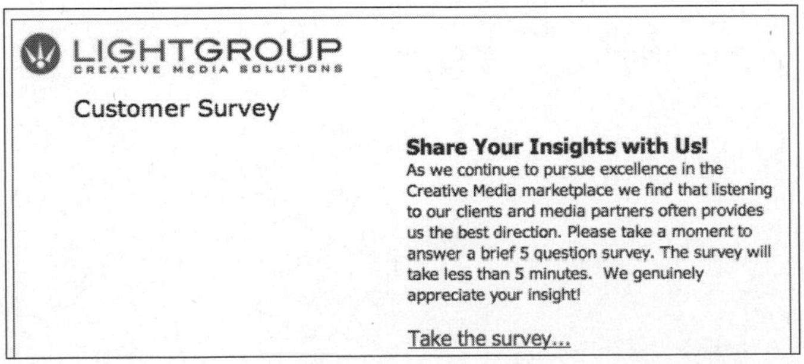

Figure B-14:
A survey
invitation.

Index

• I •

• J •

BUSINESS, CAREERS & PERSONAL FINANCE

0-7645-9847-3

0-7645-2431-3

Also available:
- Business Plans Kit For Dummies
  0-7645-9794-9
- Economics For Dummies
  0-7645-5726-2
- Grant Writing For Dummies
  0-7645-8416-2
- Home Buying For Dummies
  0-7645-5331-3
- Managing For Dummies
  0-7645-1771-6
- Marketing For Dummies
  0-7645-5600-2

- Personal Finance For Dummies
  0-7645-2590-5*
- Resumes For Dummies
  0-7645-5471-9
- Selling For Dummies
  0-7645-5363-1
- Six Sigma For Dummies
  0-7645-6798-5
- Small Business Kit For Dummies
  0-7645-5984-2
- Starting an eBay Business For Dummies
  0-7645-6924-4
- Your Dream Career For Dummies
  0-7645-9795-7

HOME & BUSINESS COMPUTER BASICS

0-470-05432-8

0-471-75421-8

Also available:
- Cleaning Windows Vista For Dummies
  0-471-78293-9
- Excel 2007 For Dummies
  0-470-03737-7
- Mac OS X Tiger For Dummies
  0-7645-7675-5
- MacBook For Dummies
  0-470-04859-X
- Macs For Dummies
  0-470-04849-2
- Office 2007 For Dummies
  0-470-00923-3

- Outlook 2007 For Dummies
  0-470-03830-6
- PCs For Dummies
  0-7645-8958-X
- Salesforce.com For Dummies
  0-470-04893-X
- Upgrading & Fixing Laptops For Dummies
  0-7645-8959-8
- Word 2007 For Dummies
  0-470-03658-3
- Quicken 2007 For Dummies
  0-470-04600-7

FOOD, HOME, GARDEN, HOBBIES, MUSIC & PETS

0-7645-8404-9

0-7645-9904-6

Also available:
- Candy Making For Dummies
  0-7645-9734-5
- Card Games For Dummies
  0-7645-9910-0
- Crocheting For Dummies
  0-7645-4151-X
- Dog Training For Dummies
  0-7645-8418-9
- Healthy Carb Cookbook For Dummies
  0-7645-8476-6
- Home Maintenance For Dummies
  0-7645-5215-5

- Horses For Dummies
  0-7645-9797-3
- Jewelry Making & Beading For Dummies
  0-7645-2571-9
- Orchids For Dummies
  0-7645-6759-4
- Puppies For Dummies
  0-7645-5255-4
- Rock Guitar For Dummies
  0-7645-5356-9
- Sewing For Dummies
  0-7645-6847-7
- Singing For Dummies
  0-7645-2475-5

INTERNET & DIGITAL MEDIA

0-470-04529-9

0-470-04894-8

Also available:
- Blogging For Dummies
  0-471-77084-1
- Digital Photography For Dummies
  0-7645-9802-3
- Digital Photography All-in-One Desk Reference For Dummies
  0-470-03743-1
- Digital SLR Cameras and Photography For Dummies
  0-7645-9803-1
- eBay Business All-in-One Desk Reference For Dummies
  0-7645-8438-3
- HDTV For Dummies
  0-470-09673-X

- Home Entertainment PCs For Dummies
  0-470-05523-5
- MySpace For Dummies
  0-470-09529-6
- Search Engine Optimization For Dummies
  0-471-97998-8
- Skype For Dummies
  0-470-04891-3
- The Internet For Dummies
  0-7645-8996-2
- Wiring Your Digital Home For Dummies
  0-471-91830-X

* Separate Canadian edition also available
† Separate U.K. edition also available

SPORTS, FITNESS, PARENTING, RELIGION & SPIRITUALITY

0-471-76871-5

0-7645-7841-3

Also available:
- Catholicism For Dummies
  0-7645-5391-7
- Exercise Balls For Dummies
  0-7645-5623-1
- Fitness For Dummies
  0-7645-7851-0
- Football For Dummies
  0-7645-3936-1
- Judaism For Dummies
  0-7645-5299-6
- Potty Training For Dummies
  0-7645-5417-4
- Buddhism For Dummies
  0-7645-5359-3

- Pregnancy For Dummies
  0-7645-4483-7 †
- Ten Minute Tone-Ups For Dummies
  0-7645-7207-5
- NASCAR For Dummies
  0-7645-7681-X
- Religion For Dummies
  0-7645-5264-3
- Soccer For Dummies
  0-7645-5229-5
- Women in the Bible For Dummies
  0-7645-8475-8

TRAVEL

0-7645-7749-2

0-7645-6945-7

Also available:
- Alaska For Dummies
  0-7645-7746-8
- Cruise Vacations For Dummies
  0-7645-6941-4
- England For Dummies
  0-7645-4276-1
- Europe For Dummies
  0-7645-7529-5
- Germany For Dummies
  0-7645-7823-5
- Hawaii For Dummies
  0-7645-7402-7

- Italy For Dummies
  0-7645-7386-1
- Las Vegas For Dummies
  0-7645-7382-9
- London For Dummies
  0-7645-4277-X
- Paris For Dummies
  0-7645-7630-5
- RV Vacations For Dummies
  0-7645-4442-X
- Walt Disney World & Orlando
  For Dummies
  0-7645-9660-8

GRAPHICS, DESIGN & WEB DEVELOPMENT

0-7645-8815-X

0-7645-9571-7

Also available:
- 3D Game Animation For Dummies
  0-7645-8789-7
- AutoCAD 2006 For Dummies
  0-7645-8925-3
- Building a Web Site For Dummies
  0-7645-7144-3
- Creating Web Pages For Dummies
  0-470-08030-2
- Creating Web Pages All-in-One Desk
  Reference For Dummies
  0-7645-4345-8
- Dreamweaver 8 For Dummies
  0-7645-9649-7

- InDesign CS2 For Dummies
  0-7645-9572-5
- Macromedia Flash 8 For Dummies
  0-7645-9691-8
- Photoshop CS2 and Digital
  Photography For Dummies
  0-7645-9580-6
- Photoshop Elements 4 For Dummies
  0-471-77483-9
- Syndicating Web Sites with RSS Feeds
  For Dummies
  0-7645-8848-6
- Yahoo! SiteBuilder For Dummies
  0-7645-9800-7

NETWORKING, SECURITY, PROGRAMMING & DATABASES

0-7645-7728-X

0-471-74940-0

Also available:
- Access 2007 For Dummies
  0-470-04612-0
- ASP.NET 2 For Dummies
  0-7645-7907-X
- C# 2005 For Dummies
  0-7645-9704-3
- Hacking For Dummies
  0-470-05235-X
- Hacking Wireless Networks
  For Dummies
  0-7645-9730-2
- Java For Dummies
  0-470-08716-1

- Microsoft SQL Server 2005 For Dummies
  0-7645-7755-7
- Networking All-in-One Desk Reference
  For Dummies
  0-7645-9939-9
- Preventing Identity Theft For Dummies
  0-7645-7336-5
- Telecom For Dummies
  0-471-77085-X
- Visual Studio 2005 All-in-One Desk
  Reference For Dummies
  0-7645-9775-2
- XML For Dummies
  0-7645-8845-1